BEYOND
YOUR EGO

BEYOND YOUR EGO

A TORAH APPROACH TO SELF-KNOWLEDGE, EMOTIONAL HEALTH AND INNER PEACE

DR. JUDITH MISHELL

based on the creative insights of

DR. SHALOM SREBRENIK

CIS
P·U·B·L·I·S·H·E·R·S
New York · London · Jerusalem

Published and distributed
in the U.S., Canada and overseas by
C.I.S. Publishers and Distributors
180 Park Avenue, Lakewood, New Jersey 08701
(908) 905-3000 Fax: (908) 367-6666

Distributed in Israel by
C.I.S. International (Israel)
Rechov Mishkalov 18
Har Nof, Jerusalem
Tel: 02-518-935

Distributed in the U.K. and Europe by
C.I.S. International (U.K.)
89 Craven Park Road
London N15 6AH, England
Tel: 81-809-3723

Book and cover design by Deenee Cohen
Typography by Chaya Bleier
Cover photography by Solaria Studios

ISBN 1-56062-083-8

Library of Congress Catalog Card Number
91-073665

Printed in China

This book is dedicated to
my beloved granddaughter

KALIA

*May the Lord make you like Sarah, Rivkah, Rachel
and Leah
and bring you to Torah, chupah and good deeds.
May Hashem bless you and guard you.
May Hashem shine His countenance upon you and
be gracious unto you.
May Hashem turn His countenance toward you and
grant you peace.*

Dr. Judith Mishell

This book is dedicated to

MY PARENTS

*They are the source of
my striving for truth and spirituality.*

Dr. Shalom Srebrenik

In honor of my outstanding friend, who is involved in great works in the field of kiruv rechokim, R' Shalom Srebrenik.

Many Blessings!

It was my honor to read your inspiring manuscript. I delved into the sources as much as time allowed, and I have not found anything contradictory to the thoughts of our Sages. Furthermore, it was also obvious to me that you have endeavored to provide illumination based on the reliable sources of Chazal, Rishonim and Achronim. I must also tell you that I am apprehensive about the phraseology being in psychologic terminology, but I know that your intentions by this are to attract many of those who do not understand another language. Therefore, I cannot but bless you that Hashem will ensure the success of your undertakings henceforth, to enlighten many to the truth of our Torah.

May it be His will that the words of the Rambam will be speedily fulfilled. "Torah has promised that at the end of exile Israel will repent, and immediately, they will be redeemed."

With love and great respect,

י"ט אדר תשנ"א לפ"ק, Gateshead

לכבוד ידי"נ גדול המזכה את הרבים הר"ר שלום שליט"א,

I have read your manuscript from cover to cover and must tell you how impressed I have been not only by the clarity of presentation by which the most profound thoughts become simple ideas but also by the broad scope of subjects that you manage to cover within its chapters.

I also want to compliment you on the magnificent way in which you have managed to project the undiluted Torah viewpoint as the only answer to the problems of our times. This work by its very nature calls for secular sources to be quoted comprehensively—you have skillfully refuted and rejected all those that challenge Torah concepts and have succeeded admirably in presenting only conclusions that concur entirely with the teachings of our Sages.

In your introduction you describe your work as a Torah psychology book. This is truly an understatement, for it is a lot more than that. This is a handbook for the proper development of the personality based on authentic Torah sources, a veritable mussar sefer—a "Chovos Halevavos" in the modern scientific language, so well articulated that the simplest layman can study it, comprehend it and eventually succeed in molding his character to become a true Torah personality.

May this book help to expand the inspiring successes of your kiruv program by providing you with a much enlarged audience to benefit from your herculean efforts להגדיל תורה ולהאדירה.

הכו"ח בידידות נאמנה לכבוד המצוה הגדולה של זכוי—ומצדיקי הרבים ככוכבים לעולם ועד.

ממית חיים בולמאן

בע"ה אייר תשנ"א

"והנפש לא תמלא"

"And the soul is not fulfilled."

The anguish of contemporary existence drives many to psychologists and psychiatrists, who generally view the soul as a function of biology-emotion-reason, not as G-d-given and independent. Their axiology is "faith-oriented" on a secular-humanist world view, despite the pretense of scientific objectivity.

Their data base and technique seem compellingly impressive. Their results largely fall short of the promise envisioned.

Torah-psychology, by contrast, has not been given formal systematic exposition, despite the depth of its truthfulness and power. Nor has it found expression in a current idiom, or encountered prevalent psychological theory and practice—though many cry out for the healing of Torah in their travail of soul.

Judith Mishell and Shalom Srebrenik have collaborated in a massive study on the subject.

It is the hope of the undersigned that their effort will be both path blazer and beacon in lighting up the road of Torah-healing and guidance for our present travail.

Their Torah sources are painstakingly researched and faithfully applied against a background of superb credentials in the knowledge and practice of contemporary psychology.

The authors have given their exposition on G-d, Torah, soul, freedom-of-will; the elemental, social, religious, transcendent levels of souls and their elevation from rung to rung; the practical application of Torah psychology to life. Felicity and grace of style are accompanied by precise and clear diagrammatic models.

The entire work breathes rich learning and reverence. Many will be its grateful beneficiaries. It is a moving testament to the words of our prayer: "אלוקי נשמה שנתת בי טהורה היא, My Lord, the soul you have placed in me is pure."

הכותב למען כבוד התורה

נחמן בולמן

ACKNOWLEDGMENT

I am profoundly grateful to *Hakadosh Boruch Hu* for bringing me to Torah and giving me the opportunity and *koach* to write this book. My heartfelt prayer is that the book will help others to see that Torah is the source of the most profound insights into the human personality.

I am also deeply grateful to my beloved husband Don for his unflagging support and dedication. He has generously and selflessly provided all my needs so that I could devote myself to research and writing over the past five years.

Special thanks to Dr. Shalom Srebrenik for the very great privilege and pleasure of working with him. This book is based on his brilliant model of the soul/psyche and his penetrating insights into Torah. From his wellspring of creativity come most of the metaphors, parables, and analyses contained within. My life has been immeasurably enriched by my contact with him and his wife Eliana, whose life teaches the meaning of *chessed*.

I want to express my abiding gratitude to Rabbi Nachman Bulman for his support and encouragement throughout the writing of this book. At a time when he was plagued by ill health, he somehow managed to read the final manuscript and make many sensitive suggestions and substantive emendations.

Thanks also to Liz Danziger, whose encouragement, lucid thought, and gentle but incisive editing contributed enormously to this work. Liz taught me the craft of putting a book together. She deserves the credit for whatever stylistic grace and clarity can be found in the writing, but where grace and clarity are lacking, the reader can assume that she was not consulted.

A particular note of thanks goes to my "technical advisors" Judd Magilnick, Charlie Kaufman, and Robert Lipman. They set up equipment, installed programs, and patiently "walked me through" commands when I couldn't get the computer to cooperate. With their patient help the computer became my friend rather than my enemy. In addition, Judd generously allowed me to use his more advanced equipment to expedite the final editing and printing of the manuscript.

I want to thank Ziva Rifkind, Ph.D., for the many hours she devoted to painstakingly translating Hebrew manuscripts into English. And, also, Miriam Samsonovitz, for taking time out of her harried schedule to translate passages for me whenever I was in Israel.

Thanks also to Rabbi Mordechai Plaut who kindly allowed me to use his computer when I was in Israel, and to Ellene Newman for her assistance with the graphics I used while writing.

Very special thanks to the staff at CIS Publishers whose

time and talents turned the manuscript into a handsome book—to Rabbi Yaakov Yosef Reinman and Raizy Kaufman for their enthusiastic encouragement; to Chaya Bleier who did an excellent job coordinating the countless details involved in executing the production of the book; and to Deenee Cohen for her clean, crisp design, which both clarified and beautified the book.

Last, but not least, I want to thank Rabbi Avraham Marmorstein for his perceptive final editing. His astute eye discerned the inconsistencies and rough "seams" that had crept in after many years of work. His intelligent revisions ironed out the rough spots and improved the overall quality of the book.

Judith F. Mishell
March, 1992

ACKNOWLEDGMENT

I want to thank the rabbanim whose encouragement and dedication helped me develop the model on which this book is based. Over a period of many years, Rabbi Shlomo Fisher, Rabbi Moshe Shapira, Rabbi Shlomo Wolbe and Rabbi Dov Yaffe gave me deep instruction on the meaning of the sources. Without their continuing and very intensive guidance, this book, which is a translation of a profoundly religious model into practical terms, could never have been realized.

I also want to thank Chanah Katz, who worked for many years researching the sources and helping me develop the model.

Words are inadequate to thank my wife Eliana. She inspires me, evokes my sensitivity and makes my work possible.

Thanks also to Don Mishell, whose support of this project has taken the form of trips to Israel so that Judy and

I could work on the book, for the transportation, middle of the night breakfasts, editing, faxing and mailing.

But finally, this book had to be written. After developing the model, I still had to find a person with three particular attributes: Torah observant psychologist who could write. Without Judy Mishell's devotion and belief in my dream that this book was worthwhile it would still only be an idea in my head. I thank her for the many years of work in writing and the hours of research and revisions and the thousands of miles traveled . . . and now I am dreaming of the next book.

Shalom Srebrenik
April 1992

THE LADDER OF THE DIVINE SOUL

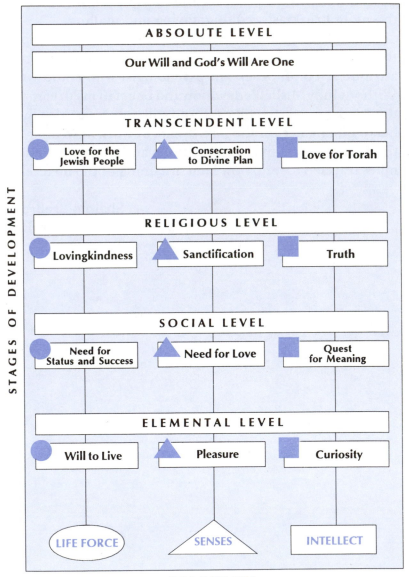

TABLE OF CONTENTS

THE SOCIAL LEVEL

THE RELIGIOUS LEVEL

THE HIGHER LEVELS

AFTERWORD

APPENDICES

INTRODUCTION

T he secular world around us is plagued by increasingly serious problems, and no one seems to know why. Drug abuse is at an all-time high, despite drug education programs and highly publicized deaths attributable to drug use. Divorce, with its aftermath of broken-hearted, confused children, shatters approximately fifty percent of marriages.

The streets are not safe, and even being at home can be dangerous (approximately twenty-five percent of households were touched by crime in 1984). The number of teenage pregnancies is alarmingly high, producing a bumper crop of babies, many of whom will not receive the nurturing, nutrition or education necessary to lead productive lives.

Amidst unprecedented affluence and

comfort, many people feel empty, alienated, dissatisfied and unhappy. They desperately search for "highs," thrills and excitement to fill the emptiness of life lived without purpose and meaning.

WHAT WENT WRONG?

What went wrong in the brave new world? Why are the young dying of drug overdoses? Why are marriage and family life so unstable? Why are elaborate security procedures necessary to prevent violation of person and property? These evils can fairly be attributed to some of our society's widely-held views. Here are ten of the assumptions on which that world view is based:

1. The world is a chance phenomenon; it exists with no plan or design.
2. There are no absolute rights and wrongs.
3. Truth is in the eye of the observer; truth is, therefore, relative and does not exist in "absolute reality."
4. Human beings are merely a link in the evolutionary chain; they are not of divine origin, and they do not have any particular purpose.
5. People have inherent rights, and the world is obligated to fulfill them.
6. Human behavior is determined by genetics and conditioning; therefore, people are not responsible for their behavior.
7. All phenomena can ultimately be explained and controlled by science.
8. Being happy is the most important thing in life.

9. Freedom means having as many options as possible.
10. If there is a God, His existence has nothing to do with the way the affairs of men are conducted.

These ten assumptions have been repeated so often and with such authority in professional and lay publications and by the mass media that they seem to be unquestionably true. They organize and guide public policy and action, and they have become part of the common consciousness. If any of these assumptions ring true for you, it is because almost everyone in our society has internalized them as truth.

It is the contention of this book that these assumptions are incorrect, and that belief in them and action based on them inevitably leads to the kinds of problems which exist in the world today. I further contend that if you accept these assumptions as true and use them as guidelines for your decisions, you may be ruining your life. I make this claim on the basis of personal and professional experiences, and with the support of a body of wisdom which has existed and been effective for thousands of years.

The foundation for this entire book is the ancient but very relevant wisdom found in the Torah. Torah, a word which I will be using frequently, includes both the Written Torah, or Five Books of Moses (Genesis, Exodus, Leviticus, Numbers and Deuteronomy), and the Oral Torah,*which is the oral transmission from generation to generation.

It is a principle of this position that the Torah is of Divine origin. The Torah contains profound insights into the very essence of the universe and life. It answers the fundamental

---

* After the destruction of the Second Temple the Jews were dispersed, and the oral transmission process could no longer be assured. Therefore, the Oral Torah was written down in the Talmud (*Mishnah* and *Gemara*).

ontological questions which men have been asking for centuries: What is the origin of the universe? What is the origin of life? Does life have a purpose, or is it all a meaningless void? If there is a purpose, what is it? What is the best way to live in order to fulfill that purpose?

The world view that emerges from studying Torah is radically different from the currently accepted world view described above. To begin with, its fundamental, unifying principle is that there is one omnipotent, omniscient, living God. The second principle is that God created the universe and everything in it. The third principle is that the entire universe, including human life, was created by God with plan and purpose. Nothing is random. The fourth principle is that the entire universe was created as an arena in which human beings could face the challenges of spiritual elevation. This challenge is the purpose of creation. The fifth principle is that the God-given Torah contains all the information we need to be able to fulfill His purpose.

This book is focused on the spiritual and psychological insights found in the Torah. Its purpose is to provide information on the psychological benefits of living in accord with God's plan. The book is about God's view of human nature and the ultimate spiritual and psychological development of the human personality. It is about the Torah system, which teaches us how to achieve inner integrity by living in harmony with our deepest needs.

The Torah system has worked for its adherents around the globe for thousands of years. Every generation which has lived according to Torah principles has reaped the benefits of stable families, outstanding intellectual achievements and exemplary moral behavior.

There are, of course, problems among Torah-observant

Jews; problems are part of human life. Without problems we couldn't fulfill our purpose in life of improving our characters by facing the challenges inherent in living and making choices. Some of our problems come from exposure to the secular world, and to the extent that secular ideas and life styles infiltrate Torah society, we suffer the same problems as secular society, for example, a rising divorce rate. Other problems result from our interaction with secular society; we can be tormented by conflict between secular and Torah values. Another reason for problems in Torah life is that, since we are in exile, Torah is veiled and the full power and beauty of Torah life is attenuated. We don't have a complete Torah society, and we cannot elicit the full potential of Torah Judaism.

But there are major differences between the problems of Torah Jews and those of other people. One of the differences lies in the types of problems encountered. The Torah world is not ripped apart by drug abuse, promiscuity, crime and broken families. One may hear about the breakdown of a Torah family, but not of the Torah family system.

The differences exist because the Torah provides consistent ethical guidelines for living, and because character training is an essential part of Torah education. Secular society, on the other hand, lacks a coherent ethical framework for problem solving and thus produces an endless array of "solutions" which lead to new sets of problems. The "me" generation has been replaced by the "no" generation which will be replaced by whatever "seat of the pants" solution emerges next. This trial-and-error approach leaves enormous human suffering in its wake.

In fact, many of the problems which do exist in the Torah world come from imitating the values of the secular world.

When Jews abandon Torah, or alter Torah values and laws to suit their convenience, they end up with the same kinds of problems found in the societies they copy. The only thing that distinguishes Jews and Jewish society is living according to Torah.

The Torah system has integrity. It does not change according to fad and fancy or according to the whims of charismatic leaders. The Torah's cohesive world view and code of behavior have been a rudder to the Jewish people in the violently stormy seas of history. They have been a wellspring of renewal for Jews during their darkest days. The awesome power of the Torah system can be seen from the fact that the Torah and the Jewish people have survived and transcended the best efforts of those who have attempted to eradicate them.

Of course, there may be some secularized Jews who have concluded that Torah Judaism is not for them. Perhaps they, or their parents, or their grandparents, rejected Torah Judaism long ago because it seemed hopelessly obsolete and completely irrelevant to modern life. Torah Judaism seemed to be a life hemmed in by meaningless rituals and stifling restrictions. It seemed that life could be better without it. Instead of following rules, one could make one's own decisions. If one chose to, one could taste all the pleasures of the world; the only guide one needed was the rational mind. If the human mind could not find a rational reason to do or not do something, then why do or not do it?

In fact, there certainly is good reason *not* to follow the dictates of the so-called rational mind. In our culture, we have a belief in the supremacy of the rational mind, but this belief may be irrational itself. In his book *The Mind's New Science*, the renowned cognitive psychologist Howard

Gardner concludes that human beings do not approach complex cognitive processes "in a manner that can be characterized as logical or rational . . ."[1] Our conclusions, which usually seem so "right" to us, are often *not very logical and rational at all.* To use a computer metaphor, the solution is only as good as the program and the data provided. Our programs are imprecise and biased, and our data is often flawed and almost always incomplete. Who can say they know all there is to know about the simplest things, much less about the fundamental questions of life?

When we try to be rational about our own lives we face two major cognitive problems: We are particularly subject to bias when dealing with emotionally charged topics; and we all have blindspots about ourselves. This is why it is so important to set aside, at least during the time you are reading this book, the idea that you already "know" about Judaism and about the Torah system. Perhaps you do, but there may be much more that you need to learn. I know this from my own experiences.

MY OWN EXPERIENCES

I am Jewish, but the Judaism I knew as a child created more problems for me than it solved. My early experiences with religion were empty and shallow. There was no Torah learning, no warm glow of *Shabbos* candles, no enticing smell of *challah* baking in the oven, no joyous meals in a *Sukkah*. I went to the synagogue only on the High Holidays and did not understand the significance of the holidays or one word of the services. I attended *bar-mitzvahs* and *bat-mitzvahs* where all that seemed to matter was the "show" (the elegance of the hall, the amount of food, the band and the new clothes). I was told that being Jewish meant that I was better than non-Jews, but what it meant to me was that there was an invisible wall between me and my dearest friend (who was Christian). And it meant to me that I had to feel a little guilty and alien when we sang Christmas carols in school.

Gradually, over many years, I became more and more atheistic, finally disavowing "organized religion" entirely and becoming a devout secular humanist. In time, I became a clinical psychologist. I have been engaged in the practice of psychology for twenty years. I became a psychologist because I was intrigued with the human mind and personality and because, for as long as I can remember, I have wished to have a good life and to help others to do so. For more than two decades I have struggled to understand human nature and behavior. I have tried to be conversant with every theory of personality, every method of therapy and every avenue of change which promised beneficial results.

I grew up during the period when psychological thought seemed to permeate the air. I remember going to movies as a child and seeing scenes in which therapists, by the use of techniques such as word-association, uncovered the deep, dark secrets of a person's psyche. Miracle cures ensued. Bad boys became heroes, strange people became normal, and everyone lived happily ever after. The lesson was: Problems are caused by cruel mistreatment or terrible living conditions. Problems are cured by giving people an opportunity to explore and express their innermost experiences. People are not to blame for their problems, and hence they are not responsible for them or their consequences.

This was extrapolated to the prevention of the ordinary problems of ordinary people by the following logic: If therapy can cure such serious problems, then applying its methods to child rearing, education and relationships in general will prevent psychological damage. I didn't see the flaw in the logic at the time, but I now understand that it was like concluding that since radiation therapy is effective in treating cancer, a good way to prevent cancer is to have an X-ray every week.

PSYCHOLOGY AS THE NEW WORLD RELIGION

From what I read and saw and heard, psychology seemed to be the way to save the world. And as far as I could see, the world really needed saving. Everywhere I looked, there were problems, some on a global scale, some much closer to home. Looking back on my life, it seems inevitable that I would have turned to psychology in search of personal and social redemption. For redemption no longer seemed possible through religion; man's great new hope was the "science" of psychology.

It seems that as the psychological world view waxed, the religious world view waned. Freud and his psychological heirs had produced a revolution in the way people thought. People now viewed life from a psychological rather than a religious perspective. In fact, psychology had become the religion of the Western world, and psychologists had become its high priests. The language of psychology was woven into everyday speech, and even people who never set foot inside a therapist's office used psychological jargon. People talked about repression, complexes and defense mechanisms as if these concepts had intrinsic reality rather than being terms to describe processes of questionable validity.

Throughout my lifetime, psychology has remained in vogue. During the two decades that I have been practicing psychology, many psychological "change methods" have been spawned, each of which held out the promise of a better life. I have tried many of those approaches, both for personal growth and for application in my work. Every path, though exciting and promising at first, proved to be ultimately unsatisfying. Each approach emphasized one or, at most, a few aspects of existence, but ignored many others. Though each was effective to a limited extent, the overall price paid for the gain was too high.

When attention was focused on self (self-fulfillment, self-expression, self-esteem), relationships with others often deteriorated. When relationships were emphasized, personal growth and development often suffered. Behavioral methods left out feelings, analytic approaches left out behavior, and both approaches left out values. Somehow, even though I was living at the cutting edge of the mental health movement, my life and the lives of many of my clients and friends felt incomplete. There was a distinct feeling that something very important was missing from our lives.

I searched assiduously for an answer within the promised land of psychology. There was often an initial feeling that I had found "the answer," and I had the thrill of exhilaration that goes with challenge and accomplishment. I learned a great deal, but time and time again, I came to the conclusion that I still did not have "the answer." A nagging doubt gnawed away at me. Maybe, as one therapist had told me, there was no "answer." Even though I got discouraged, I never gave up completely. A restless stirring deep inside propelled me, and I thought, "I have to keep searching. There must be more."

I have written this book because there is more. I finally

found a way of life that has brought me the kind of deep satisfaction and peace of mind I sought. I have been on the same path for more than ten years, and there are no signs that it will prove to be a temporary and ultimately unsatisfying "high." Rather, there is an ever-expanding sense of infinite potential for growth and enrichment. There is constant intellectual, psychological and spiritual challenge, and the benefits of meeting the challenges are cumulatively deepening and fulfilling. My life is immeasurably better, and my work is more gratifying and more effective.

THE EXCITEMENT OF MY DISCOVERY

What did I find? What could possibly be so powerful? Much to my own amazement, I found Torah Judaism.* How could this be? How could Torah Judaism be so startlingly new and revealing to me? Why had I never considered it before? Why, in all my searching, had I not heard of the awesome power, nay the magic, of Torah?

I, who had turned to Zen when I began to sense that my quest was a spiritual, not a psychological one, had never considered "trying" Judaism. I was blinded by my belief that I knew what Judaism was. I thought that I had "tried" it while I was growing up, but soon after I started learning and living Torah I realized that I had been completely ignorant of what

---

* I am deeply grateful to Rabbi Daniel Lapin of the Pacific Jewish Center for the time and energy he devoted to establishing a Torah community in which *baalei teshuvah* could be nurtured. He opened the door to Torah for me, and helped me to appreciate the splendor that lay beyond. Thanks also to Rabbi Avraham Chaim Lapin *zatzal*, whose *mussar shiurim* added another dimension to my undertaking of Torah.

Torah Judaism really is. As I gradually opened to the radically different view of life that emerged from the study of Torah, I began to see a unifying theme in the world which made sense of things that had seemed incomprehensible before. And as I incorporated more and more Torah into my way of living, I began to experience a sense of balance and clarity of direction that brought me peace of mind.

When I began to be aware of the profound changes occurring in me, another staggering insight came to me. Torah Judaism was doing for me (and my Torah observant friends) what I had for so long believed only psychology could do. I was finally achieving the "mental health" goals which had eluded me for so long. I realized that I had found a remarkably profound source of psychological knowledge and a healing way of life.

MY PATH TO A TORAH PSYCHOLOGY

As a psychologist, I wanted very much to understand what was happening to me. I had many questions. What was helping me to change in such a positive way? Could I incorporate these effective change methods into my work? Was it even legitimate to try to practice psychology within a Torah framework? If so, what modifications, if any, would be necessary in order to apply Torah insights in a psychological setting?

I have been working on answering these questions for ten years. My work has taken the form of integrating and applying the psychological insights found in Torah to the problems-in-living faced by all people. I have found the methods to be very effective and to have wide applicability. The name given to this approach is Torah psychology.

This Torah psychology book was written for those who want to live life with a sense of balance and proportion, who want to face life's inevitable challenges with a clear sense of direction, who want to experience peace of mind and self-fulfillment, and who want harmonious relationships. It is for those who want to live in such a way that they can feel true self-respect and self-esteem, rather than living in a way that produces self-contempt. It is my way of saying, "Don't despair. There *is* more."

But why should you listen to what I say? Many people claim to have found answers to the big questions of life. The fact that I am a psychologist with a great deal of experience tells you nothing about the validity of what I say. Many other psychologists with a great deal of experience disagree vehemently with me. I told you a little about myself only so that you could form some impression of my credibility as a filter for the truth. What I say is important and valid only if it is true. All I do in this book is to transmit Torah teachings and add our* applications of Torah to living and emotional well-being.

This is not a step-by-step "how-to" book. It does not provide easy answers, but it does open up new horizons and lay out a path to follow.

May I start by asking you to accompany me on a hypothetical journey via a parable whose idiom is religious but whose application is universal? Consider the following story:

> Three men were doing the same work on a construction project. A visitor to the construction site asked the first man what he was doing. The worker said that he was hammering

* The plural personal references refer to Dr. Srebrenik and myself.

nails in boards. The visitor then asked the second worker what he was doing. This worker said that he was making the frame for a building. The visitor then asked the third worker what he was doing. The third worker said that he was constructing a synagogue for the glory of God.

How do you see your life now? Are you hammering nails in boards, just getting through each day, putting one foot in front of the other, killing time? Or are you making a frame? If so, you know that your life must have some purpose, but you are not sure what the purpose is. Or are you constructing a synagogue for the glory of God? In other words, are you living your life in such a way that every moment has meaning, every word and every action is sanctified by being linked to the Eternal?

The way you answer these questions is one of the most important determinants of your mental, physical and spiritual well-being. If you reduce all your activities to the mundane level, you rob your life of purpose and significance. The meaning you ascribe to your life has a profound impact on how you are affected by everything that happens to you. The same set of circumstances can be demeaning or uplifting, discouraging or motivating, joyous or boring, a burden or a blessing.

But, we might ask, how does acting for the glory of God give our lives meaning? Does God need our glorification? What does it do for us? The parable of the King and the simple man can help us to understand this.

Once upon a time there was a King of extraordinary wisdom and kindness. His strength and abilities were unlimited. All his subjects longed to be close to him, to learn from him, and to win his favor.

The generous King wanted to bestow the greatest possible kindness on his subjects, so he decided to go to the simplest person in his kingdom and ask him what he wanted. The man said he wanted children, health, wealth, wisdom and permission to visit the King and be enriched by his wisdom.

"I grant you this, but I can think of even more," the King said. "I want you to become my partner, second only to me. I will crown you and you will sit beside me, and together we will rule the kingdom."

The simple man fainted, but when he was revived he said, "My dear King, I appreciate the great honor you bestow upon me, but I cannot accept your offer. If I sit beside you I will be overcome with shame because of my ignorance and insignificance. The crown is not an honor for me because I have not earned it and do not deserve it."

"You are right," the King said, "but I will give you a training program that will prepare you for the honor. If you successfully complete the training, you will have earned the honor."

The King brought the man to the palace and showed him the royal treasures and the Book of Wisdom. The man was filled with such delight that he never wanted to leave the palace, but the King explained to him that in order to earn the honor of sitting beside the King, he would have to leave and go back and train himself for his great duty.

In the meantime, the King would go far away to another palace hidden in a cave. Only the man would know where the King was. The man would have the job of revealing the hiding place of the King to the world, and if he succeeded, he would have earned the right to sit beside the King and rule.

The King warned the man that the journey would not be an easy one. There would be many tests of his courage;

people would ridicule him and tell him that the King never existed or that he had deserted him. Many seductive temptations would be placed in his path. There would also be many obstacles to overcome. "But I have designed every difficulty to train you for your mission. Every difficulty is tailored to you, so with every one that you overcome, you have made yourself more worthy of sitting beside me."

The King gave the man three things to help him stick to the task: a training system, the Book of Wisdom and the *memory* of the delight of being in the palace. By following the training system and studying the Book of Wisdom, the man's memory would be enhanced. Again and again, he would feel a little of the delight and his longing would be intensified, thus giving him the strength and courage to meet the challenges before him.

In this parable, the "simple man" is the soul. Its job is to urge us to keep seeking the hidden "King" in spite of the obstacles along the way. If we stay on the path, we can reach the "palace" and elevate ourselves to a position of honor and delight. The "King" does not need us to serve him, but he gives us the opportunity to earn the ultimate good by training us to be like him.

Absorbing the information presented here requires an open mind and an open heart. You have to be like a sponge that is damp enough to absorb water—not like one that is so dry that the water runs off the surface, and not like one so saturated that there is no capacity for more. If you either already believe, or can entertain as a working hypothesis the idea that God exists, that there is a Divine plan, and that living according to His plan might be a good idea, you are open to the message in this book. In order to derive benefit from this or any other book, you have to be receptive to its fundamental principles. If your heart and mind can unfold to new possibilities, if you think that there just might be helpful insights to be learned from Torah Judaism, read on!

CHAPTER 1

Beyond Psychotherapy: Going to the Source

We can call God the "ultimate psychologist" because as our Creator He knows us best. Only He, with His Divine perspective, knows the deepest needs of our souls. And only He, as Creator of the universe, has a comprehensive view of not only the spiritual, but also the psychological, physical, social and political factors which affect us.

We are very fortunate that God not only created us but also gave us an "instruction manual" for life, a manual complete with the most penetrating psychological and spiritual insights. This instruction manual is the Torah. In the Torah we have all the information we need to live in a way that is harmonious with our divine essence and which enables us to satisfy our deepest needs. In fact, it is only by living in accordance with the eternal wisdom of Torah that we can find real satisfaction and develop to our highest potential.

If the idea of living strictly in accordance with Torah sounds too limiting, please consider the following: If you were presented with a complicated piece of technology with which you were completely unfamiliar, such as a VCR or a computer, would you be better off learning how to use it by trial and error or by carefully reading the manual?

I once had a friend who felt sure he knew how to assemble his expensive new stereo equipment. He thought it would take too long to read the manual, and he was impatient to listen to music. He removed all the components from the cartons, carefully discarding packing materials, setting aside little bags of screws and cutting off the "rubber band" which was holding the turntable in place. He then assembled the components, and with eager excitement, he plugged it in and turned it on. The power indicator light went on.

Thinking everything was in order he selected his favorite record, placed it gently on the turntable and pushed the button to activate the turntable. To his dismay, nothing happened. After checking the wiring, he tried again, but still, the turntable didn't turn. Full of indignation, he called the owner of the stereo shop, who said he would send a serviceman over as soon as possible. When the serviceman arrived the next day he could tell at a glance what went wrong. It seems that the "rubber band" that my friend had cut off the turntable was actually the drive mechanism. My friend was lucky. The part was replaceable, and all he had to do was pay the bill for parts and service, and then he was able to enjoy his new stereo.

When it comes to our precious lives, trial and error can be exorbitantly expensive. Not all parts are replaceable, and not all damage can be repaired. For example, the cost in human terms of trying to figure out by trial and error how to have a successful marriage is staggering. And the divorce rate tells us that after decades of promising "breakthroughs" in relationships—such as open marriage, fair fighting, gender role equality—we still haven't figured it out. The cost to the divorced couple, the pain of disappointment, failure, loss and loneliness, is great. To children, however, the cost is overwhelming.[1] To them, the parents are an indivisible unit, and the home is inviolable. Can a child whose secure world is split apart by divorce ever fully recover from the wrenching shock? I think not. No one can afford the untold suffering inflicted by divorce.

TORAH DOES NOT FEEL CONSTRICTIVE

It may sound strange to some readers, but I have discovered to my own amazement and delight that living according to the manual for life, the Torah, is not constricting at all. Just as great music soars and stirs the soul when it is performed by an orchestra in which the musicians subordinate their individual virtuosity to the demands of the score and the conductor, we human beings live with the greatest joy and harmony when we subordinate our impulses and drives to the demands of higher goals. What happens in an orchestra if the first violinist decides to display his own talents by playing Paganini while everyone else is playing Mozart? It sounds terrible. Similarly, we are likely to destroy the harmony of our own lives if we live without an overall plan.

Living according to Torah means that we raise ourselves above the level of pure instinct; we become less like animals and more fully human. Instead of seeing ourselves as beings who evolved out of primordial slime, we see ourselves as beings intentionally created according to a divine plan. Instead of the "existential angst" and alienation that go with believing that life is meaningless and absurd, we have the serenity and connectedness that go with knowing how meaningful and precious life is. This is what Torah psychology provides.

Any personality theory which is not derived directly from Torah is nothing more than a speculation about the human mind by the human mind. Such theories are bound to be deficient because the human mind is not capable of fully knowing itself. We think we are aware of ourselves, but the deep roots of our motivation are hidden from us. Many psychologists have recognized this and attempted to explain the "unconscious" forces operating within us. Most of them have failed to include the awesome, uplifting power of the soul as part of the "unconscious." To see the "unconscious" roots of our behavior as nothing more than a cesspool of seething darkness degrades all of us—and it's not even true.

The Torah view of human nature goes far beyond the most positive secular psychological view. Even Abraham Maslow, who made a real contribution to psychology by being one of the first personality theorists to focus on healthy growth and development rather than focusing on sickness, was unable to fully conceive the greatness within each of us. In his book *Toward a Humanistic Biology*,[2] Dr. Maslow introduces the idea of studying the "good specimen" in order to promote superior development. In many of his other works, e.g., *Toward a Psychology of Being*,[3] he discusses the concept of self-actualization. Self-actualizers are people who, having satisfied their basic needs, have gone on to try to satisfy higher needs (metaneeds). Dr. Maslow noted that people not committed to metaneeds seem to fall prey to meaninglessness or the "existential vacuum." In studies of self-actualizers, Maslow found that they were, without exception, devoted to a calling beyond themselves. In his article *The Farther Reaches of Human Nature*,[4] Dr. Maslow talks about a "fourth force" in psychology, a force that goes beyond behaviorism, freudianism and humanism. This fourth force is "transhumanistic psychology" which deals with transcendent experiences and transcendent values.

It is clear that Maslow was trying to understand the spark of the Divine in the human being when he arrived at the conclusion that there was a "fourth force" at work in the human psyche. But even his "self-actualized" human being is at a very low level of development compared to the "actualized" Torah personality which I will describe in the coming chapters.

What is missing in Maslow's view? Why was there a ceiling on his view of human potential? Why did the true greatness of man elude him? He failed to grasp man's true potential because he limited his view to the "good specimens" produced by secular living. Maslow's "self-actualizers" are indeed good examples of the best that can be produced by a secular world view, but the Torah world view has produced many more refined, elevated and insightful personalities. A good example of such a personality is Rabbi Moshe Feinstein. People who encountered him describe every aspect of his rich and multi-faceted personality in superlatives. They saw him as possessing spiritual grandeur, incredible wisdom, boundless compassion, great generosity and unshakable faith. We must look to men like "Reb Moshe" if we want to know what men can be.

Maslow's view of human potential fell short because he believed that man's higher, transcendent nature evolved from his biological nature, not from a Divine source.[5] He made the mistake of studying an organism detached from the real source of its motivation. We have a wonderful analogy in the behavior of the termite or white ant. After ten years of study, the scientist, poet and scholar Eugene N. Marais concluded that

> the power of the queen [termite] is the mainspring of the collective activity of the soldiers and workers. The queen is the psychological center of the community; she is the brain of the organism which we call a termitary.[6]

While the queen is alive each termite performs its role perfectly. A drop of sand at a time, the termite community constructs an amazingly complex termitary complete with shafts which penetrate as deeply as sixty-five feet into the earth and towers which reach up to forty feet high. Given the size of the termite, this is comparable to a skyscraper as high as the Matterhorn (14,760 feet high) built by human hand. What happens if the queen is killed? "Immediately the whole community ceases to work; destroy or remove her and their activity is at an end."[7]

It would be absolutely futile to try to fathom the behavior of individual termites or the community of termites without knowing the power of the queen; yet this is exactly the error that secular psychologists make when they try to comprehend human behavior without knowing the powers of the divine soul. Human nature cannot be understood without an acknowledgment of the divine soul and its connection with God.

The more I studied Torah and continued my practice of the science of psychology, the more I came to believe that psychology was not answering the world's problems because of a basic deficiency. It was trying to understand life without acknowledging the real source of life. To really understand and serve mankind, psychology must acknowledge God and turn to His Torah for the truth about the nature of man. It must see man as a spark of the Divine and strive to understand the awesome powers of the soul in man. Psychology must deal with what man could and should be, not only with what man is. We cannot know our true potential without knowing the Torah view of man.

Let's try a little experiment to illustrate the point that certain aspects of our existence can be beyond our grasp. Look around the room you are in and notice all the colors. Notice the reds and greens and blues and yellows and blacks and whites, and all the blends, such as turquoise, pink, orange and brown. Now imagine someone born without color vision. He can see perfectly, but he sees in black and white. Can you explain color to him? Can he ever experience the pleasure you feel when you stand in a rose garden and marvel at the array of reds, pinks and corals?

The divine dimension is like color, and the human mind is like a black and white receiver with a "port" for a color adapter. Torah is our color adapter. With Torah we can tune into the divine channel; with it, we can see the spiritual colors of the universe. Without Torah, the divine dimension is off the scale of what the human mind can accurately perceive. Without Torah, we may have the illusion of seeing it all, but we are missing most of the beauty.

Because of the limits of the human mind, non-Torah personality theories contain, at best, a bit of the truth; none of them are comprehensive. All are fragments of the total picture of what it is to be human, fragments defined and delineated by the particular human mind which formulated the theory. Each theory distorts the human being by assuming that a narrow band of the complete psyche dominates the personality. In these theories, personality development is viewed from the perspective of how the person handles the central theme, e.g., pleasure or power-seeking. In other words, man-made theories are like filters which let in only a small part of the already limited black and white picture. It's not surprising, then, that they frequently contradict each other.

Let's see what happens if we try to follow the advice of three well-known contemporary mental health experts. We'll start with Garth Wood, a psychiatrist. In his book *The Myth of Neurosis: Overcoming the Illness Excuse*,[8] Wood states that a basic error is being made by psychiatry in extending the boundaries of mental illness to include normal life problems and problems of morality. He proposes a new approach to these problems which he calls "moral therapy." In essence his proposal is that friends, family and clergy help people discover and live in accordance with their own value systems.

Although Dr. Wood sees the problem clearly, he ends up in a moral morass because his solution depends on the presence of an internalized value system shared with members of the society. Dr. Wood states that his approach will work because our civilization tends to produce a "relatively uniform morality, commonly known as the Judeo-Christian ethic. We may differ on specific issues, but most of our consciences are relatively the same." *(Insight, Dec. 1, 1986)*

But, Dr. Wood, what happens when the "Judeo-Christian" ethic is no longer being taught? Many parents and teachers have abandoned the teaching of ethics, and children are left to formulate their own value systems—if they want to. There is no uniform moral code, and there are vast differences of opinion on every issue. Obviously, we need another "expert" opinion.

Behaviorist B. F. Skinner states that there is an "identity crisis" in psychology. He believes the problem is that psychologists mistakenly keep searching for internal determiners of behavior in spite of the fact that "no feeling or state of mind has ever been unambiguously identified."[9] Questions about these internal states "should never have been asked." Skinner believes that an organism's (including a person's) behavior can be better explained by studying external, physical events: stimulus, response and consequence; and he believes that treatment should take the form of modifying behavior via manipulation of these external events. In other words, never mind what we think or feel or value. All we need is to modify our behavior.

Since we are getting such conflicting advice from Dr. Wood and Dr. Skinner, let us turn to someone who disagrees with both of them. Unlike Dr. Skinner, psychologist Albert Ellis believes in internal events. In fact, he believes that the internal events called "beliefs" are the primary determining factors in mental health; rational beliefs lead to good mental health and irrational beliefs lead to poor mental health. Rather than doing what Dr. Wood recommends, which is helping people to live according to their own values, Dr. Ellis teaches them to identify their irrational beliefs and to replace them with rational ones.

His basis for what is and is not rational is, of course, his own system of beliefs. According to Dr. Ellis, "most clients are natural resisters who find it unusually hard to resist their resistances"[10] and think the way Dr. Ellis thinks. In an article entitled "The Impossibility of Achieving Consistently Good Mental Health" (originally presented at the 1986 APA Convention as winner of the 1986 APA Distinguished Professional Contributions to Knowledge Award), Dr. Ellis stated his belief that humans have a "strong biological tendency to needlessly and severely disturb themselves and to fight like hell against giving it up," thus making good mental health almost impossible "even when helped by the most efficient forms of psychotherapy."

Dr. Ellis doesn't seem to consider the possibility that there might be something wrong with the therapy, not with the people. Perhaps not everyone agrees with Dr. Ellis that "musts" and "shoulds" lead to mental distress. Perhaps what people naturally resist is accepting beliefs which they recognize to be untrue. Perhaps the therapy overlooks or even denies fundamental truths about human life. Perhaps a method which purports to be based exclusively on rationality and the scientific method fails to tap into the greatest source of potential for growth and change—the human instinct for spirituality.

What are we to do? We have three prominent, well-trained professionals giving us contradictory advice. Wood recommends that we look inside to discover our own morality and then live in accord with it; Skinner says we shouldn't bother about internal states of mind like feelings and values, we should just change our behavior; and Ellis tells us to change our internal state to match his. Whose advice are we to follow? Wood's? Skinner's? Ellis's? If we follow Wood's advice, how do we determine what our values are and if they are correct? If we follow Skinner's advice, what values will we use to select the desired behavioral goals? And if we follow Ellis's advice, what if we think a belief is rational and he doesn't? Do we then have to believe that we are "natural resisters" with a biological tendency to think irrationally?

This is just a small example of the inevitable confusion in the field of mental health. Inevitable because without the comprehensive divine perspective we wander endlessly in a maze that has no exit. Inevitable because although a given "change method" might be very powerful, it will be resisted if it is used to produce behavior which violates a person's basic sense of right and wrong. Inevitable because even with the best intentions and most honorable purpose it is impossible for human beings to see the human condition clearly.

We simply do not have a vantage point which gives us the whole picture and frees us from our human limits and personal biases. At best we can describe only a part of the whole: the world as seen by Wood, Skinner, Ellis, you or me. I would feel as pessimistic as Dr. Ellis if I thought there was nothing beyond the limits of human perception.

However, there *is* something beyond the human range. There is a cohesive framework for maximum spiritual and psychological development derived not from the human mind but from the infinite wisdom of the ultimate psychologist—God. This model of human personality development is based on the timeless truth given to us by God in the Torah. It provides us with a *comprehensive* view of human nature which includes the body, mind and emotions, as well as the divine soul and its development. Moral training and growth are seen as intrinsic and essential parts of personality development.

God created us. Only He has the divine perspective, and

only He can give us complete and correct guidelines for living. When we have questions about how to live our lives, whom else should we ask but the "ultimate psychologist"?

Free Will: Finding Yourself

Only one thing, one detail really constitutes "me," and that is the free will given by God to man. Free choice is what constitutes the self, the "I" in its entirety. Without this choice, the "self" does not exist.

T hese words by Rabbi Yechiel Michel Tucazinsky[1] sum up the Torah view of free will. Free will is a fundamental principle of Torah Judaism. The divine soul gives us the power to choose freely; with that power we shape our own lives. By making choices, we have a way to "give birth" to ourselves, to become the "self" we wish to be. This is a thrilling opportunity. We can make choices that elevate us or choices that degrade us.

Ruth is a young wife and mother whose choices illustrate how we can create our "selves." Ruth is a successful writer. She enjoys being a wife, mother and writer and finds her busy life very fulfilling. Her "busyness," however, led to a difficult dilemma.

The dilemma was that Ruth didn't feel she had enough time and energy left to be a daughter. Ruth has always been very close to her parents. They are both very devoted to her and her new family, and they take great pleasure in their little grandson. The problem is that Ruth often finds their calls and visits inconvenient. Sometimes, they call during the time she has set aside for writing during the baby's nap. At other times, she knows they would love a visit, but what she really wants to do is get a baby-sitter so she can catch up on her work.

Ruth is very grateful to her parents for all they have done for her (which she understands much better now that she is a parent), and she knows that her gratitude is meaningless if it is not expressed. Also, she considers it very important for her son to spend time with his grandparents. She finds herself in a very distressing conflict. On the one hand she thinks, "I have to get my work done. If I don't do it while the baby sleeps, I'll never get it done. If I have to spend every Sunday afternoon visiting, I will never catch up." On the other hand she thinks, "I owe my very life to my parents. They have always been good to me. I wouldn't have such a wonderful life today if they hadn't taken such good care of me. The least I can do is be gracious when they call and visit them on Sunday afternoon with the baby."

After an agonizing struggle between her desire for more time for work and her personal "truth," or moral conviction, that she should be good to her parents, Ruth made two choices: 1) to set aside time each week for a visit with her parents and 2) to discipline herself so that she doesn't sound abrupt or annoyed if they call at an inconvenient time. No matter how hurried she feels, she resolved to take a minute or two to greet them in a warm and friendly way and see how they are, before asking if she can call back later.

What kind of person does Ruth "give birth" to by making these choices? First, she earns self-respect. She can genuinely like the person she is creating, because that person lives according to truth rather than impulse. Second, but closely related to the first, she creates a person who is free of the self-contempt we feel when we violate our own moral codes. She creates a person who feels harmony and inner peace rather than discord. Third, she becomes a more loving and appreciative person, because our love and gratitude grow when they are expressed in deeds.

Ruth elevated her "self" by choosing to honor her parents actively. She created a very different "self" than she would have if she had chosen to neglect her parents. In order to do that she would have had to trespass on her own commitment to the truth and the values she tries to live by. If she did that she would either have to live with internal conflict or lower her standards to match her behavior. She would have become a less harmonious and loving person.

Ruth's resolution of her dilemma illustrates one of the main principles of free will: We exercise free will only when we make choices between the truth and what feels good because it fills some personal need, preference or value. Ruth believed that it was true that she should respect and honor her parents. Her need for success as a writer and her desire to spend more time writing competed with the demands of her truth. She chose her truth.

What happens when someone has a very flexible definition of truth? Let's say that Ruth believed that it was true that she *should* honor her parents, but not that she *must* honor them. In this case, her truth is defined so loosely that she is not doing anything wrong if she doesn't spend more time with them. It would just be better if she did. This definition of the truth is so loose that it can justify any course of action that feels good. At this point, however, Ruth runs into a problem. The "should" in her truth causes her to suffer guilt feelings. She can try to soothe any discomfort she feels by sending her parents gifts and cards on Mother's Day and Father's Day, sending them pictures of the baby and inviting them to the baby's birthday party.

But what if Ruth is too busy or just doesn't feel like taking time to remember her parents? If she follows her own flexible truth she will still be choosing, but if she decides to change the truth in order to relieve herself of guilt, she loses her power to choose. If she changes the truth to fit her needs— "It is true that I should honor my parents, but honor is just a feeling. I don't really have to do anything"—she nullifies her capacity for the exercise of free will. (For a fuller discussion of these principles, see Chapter 17.)

Let's look at the difference between a computer and a person. The computer is a machine with a memory (hardware). It needs a program (software) and data (input) in order to give results (output). Suppose that with exactly the same hardware, software and input, the output is different. One time $2 + 2 = 4$, and another time $2 + 2 = 5$. Could you forgive the computer? No! The computer is out-of-order. A computer has to follow the logic of its program. No matter how sophisticated the program, the output is still determined by the program. Even when the computer seems to be making choices about complex phenomena like the stock market, it is just making mathematical calculations based on the input and following the rules laid down by the programmer. The computer cannot choose to change the logic.

Now we turn to a person. Suppose a murderer is brought to trial. A physician testifies that, on the basis of a complete physical examination, the criminal was compelled to do what he did because of a massive brain tumor that had profound effects on his emotions and judgment. His behavior was completely determined by his physical condition. Could the judge be lenient to this man? Yes! The judge could be lenient, because the man had not chosen to commit murder.

This metaphor shows us that computers and people are exactly opposite. When a computer's output is determined, the computer is in working order. But when a human being's output is determined, he is out-of-order. This is shown graphically in the following chart:

	DETERMINED	UNDETERMINED
COMPUTER	WORKING ORDER	OUT-OF-ORDER
PERSON	OUT-OF-ORDER	WORKING ORDER

So, when do we choose? We choose when things are not on the same scale, when we cannot just give weights to the alternatives and compare the outcomes. We choose when we have two essentially different things to compare: truth vs. what feels good because it satisfies a need, preference or value.

If we did not have free will, if the "self" was nothing more than a string of predetermined responses, if the "I" were nothing more than a name for an operating "program" in the brain, we would have neither the opportunity to elevate ourselves nor the responsibility to do so. We would be nothing more than puppets who had the illusion that we were pulling our own strings.

As political philosopher Isaiah Berlin said in his book *Four Essays on Liberty*,[2] "If all things and events and persons are determined, then praise and blame do, indeed, become purely pedagogical devices (p. xv) . . . if I literally cannot make my character or behavior other than it is by an act of choice . . . then I do not see in what normal sense a rational person could hold me morally responsible either for my character or for my conduct. Indeed, the notion of a morally responsible being becomes, at best, mythological (p. xvii)." Puppets cannot be blamed or praised, and they are not responsible for themselves.

Deep down, however, we know that we are not puppets. We may sometimes feel like puppets, pulled by the strings of our own desires or "conditioning," but fundamentally, we know that we have free will. It goes against our most abiding sense of ourselves to be told that we are nothing more than a set of conditioned response patterns.

Our analysis of free will enables us to go on to a higher level definition. There are two kinds of choice, *psychological choice* and *spiritual choice*. In many of the situations in which we usually think of ourselves as making free will choices, we are really only expressing preferences. We can express esthetic preferences ("I'll buy the pink sweater because I look better in pink than blue") or preferences between needs ("I'm tired and hungry, but since I won't be able to sleep on an empty stomach, I better put off going to sleep until I eat"). *We go up to the level of choice only when one branch of the conflict involves truth.* It is psychological choice when we express preferences between needs and personal truth of values ("I think I should work to save the whales, but I really need more time for exercise. I'm getting out of shape") or between competing values ("I'll have only enough time to devote to one worthwhile cause, so I'll work to save the whales rather than to reduce smog").

Now we can begin to understand that what we called choice before—Ruth's choice to follow the dictates of her personal truth and spend more time with her parents—is *psychological choice*, or choice between a personal value and a need. It is choice because it is based on a firm conviction of personal truth.

But, as we saw, personal truth can be compromised. Once truth is defined in a flexible way, it is no longer truth. *We really choose only when we know we can't fool around with the truth.* And the only truth we can't fool around with is the absolute truth of Torah. *Only choice involving Torah truth is spiritual choice.* For example, if Ruth believed that she should be good to her parents because it is a *mitzvah* to honor her parents, it would be *spiritual choice*.

Let me try to explain the difference between spiritual choice on the one hand and psychological choice and expressing preferences on the other hand. We were given free will so that we could choose between truth and falsehood, right and wrong. We are not exercising this sublime power unless absolute truth is involved, unless the struggle is between absolute Torah truth and what seems good because it fills some personal need, preference or value.

But how can we, with our great powers of self-deception, know the difference between what is true and what we need or want? Rabbi Shlomo Wolbe addresses this question in his work *Alei Shur*:[3]

> How can a person decide which he should choose? Evil is alluring, doing good doesn't arouse him. The pleasure that a *mitzvah* confers is a real pleasure, but one which he has never experienced.
>
> How will he decide which to choose? He must differentiate between truth and falsehood. But how?
>
> By means of his common sense. It is capable of discerning between truth and falsehood. It perceives the truth inherent in the *mitzvah* and the falsehood inherent in the transgression.

In other words, the choice is between the truth of the *mitzvah* (commandment) and the attraction of the falsehood. We are not initially drawn to the *mitzvah*, but intellectually, we can recognize its inherent truth. If we choose the truth, we will experience real pleasure and eventually we will be more attracted to truth than to falsehood. (See Chapter 17 for further discussion of truth.)

If we can discern between truth and falsehood, and if we are responsible for the "selves" we create by our choices, does that mean that there are no other influences on who we are and who we become? Is it all up to us? Does it mean that the child born into a life of deprivation and abuse has the same choices as the child born into a life of comfort and loving support? Of course not. They do not have the same choices, but they *do* have the same power to choose. In other words, the content of their choices will be different, but the *act of choosing* will be the same.

Let me try to make this clear with an example. Jimmy is sixteen years old. He grew up in an impoverished, ghetto home. He never knew his father, but his mother worked hard to feed and clothe her family of four children. Jimmy and the other children were often left alone, and they wandered around a neighborhood where drugs and alcohol were used openly, and crime and violence were common. They learned how to fight, but they were often terrified of bigger kids who would rough them up and demand "favors." They went to school sporadically but didn't learn very much there. By the time Jimmy was fourteen he had become one of the "bigger kids." He was tough and mean; he used drugs and alcohol; when he wanted something he stole.

David is also sixteen. He grew up in a middle-class Jewish home on a pleasant suburban street. His parents adored him and gave him every opportunity for growth and enrichment. He had music lessons, went to camp and attended the best Jewish Day School available. His parents showed an active interest in his progress: they helped him with his homework, attended parent-teacher meetings, and went to all of his school performances. David was a good son and a good student.

Obviously, Jimmy and David do not have the same choices, *but they both have the power of choice.*

Suppose that one day Jimmy needs some money to buy drugs. He notices that his mother, who went to visit a neighbor, has left her purse at home. He looks inside and finds about eighty dollars. But his truth is that he shouldn't steal from his mother. He considers taking only half of the money, but that would still be stealing from his mother. He is caught in a big conflict. He really wants drugs, but he knows that his mother works very hard for the few dollars she makes, and she would be extremely upset if her money was stolen, especially by Jimmy. He just will not dishonor his mother, so he *chooses* not to steal the money.

David also finds himself in a conflict. It is a beautiful spring day and some of his friends have decided to give in to "senioritis" and skip school and go to the park. It's just innocent fun, and some of their parents even agreed to write "excuses" for their sons the next day. But David knows that his parents don't approve of his missing school. He is in a real bind, because the kids are teasing him about being a "goody-goody" and challenging him to be a man and go. It sounds like great fun, and he hates missing a good time, but he decides against it because he just can't violate his truth—that he should honor his parents.

Both Jimmy and David made psychological choices; they chose between their truth and what was attractive to them. Both of them were in conflict and both of them chose freely. The only thing that was different was the content of the choice.

What effect does Jimmy's choice have on him? Can he transform himself by making one righteous choice? According to *Alei Shur*:[4]

> Man does not have such absolute free will that he can change himself in one instant from being a totally evil person to a complete *tzaddik* (righteous person). The decision to change can be made at once, but the actual process of changing from a wicked to a righteous person can stretch out over years.

Alei Shur is telling us that Jimmy can't transform himself by a single choice, but he can start a process of self-creation that will eventually transform him.

To shed further light on the subject of free choice, we

will turn to the wisdom of Rabbi Eliyahu Eliezer Dessler.[5] Rabbi Dessler* teaches us that there is a *free will point*. The *free will point* is the point where there is an awareness of conflict between impulse or desire and moral principle. Without awareness of conflict there is no choice. Areas above and below this point lie outside the range of free will. Rabbi Dessler explained it this way:[6]

> When two armies are locked in battle, fighting takes place only at the battlefront. Territory behind the lines of one army is under that army's control, and little or no resistance need be expected there. A similar situation prevails in respect to territory behind the lines of the other army. If one side gains a victory at the front and pushes the enemy back, the position of the battlefront will have changed. In fact, therefore, fighting takes place only at one location.

In other words, free will is exercised only on the battle-line between competing wills, or, as Rabbi Dessler says, "when one is tempted to go against the truth as one sees it, and the forces on either side are more or less equally balanced." (p. 54) Areas *below* the free will point are part of an already established moral behavior-pattern; they are territories already under control. For example, no matter how much Jimmy needs money for drugs, he won't kill for it. His mother taught him that you never kill. Areas *above* the free will point involve questions of right and wrong which the person's moral sense cannot yet tackle; they are like territories behind the enemy's lines. Above the free will point for Jimmy are all those things he has not yet even considered, e.g., working for money or giving up drugs.

*for more information on Rabbi Dessler see biographical notes (p. 421).

For David, the free will point was the struggle between being "one of the guys" and deceiving his parents. The area already under control, i.e., below the free will point, would include things like dropping out of school; he would never consider that. In the area "behind the enemy's lines" or above the free will point might be talking one of the other guys out of skipping school because he knew that his parents would also disapprove.

Some might say that David's choice was at a higher level than Jimmy's, because Jimmy would still go out and steal the money from someone else, while David would never consider stealing. Others might say that Jimmy's choice was at a higher level because he had such disadvantages that not stealing from his mother really took a lot of guts, while David was doing something easy by comparison. From a Torah point of view, however, the important thing is the act of choosing, not the level of choice. Both boys elevated themselves by making the moral choice; both would have degraded themselves if they had chosen the other way.

The level of the free will point is set by many factors which can be summarized in two categories:

Innate characteristics and life circumstances. These conditions include health, intelligence and environmental factors.

Our own previous choices. Every choice either elevates or lowers us, leaving us in a different place than we were before the choice was made. With each choice for the truth as we know it, we rise to a higher spiritual level; issues that were on the battlefront go into conquered territory. And each choice against the truth as we know it pushes the battleground back; the enemy gains some of our territory. We lose the power of choice in that area.

It is very important to know that these two factors affect

the level of the free will point, but they do not affect the act of choosing. As Rabbi Dessler says, "Every human being possesses the power of perceiving the truth available to him at his particular level, clinging to it and refusing to be deflected from it by the seductive illusions of falsehood."

Regardless of what level we are starting at, we are free to choose. And because we are free to choose, we are actually given the power to create our "selves." In the words of Rabbi Tucazinsky:[7]

> Every deed, every word or thought wrought from every turn, influences one's character, the effect being cumulative. Moreover, every resulting change in character will itself bring about great changes in one's manner of living and in the events of his life . . . Only the gift of free will gives one the ability to shape one's own destiny.

What a tremendous challenge we have! Ours is the power to choose—and with this power we can either ennoble or defile ourselves.

The Divine Soul: The Seeing "I"

CHAPTER 3

Why speak of the soul in an age of science? Why suggest that there is some aspect of the psyche that is not subject to the limitations of space and time and which might precede the birth of the body and survive its death? The main reason is that something vital has been left out of almost all the modern efforts to understand our mental life, something that counts as a first principle, without which everything is bound to be incomplete and off base.[1]

Do you have a soul? Do you have a mind? Are you more than your physical body? Or are your thoughts, values, beliefs, feelings, motives and goals nothing more than a linguistic system for expressing the neurochemical patterns of your brain? In other words, is there a spiritual side to your existence which is separate and distinct from the purely physical side of your existence, or are your mind and your brain just different aspects of the same physical process? Is there a "you" who reads these questions and answers them? Or is there just a physical/chemical/electrical system encapsulated and operating in your body that happens to call itself "I"?

These questions reflect a philosophical controversy that has been raging for centuries, the so-called "mind-body" problem. There are two basic views on it: dualism and monism.

A simplified version of the dualist position is that mind and body are *fundamentally* different from each other, that the mind has reality which is separate from, although closely related to, the body. An equally simplified version of the monistic position is that mind and body are *fundamentally* one and the same entity. This implies that any mental or spiritual event can ultimately be boiled down to a physical explanation.

The monistic position has been ascendant in psychology for many years. After the incredible success of the physical sciences in the eighteenth and nineteenth centuries, social scientists were eager to adopt the concepts of the "hard sciences" for themselves. Many nineteenth and twentieth century scientists disdained "soft" mentalist explanations, i.e., explanations based on the existence of a mind separate and distinct from the body. Listen to the words of physiologist Emil DuBois-Reymond:[2]

> Brucke and I *pledged a solemn oath* to put into effect this truth: "No other forces than the common physical-chemical

ones are active within the organism. In those cases which cannot at the time be explained by these forces one had to assume new forces *equal in dignity to the chemical-physical forces* inherent in matter . . ."(italics added).

The implication is that chemical-physical forces have dignity; non-material or supernatural forces are at best unnecessary and at worst ridiculous and embarrassing concepts.

Dubois-Reymond and Brucke* had a dogmatic attachment to the basic principles of their "religion" of science. This *faith* in science certainly ran contrary to their claim to be fervent searchers for truth. They had *faith* that the methods that worked so well in physics, chemistry and biology would work equally well when applied to the study of human nature. As a result of this kind of *faith* in rigidly physicalist explanations, "mental" phenomena came to have such low status in the scientific community that the controversy seemed finally resolved. Mental events were considered nothing more than the inconsequential by-products of processes in the real material world.

Many scientists reviled the concept of mind. Gilbert Ryle called it the "Ghost in the Machine"[3] and Richard Rorty said that it is "the blur with which Western intellectuals became obsessed when they finally gave up on the blur which was the theologian's concept of God. The ineffability of the mental

---

*A fascinating footnote to this story is that the "Brucke" mentioned in the quote above was one of Freud's early teachers and one of the formative influences of Freud's thought. Freud, of course, went on to become a major influence on psychological and psychiatric thought. He carried out Brucke's pledge of seeing the psyche in physical terms as a dynamic energy system in which tension was created by repressed desires.

serves the same cultural function as the ineffability of the divine—it vaguely suggests that science does not have the last word."[4] This angry insistence on reality being limited to physical matter held sway in psychology for many decades. (It went so far to the extent that in one of my graduate psychology classes I was told that I could talk about the mind only if I brought a pound of it to class.)

For those who held this monist-materialist creed, the only topics suitable for discussion and research were those which could be readily observed and reliably measured. Invisible internal events such as "ideas," "plans" and "values" were not considered amenable to scientific study and were, therefore, treated with contempt. There were even those who tried to restrict the field of psychology exclusively to the study of behavior.

In the past few decades, advances in mathematics and science have opened new paths to the study of internal events, and the "mind" has become an acceptable scientific construct. The mind-body controversy has been reopened at a new level of sophistication and with a new name—the mind-brain problem.

But the issues remain basically the same: Is there a fundamental duality to human existence? Is there non-material as well as material reality? Are there "mental" phenomena which cannot be explained in terms of chemistry, electricity or physiology? Is the mind truly different from the brain? Or is human existence monistic, made up of only one basic existential material which has different manifestations? Highly qualified scientists hold widely differing views; many reject the monistic view.

Neuroscientist and Nobel Laureate Sir John Eccles comes out strongly on the side of dualism. He says, "It is a mistake to think that the brain does everything and that our conscious experiences are simply a reflection of brain activities."[5] His view is that we are a combination of two entities: our brains and our conscious selves. The brain is an instrument that has been our "lifelong servant and companion."[6] It is the self-conscious mind, not the brain, that produces the unity of conscious experience we call *self*.

Our sense of self links us from our earliest conscious experiences to the present. It lapses during sleep, except for dreams, and it recovers the next day by the continuity of memory. "It is my thesis," says Sir John, "that we have to recognize that *the unique selfhood is the result of a supernatural creation of what in the religious sense is called a soul.*" [7](italics added).

Other great scientists also believe in the fundamental duality in the cosmos. The scientist K. R. Popper[8] says, "I intend to suggest that the brain is owned by the self." (p.120) The famous neurosurgeon Wilder Penfield stated that the mind is a basic element in itself, which cannot be accounted for by any neuronal mechanism.[9] He agrees with Hippocrates that the brain is a messenger to the mind, *that purpose comes to the brain from outside its own mechanism.* The mind directs, and the brain executes. Penfield writes:

> The physiological basis of the mind is the brain action in each individual; it accompanies the action of the spirit, but the spirit is free; it is capable of some degree of initiative. The *spirit* is the man one knows.[10] (italics added).

Penfield formed his conclusions about brain function on the basis of research and observations on patients undergoing brain surgery. He noticed that patients could be aware of what was going on in the operating room, and at the same time, when their brains were stimulated with electrodes, they could have vivid flashbacks of the past. These patients would essentially relive past events as if they were happening right then. Yet they were not confused by these simultaneous occurrences. They could say to Dr. Penfield, "You made me do (or think) that."

Penfield was struck by the independent functioning of the patients' "minds" while they were going through these experiences from the past. The brain could be forced to remember, but the mind could not be forced to believe or to decide. There was clearly a "self" that was aware and knew what was happening, and there was a brain, or data bank, which was being activated to make people remember events from the past. Penfield did not find any place in the cerebral cortex where electrode stimulation caused a patient to believe or decide something. According to Penfield, *belief and decision-making are functions of the mind*. They cannot be accounted for by any neuronal mechanism. The mind programs the brain continuously to suit the person's individual purposes and interests.

Here is Penfield's list of seven functions performed by the mind:
1. Focuses attention
2. Is aware
3. Reasons
4. Makes new decisions
5. Understands
6. Acts as though it had been endowed with an energy of its own.
7. Puts decisions into effect by activating neuron-mechanisms.

Penfield adds these meaningful words:

> What a thrill it is, then, to discover that the scientist too can legitimately believe in the existence of the human spirit! (p. 85)

The subject is still controversial, of course; the monistic position has its adherents (e.g., Pribram[11]). The monist-dualist dispute will continue as long as there are scientists who deny the possibility of purely spiritual phenomena, who presume that anything which cannot be verified by the scientific method is either false or not worth considering. Keith Campbell expresses this position when he says that since the spirit is "methodologically elusive"[12] we should search for a more adequate explanation for the soul. In other words, if we can't observe it and measure it, we should ignore it. Isn't it amazing that even before starting the search he has excluded a whole realm of possibilities?

This is like the story of the man who lost his keys late at night on a dark street. For many hours, he searched the ground in the circle of light under a street lamp further down the street. A person who lived nearby and saw him searching endlessly asked, "Are you absolutely sure you lost them here?"

The man pointed down the street and said, "Actually, I lost my keys down the street over there, but the light is better here."

Since the spiritual universe is by definition non-material and thus non-measureable, the person who demands quantitative answers will never be satisfied with dualistic explanations.

Despite some scientists' contention that "If I can't kick

it, it doesn't exist," many of the greatest scientists of this century have acknowledged that the answers to the deeper questions of life cannot be found within the finite circle of light shed by science.

In the words of Sir John Eccles, "The coming-to-be of each unique selfhood lies beyond scientific enquiry . . . all monist-materialist explanations are mistaken simplifications."[13] Sir John believes that we have to be open to the possibility of some deep, dramatic significance to life. He sees in the cultural achievements of mankind a search for absolute values, and he believes the aim of science is to come closer to absolute truth.[14]

Max Planck, Nobel Physics Laureate (1919), said, "There can never be any real opposition between religion and science; for the one is the complement of the other. Every serious and reflective person realizes, I think, that the religious element in his nature must be recognized and cultivated if all the powers of the human soul are to act together in perfect balance and harmony."[15]

Another physicist, Werner Heisenberg, in his book *Physics and Beyond*,[16] wrote the following: "The word soul refers to the central order, to the inner core of a being whose outer manifestations may be highly diverse and pass our understanding."

Fortunately, we have a way to approach those things that "pass our understanding." As Maimonides said, "The foundation of foundations and the pillar of all sciences is to know that there is a Prime Being."[17] In other words, if we start with the fundamental knowledge of God, we will be able to understand things that are otherwise inaccessible to the human mind.

THE TORAH VIEW ON HUMAN EXISTENCE

Now we turn to the teachings of the Torah for answers to the questions with which we started this chapter. Is there a *you* reading this book, or is it just being processed by a physical/chemical/electrical system with an illusion of "I-ness"? Is there a fundamental duality to human existence? Is there non-material as well as material reality?

According to the Torah, there is a fundamental duality in life. We are composed of two opposite parts, the spiritual soul and the physical body. One way to think about this is to picture the body as a horse and the soul as the rider. The main question is, who is leading this tandem? Ideally, the soul (the "rider") should be the one that leads, counsels and makes choices; the body (the "horse") should be the one that follows. When we say "I," we should be referring to the choosing soul. I *am* a soul; I *have* a body.

When you know you are the rider, you love your horse and take very good care of it, but you do not let it lead. Picture a horse and a rider climbing up a mountain. They climb higher and higher. There's grass and water, and they eat and drink what they need. The horse gets tired and raises its head. The rider pats the horse and gives it a sugar cube to calm it down. "A little more, a little more," he coaxes. The rider considers the horses's needs and desires and limits, but the rider sets the pace and determines the goal. The rider is in control.

Letting physical desire dominate life is like letting the horse be in control and lead the rider. We may stumble into a lot of unexpected trouble en route to a green pasture; worse yet, we will miss out on the most glorious aspects of being human. We will never know the deep joy and serenity that come from commitment to the higher goals set by our souls. Our yearning for immortality, our capacity for nobility, our ability to love selflessly and give generously, our ability to sacrifice our individual desires for a higher good, these are some of the goals of the soul. They are not sublimations of basic human impulses and they are not merely acts of self-preservation clothed in noble garb. The powers of the soul are from above, not from below.

In this Torah model, the brain is part of the horse, needing direction from the rider. The rider, or mind, is the soul. The brain is merely a machine, in some ways like a computer. As Penfield said:[18]

> Inasmuch as the brain is a place for newly acquired automatic mechanisms, it is a computer. To be useful, any computer must be programmed and operated by an external agent.

The brain and the computer are similar in that they are both devices that store data and process it according to programs supplied by a programmer. On the other hand there are also vast differences to be found between the brain and the computer. To quote the esteemed cognitive psychologist Howard Gardner:[19]

> Indeed, the computer resembles a human being who is asked to solve an algebra problem in a foreign language, of which one knows but a few words. Faced with such an enigma, both computer and foreigner gravitate to the few numbers each recognizes and make the best guess about the mathematical operations that should be carried out on those numbers.

My own doubts about the computer as the guiding model of human thought stem from two principal considerations—the community surrounding a cognizing individual is critical—it makes no sense to indicate that a computer has made a mistake or is unjustified in its beliefs. The computer is simply executing what it has been programmed to execute, and standards of right and wrong do not enter in its performance. My other reservation about the computer as a model centers on the deep difference between biological systems and mechanical systems.

In other words, the brain is much more complex than any computer. Yet the brain still needs a programmer. In his book, *Vital Lies, Simple Truths: The Psychology of Self-Deception*,[20] psychologist Daniel Goleman asks, "Where are the ghosts that enspirit this machine [the brain], that endow it with the qualities of a living mind?" Goleman writes that raw information relayed by the senses to the brain passes through an "intelligent filter." Both new data and old memories are scanned and filtered on the basis of meaning and relevance before they are admitted to consciousness. What we become aware of is carefully selected from the overwhelming mass of data that impinges on us.

Furthermore, this filtering and selection process is completely unconscious. Goleman calls these intelligent filters "schemas," or mind-sets that develop as a result of our experiences. Once we develop a schema, e.g., "I am a good mother," we try to fit all relevant data into the schema. If I then treat my children harshly, I either have to distort this information ("It was for their own good. They really needed a good beating."), "forget" it entirely, or change my schema

("I'm a good mother when I'm not overtired."). Goleman concludes that these schemas are the ghost in the machine, the intelligence that guides information as it flows through the mind. "To realize how they operate is to understand understanding."

But by concocting this schema of "schemas," he begs the question: Where do the schemas come from? We believe that the ability to form schemas comes from the soul. Schemas can express the primitive soul, or higher levels of the soul, depending on our level of development (the levels of the soul will be explained in the next chapter). If they come from the elemental soul, they will screen out anything which will interfere with satisfaction of primitive needs. If they come from higher levels of the soul, they will allow a person to be aware of ideas which serve a whole range of more elevated needs.

What difference does it make to us, you might ask, whether or not what we know as our selves can be reduced to the workings of the physical brain? It makes a big difference, because in order to live our lives well, we have to know that we can't trust our brains. The brain can operate under the influence of the elemental soul, the social soul or higher levels of the soul. It will keep processing input and regurgitating output regardless of the level of the programmer. Only the output will be different, depending on the level of the programmer. "Garbage in, garbage out."

We all know that we can use our minds to justify any action we want to take—and make it sound noble. "I haven't called my sickly, elderly neighbor for quite some time. Well, I've been very busy, she naps a lot, and I might awaken her if I call." "I haven't spent much time with my family lately, but it is very important for me to get some exercise after working all day. Better that I should be in good health. What would happen to them if I got sick?" The mind has the ability to generate these excuses as fast as we can generate noble intentions.

If we can't trust our own minds, what can we trust? We can trust the Torah and those who are qualified transmitters of the Torah. As we live and learn Torah, as we elevate ourselves and our reactions become more and more *Torahdik*, our intellects become activated by higher levels of the soul, and our awareness expands to include the needs of the higher levels of the soul. Then we can trust ourselves more and more. But, in case of doubt as to which level of the soul is in the driver's seat, the final arbiter is always the Torah. No matter what level of the soul we think is in the driver's seat, we can always determine the best course of action by referring to the Torah.

SCHEMA OR SOUL?

To help you decide where you stand in the monist-dualist controversy, consider the following story told by Miep Gies in her book *Anne Frank Remembered*.[21]

During the Second World War, Miep Gies and her husband Henk risked their own lives to protect several Jews in hiding in Amsterdam. Among these Jews was the Frank family, which consisted of father Otto, mother Edith and daughters Margot and Anne. Miep had worked for Otto Frank for many years, and she and Henk had become close friends of the Frank family.

As the war progressed, the persecution of the Jews got much worse. In the spring of 1942, the situation had deteriorated to the point that Jews were being deported, and the Franks decided to go into hiding. Miep agreed to take care of them.

Miep felt a particular kinship with Anne. She realized "how much pretty things meant to young ladies of fourteen" (p.159) and she became determined to find something grown-up and pretty for Anne. Miep found a pair of high-heeled red leather pumps and brought them up to the hiding place.

> I went to Anne and stuck them in front of her. Never have I seen anyone so happy as Anne was that day.
>
> (pp. 159-160)

The winter of 1943 was especially cold and stormy. Miep had to fight stinging rain and slippery streets in her long searches for food. The scarcities were worse with each passing day.

> I could not relax my vigilance in my searches. Eleven of us had to eat. Because I was a lifeline, I felt myself to be a kind of hunter, ever hunting for my always-hungry brood. But slowly, I was turning into an unrelenting scavenger and would make do even with small scraps. I could not allow myself to get sick. I could not allow myself a holiday. (p. 168)

Life became very difficult and Miep could not fight off sickness any longer.

> Fading into and out of sleep, chills and shivers coming in waves, I thought of my friends in the hiding place. My worry for them was like a great stone on my chest. Amidst all the sickness, a gloomy mood had settled over the hiding place. I tried to think of what might lend a little cheer as the

holiday season approached. I began to put aside any sweets that I could find. I scrounged up bits of butter and flour, careful not to let it be known that I was planning to bake a real cake. (pp. 168-169)

Despite all of Miep's and Henk's efforts, the Franks were taken into custody. It was suggested that Miep offer money to the Nazis to buy back the people who were arrested. In spite of the dreadful danger to herself, she went to Gestapo headquarters and made her offer for the release of the Frank family. It was denied.

My heart was thundering. Fearing that any second I'd be grabbed by someone, I made my way back downstairs . . . Again the thought rang in my brain, people who enter this building do not always come out again. I put one foot in front of the other, waiting for someone to stop me . . . Back out in the street, I was amazed at how easy it had been to walk back out the door. (pp. 203-204)

On June 3, 1945, Otto Frank came back to Amsterdam from Auschwitz.

We looked at each other. There were no words. He was thin, but he'd always been thin. He carried a little bundle. My eyes swam. My heart melted. Suddenly, I was afraid to know more. I didn't want to know what had happened. I knew I would not ask—finally, Frank spoke. "Miep," he said quietly, "Miep, Edith is not coming back—but I have great hope for Margot and Anne." (p. 231)

Mr. Frank settled in with Miep and Henk and took his place as head of the business. Some time later he received a letter. He opened it and said in a toneless, totally crushed voice:

> "Margot and Anne are not coming back." We stayed there like that, both struck by lightning, burnt thoroughly through our hearts, our eyes fixed on each other's . . . I sat at my desk utterly crushed. Everything that had happened before, I could somehow accept. Like it or not, I had to accept it. But this, I could not accept. It was the one thing I'd been sure would not happen. (p. 234)

Of this courageous, selfless devotion to the lives of others, Miep Gies says:

> I am not a hero. I stand at the end of the long, long line of good Dutch people who did what I did or more—much more—during those dark and terrible times years ago, but always like yesterday in the hearts of those of us who bear witness. Never a day goes by that I do not think of what happened then. (p. 11)

Can this story be understood without acknowledging the divine soul? Are the words "nobility," "love" and "devotion" a linguistic system for encoding the neurochemical reactions of Miep Gies? Or are they symbols which refer to her true spiritual state? Was the bravery of the many "good Dutch people" just a series of physical/chemical/electrical reactions, devoid of higher purpose? Can their selfless behavior be understood as a string of conditioned responses or schemas? Were they just flesh and blood robots?

Why reduce their heroism to meaningless absurdity? Doesn't it make more sense to recognize that Miep Gies and the other "good Dutch people" transcended their own biological needs, that they *chose* instead to follow the dictates of their divine souls?

We now turn to the question of how the soul manifests itself in the psyche. What do we have to see in the personality to know that there is a soul operating?

THE DISTINGUISHING FEATURES OF THE SOUL

THE ABILITY TO CHOOSE

The soul's ability to choose distinguishes us from other creatures and from machines. As we said in Chapter 2, the behavior of animals and machines is determined. Many of you might be saying, "Ah, but I know of cases where dogs have risked their lives to protect their masters." The difference is that animal behavior is either instinctive or conditioned. It does not fit the criteria for choice which we discussed in Chapter 2; we exercise free will only when we make choices involving *truth*, when we choose between the *truth* and what seems good to us. Therefore, the dog's behavior, helpful as it may be to its master, does not reflect the presence of a choosing soul.

YEARNING FOR SATISFACTION

The second distinguishing feature of the soul is the yearning for satisfaction (for a fuller discussion of this subject, see Chapter 6) that goes beyond unfulfilled needs. As Eric Fromm said:[22]

The most striking feature in human behavior is the

tremendous intensity of passions and strivings which man displays . . . [but] a large part of man's passionate strivings cannot be explained by the force of his instincts. Even if man's hunger and thirst and his sexual strivings are completely satisfied, "he" is not satisfied. In contrast to the animal, his most compelling problems are not solved then, they only begin. He strives for power, or for love, or for destruction, he risks his life for religious, for political, for humanistic ideals, and these strivings are what constitutes and characterizes the peculiarity of human life.

We hear this yearning clearly in the words of Bertrand Russell:

The center of me is always and eternally a terrible pain—a curious wild pain—a searching for something beyond what the world contains, something transfigured and infinite.[23]

The soul does not yearn for what this world contains, and hence it cannot be truly satisfied with what this world contains.

SELF-AWARENESS

The third distinguishing feature of the soul is self-awareness. Awareness is a metaphysical ability. In principle, a machine cannot be aware of itself; a camera cannot take a picture of its lens. A cow does not know that it is contented. Only we human beings have the ability to observe ourselves and say "I."

We have looked at very persuasive evidence that we do have divine souls. Why then do we need the Torah to tell us that God breathed the divine spark of life, the soul, into us? Because we are capable of remarkable cognitive dissonance. In the Appendix, we can see how the renowned scientist George Wald ignores his own scientific analyses to avoid the inevitable conclusion that the creation was a supernatural event. Now let us see how Eric Fromm wriggles out of the conclusion that there must be a supernatural part of man. After concluding the aforementioned quote with the words, "Indeed, man does not live by bread alone," Fromm goes on to say:

> This statement has been interpreted to mean that man has an intrinsic religious need which cannot be explained by his natural existence but must be explained by something transcending him which is derived from supernatural powers. *However, the latter assumption is unnecessary since the phenomenon can be explained by the full understanding of the human situation.*
>
> Man must accept the responsibility for himself and the fact that only by using his own powers can he give meaning to his life . . . If he faces the truth without panic he will recognize that *there is no meaning to life other than the meaning man gives to his own life by the unfolding of his powers* . . . (italics added).

Time and time again, honest, intelligent people see the truth of the world from the world, but they, unlike our Patriarch Abraham, run from the truth. They say, "Yes, I see that a supernatural explanation is demanded by the data, but I prefer another explanation." They see the truth, but they choose to create a more convenient falsehood. That's why we need the Torah. If God had not given us the Torah we could spend the rest of our lives arguing about whether or not we have souls. We could invent all kinds of clever philosophies and psychologies and pseudo-sciences. God gave us the Torah so we wouldn't have to waste our precious lives in inane debate. He gave us this great gift so that we could use its infinite wisdom to get on with our lives.

Now I want to ask you, my dear reader, do you have free will? Do you sometimes make choices between *truth* and what seems *good to you*? Do you long for something beyond the fulfillment of your needs? Are you aware of yourself? If so, you must have a soul, because a merely physical creature does not have these qualities.

Before we go any further, I want to introduce a note of caution. The English word *soul* has become so diluted that I feel I need to explain what I mean when I use the word *soul*. In this book, when the word *soul* is used, it means only what the Torah says it means. As you read on, you will find out more about what the Torah says about the *soul*, but in the meantime, at least while you are reading, please try to put aside any previous connotations of the word *soul*. Accept the possibility that you *do* have a soul which is linking you to the Divine right now. Read this book with your soul and see where it leads you.

CHAPTER 4

A Model for the Structure of the Soul: The Ladder of Life

We are unequivocally told by the Torah that life and consciousness are provided by a spiritual entity which enclothes itself in, and is operator of, the sophisticated computerized machine that we call the body. [1]

The soul has the power to elevate the body step by step, until even the body can derive pleasure from perfection along with the soul. [2]

To explain the essence of the soul and how that relates to psychological theory I have had to include a lot of technical material in this chapter. In so doing I have outlined why the truth of the Torah resolves issues of emotional well-being beyond the reach of any psychological theory.

The following model, which is consistent with the Torah, will help explain the structure and development of the soul and how the soul is manifested in the psyche. It provides a sound basis for understanding the human personality and makes it easier to grasp the various other theories quoted.

THE DIVINE SOUL

What we call the soul in Torah is similar in some ways to what psychologists call the self or ego. The soul or self is the unifying agent in the personality that we experience as "I." This "I" is conscious of itself and the world. It has free will: It selects and organizes stimuli into meaningful patterns. It has a memory. And it has continuity of selfhood. It has what might be called an *executive function* in the personality.

There are major differences, however, between the soul and the self or ego. The soul, unlike the self or the ego, is a pure, divinely-given spiritual entity. The soul is real. The self or ego, on the other hand, is an artificial designation which has no reality other than that of a useful abstraction. The soul has its own spiritual powers and needs, and these are often in conflict with the body's powers and drives. Furthermore, the soul has an existence which is independent of the existence of the body. When we talk about the development of the "psyche" or the "personality" in this book we are really talking about the development of the soul.

There is a major difference between the secular and the Torah views of the psyche. Let me clarify the difference with this parable. Suppose some visitors from another planet were hovering over the earth in their spaceship. They knew nothing about life on earth and were trying to understand the patterns of movement of some strange four-wheeled metal creatures (cars). They were trying to figure out what made the creatures stop and start, slow down and speed up. After much observation, they noticed that starting and stopping were controlled by green and red signal lights, while slowing down and speeding up were controlled by many factors, such as: the size of the creature, the number of creatures on the road, the distance between signal lights, and the appearance on the road of a screaming creature with red blinking lights on its head. This is the secular view of the psyche. It takes into account only the mechanical features of the creature and the external conditions. *It does not see the driver.*

The Torah view, on the other hand, focuses on the driver who activates the creature. This driver has executive power to respond to both the mechanical features of the creature and the external conditions in which it is operating. It also has the ability to make moral decisions. For example, "Shall I stop and help the distressed vehicle on the side of road?"

In other words, the Torah view of the psyche includes the body and the soul interacting with the environment. We get a profoundly different picture of the human psyche when we put the divine soul in the driver's seat. Perhaps the following model will help us understand the function and development of the soul in Torah teaching.

THE PARTS OF THE SOUL

Although I have been referring to the soul as if it were a single entity, it is more accurate to say, as Rabbi Moshe Chaim Luzzatto* did, that "there are actually a number of

*for more information on Rabbi Luzzatto see biographical notes (p. 421).

THE LADDER OF THE DIVINE SOUL

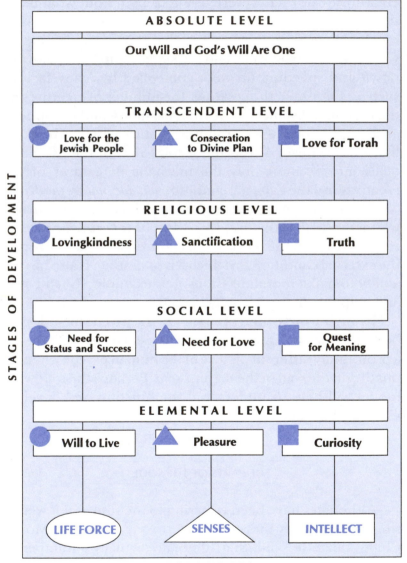

souls, bound together like links in a chain. Just as all these links comprise a single chain, so do all these levels of the soul constitute a single entity, called the divine soul. Each of these levels is bound to the one below it . . ."[3] from the very highest level, which is purely spiritual, to the lowest level, or the part of the soul that pertains to the physical body.

In the diagram-model of the soul (p. 86), it is important to note that the three parallel ladders of the soul do not represent dimensions which can be measured in physical units, such as pounds or inches. Each ladder represents a capacity of the body which is like a natural resource waiting to be harnessed. We will refer to these capacities as the resources or raw materials which the soul uses to develop the spiritual personality. Going from left to right, we see: the *life force*; the *senses* (sight, hearing, taste, smell and touch); and the *intellect*.

Next, we will look at the "rungs" of the ladders. The ladder has five rungs; each rung represents a different stage of development. The stages are marked off by degrees of spirituality.

The development of the soul is from the purely physical to the purely spiritual. The five stages of development (represented in the diagram by the rungs on the ladder) are: the elemental level, the social level, the religious level, the transcendent level and the absolute level.

The elemental level of the soul is purely physical. It is the level shared by all living creatures.

The social level is part physical and part spiritual. At this level, we are set apart from the animals by the gift of speech and awareness.

The third level, the religious level of the soul, is entirely spiritual, but it is bound to the physical body and can influence it and be influenced by it.

The transcendent and absolute levels of the soul are purely spiritual and separate from the physical body. They "do not have any detectable influence on the body . . . The only function of these souls is with respect to man's true essence and appropriate association with the highest roots."[4]

Rabbi Chaim of Volozhin[5] uses a glassblowing metaphor to explain the relationship between God and the first three levels of the soul (from the religious level down to the elemental level):

> When we examine the blowing of a craftsman making glass, we discern three stages. The first stage is when the breath is still within the mouth of the craftsman, before it enters the blowpipe. At this first stage, it can properly be called breath . . . The second stage is when the breath is already in the blowpipe, and it extends throughout its length . . . The third and lowest stage is when the vapor leaves the blowpipe, enters the glass and expands until the glass takes the shape desired by the craftsman . . . This is the final state . . . (p.178)

Rabbi Chaim goes on to explain that the religious level of the soul is like the first stage of glassblowing. The religious soul is the very breath of God. Since the religious soul is bound to the human body, we can be influenced by the breath of God within it ("reflections of the sparks of its light shine upon the head of him who is worthy," p.179) .

The social level of the soul is like the breath of the glassblower in the blowpipe—the spilling over of the divine influence from above. This outpouring of divine influence gives us a sense of spiritual motion at the social level, but it is further removed from God than the religious soul.

The breath then descends to the lowest level, the elemental soul. Here it is contained entirely within the physical, human body. At this level, its spiritual activity ceases, just as the breath of the glassblower comes to rest once the vessel reaches the desired shape.

What does all of this mean in human terms? How is the soul manifested in the human psyche? And how do we experience these stages of development of the soul?

MANIFESTATIONS OF THE SOUL IN THE PSYCHE

There are two kinds of manifestations of the soul in the psyche: specific manifestations and general manifestations.

SPECIFIC MANIFESTATIONS

At each stage of development the soul has different manifestations in the psyche. We will refer to these as the *specific manifestations* of the soul.

NEEDS AND POWERS OF THE SOUL		
LEVEL	**NEED**	**POWER**
ELEMENTAL	SATISFACTION	WILL
SOCIAL	IDENTITY	AWARENESS
RELIGIOUS	UNITY	UNIFICATION
TRANSCENDENT	FAITH	DEVOTION
ABSOLUTE	ABSOLUTE	TOTAL IDENTIFICATION WITH GOD'S WILL

The soul generates different powers and needs in us at each level. We feel the needs and are motivated to express the powers. These powers and needs of each level set the theme for that level.

One way to understand the needs and powers of the soul is to think of ourselves as cars having the potential to run at five different levels.

THE ELEMENTAL LEVEL

At the first, or the elemental level, our "engines" are turned on. We are like cars "revved" up and ready to go. In human terms, we are filled with the power of the will and the need for satisfaction (see Chapter 7 for a discussion of the power of the will and the need for satisfaction).

THE SOCIAL LEVEL

At the second, or the social level, we add a driver and motion. It is here, at the social level, that we see the intrinsic difference between humans and animals. We go beyond the physical and pick up the power of awareness and the need for identity (see Chapter 11 for discussion of identity and awareness).

THE RELIGIOUS LEVEL

At the third, or the religious level, we have a driver with a map and a destination who is searching for the right path. At the religious level, we get the power of unification and the need for unity (see Chapter 15 for a discussion of unification and unity).

THE TRANSCENDENT LEVEL

At the fourth, or the transcendent level, we are motivated by a longing for home. We feel that something very precious is waiting for us. We long to reach our destination, which gives us great momentum. We now not only use a road map with the route clearly marked but we pick up the need for faith and the power of devotion.

THE ABSOLUTE LEVEL

At the fifth, or the absolute level, we are in "radio contact" with home. We sanctify ourselves by using the car solely to obey God's will. At this level of elevation we have a need for the absolute and the power of total identification with God's will.

We have just discussed the specific powers and needs activated by the soul at each level of development. These powers and needs interact with the resources at each level and produce other specific effects. Now let's look at one ladder, the ladder of the senses, to see how the "theme" powers and needs are expressed at each level.

THE LADDER OF THE SOUL

On the elemental level of the ladder of the senses the need for satisfaction elicits desire and the need for pleasure. For the person on the social level, the need for sensory satisfaction is no longer just physical; it is combined with the social level need for identity and is thus expressed as a need for love and belonging. At the religious level, the need for sensory satisfaction is integrated with

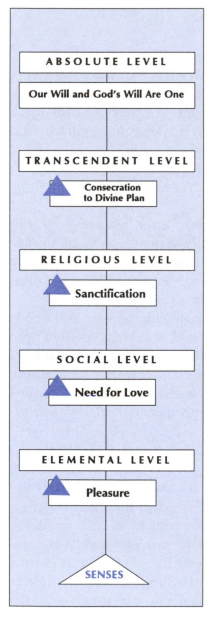

ABSOLUTE LEVEL

Our Will and God's Will Are One

TRANSCENDENT LEVEL

Consecration
to Divine Plan

RELIGIOUS LEVEL

Sanctification

SOCIAL LEVEL

Need for Love

ELEMENTAL LEVEL

Pleasure

SENSES

the need for unity between body and soul and elicits the need to sanctify love by using it as fuel for the quest for spiritual elevation. At this level, love becomes a means towards a higher end rather than an end in itself. Love creates a mutually supportive partnership for the fantastic journey back to the King (see the parable in the Introduction, p.34).

For example, a person at the elemental level would think, "I can't wait to finish work so I can go to the new club. There will be lots of new people there and I'll have a great time tonight." A person on the second level would think, "I'd really like to have a serious relationship with someone. I've been to clubs and parties but I've never met anyone who is ready to settle down. Maybe if I take a university course I'll have a better chance of meeting someone with common values and interests." A Torah-observant person on the third level would think, "I want to get married. I think I'll try to meet someone who wants to get married, share my spiritual journey and raise a Jewish family."

It is very important to understand that all three people described in the example above are responding to the same basic human need—the need for *sensory satisfaction*. However, as they move up the developmental ladder the need itself is transformed by being combined and integrated with higher level needs.

This structure may seem complicated, but the rest of this book is devoted to explaining it. There are examples that make each stage come alive so that we understand what real people are like at each stage. I write mainly about the first three stages (elemental, social and religious) because that's where most of us are.

Now that we know the structure of the soul, I want to point out that most secular psychological theories fit on the first two rungs of the ladders, the elemental and the social. There are a few that do attempt to take the third, or religious stage into account, e.g., Jungian "analytic psychology," but these theories only hint at the metaphysical part of the psyche. They do not have fully developed systems, and they are not based on the truth of Torah. Only the Torah gives us a comprehensive picture of the human psyche.

Most psychological theories not only leave out the spiritual stages entirely, but they give primacy to one or another lesser resource, thus creating a very distorted picture of human nature. Freud emphasized the pleasure principle (elemental stage); Adler focused on the will for power (social stage of the life force); and Frankl stressed the need for meaning (social stage of the intellect). Each of them identified an important part of the whole, and to that extent their words ring true. But none of them saw the totality, which is the balanced unification of all of the parts.

We have just talked about the structure of the soul and the specific manifestations at each level. Now we will discuss the *general manifestations of the soul in the psyche.*

GENERAL MANIFESTATIONS

The general manifestations of the soul in the psyche are those that are so fundamental to human life that they pervade every aspect of our lives. They are not specific to any one stage or resource.

There are two general manifestations of the soul in the psyche: the need for connection, safety and security; and the masculine/feminine dimension.

THE NEED FOR CONNECTION, SAFETY AND SECURITY

Everyone needs interpersonal connection. The need for connection is so strong that people will do anything to feel connected. They are willing to humiliate themselves—even die—for a feeling of connectedness. I have known accomplished, attractive people who were so desperate for love and companionship that they would settle for the most superficial and uncaring contact rather than be alone. It is well known that people often get depressed and even suicidal when relationships break up, and that spouses often die of "broken hearts" after the death of their loved ones.[6] Many studies have shown that how often we get sick and how long we live have more to do with the quality of our relationships than with germs, diet or environment. For example, one study showed that heart disease rates were significantly lower in a close-knit community of Italian-Americans than those in neighboring towns and the rest of the United States, *despite the fact that the residents of the community had a high-fat diet*. However, when the close ties and strong support system began to weaken as a result of changes in lifestyle among the younger generation, the heart disease rate rose substantially and began to equal national norms.[7]

The power of connection has also been demonstrated in an interesting series of experiments. Psychologists activated "unconscious oneness fantasies" by subliminally flashing the words "Mommy and I are one." They found that evoking the feeling of "oneness" had healing power. It reduced pathology in schizophrenics, reduced anxiety in people with insect phobia and helped people lose weight and reduce drinking.[8]

Why do we long to be connected? Does the longing for "oneness" originate in an elemental intrauterine memory trace of a state of symbiosis "for which deep down in the original primal unconscious ... every human being strives"?[9] Is it the aftermath of the trauma of being thrust out into the world at birth? Is it just a vestige of the period of infantile helplessness during which separation really was a matter of life and death? Is it based on a memory of the perfect happiness of the well-fed infant nestled contentedly against its mother's breast? Is it a neurotic need that resulted from unsuccessful resolution of the separation-individuation phase of development?

Each of the above explanations may be partly true, but they are all inadequate and incomplete. They are the kinds of explanations given by people who attempt to understand human nature without considering the human soul and its connection to God. If we deny God as Creator and thereby reduce the human being to a link in a purposeless evolutionary chain, these explanations make sense. But they do not make sense when applied to us. We were created by God with a divine purpose and a spark of the Divine: the soul. The desire for oneness arises from the longing of the soul to be reconnected to its Divine Source. As we shall soon see in Chapter 6, that union is the ultimate pleasure, and we are driven by our souls to search for that pleasure.

This desire for connection with God is first experienced as a desire for connection or attachment to people. Let us trace the development of the need for connection in an infant. At two months old, Naomi recognizes "Mommy" and will smile and coo in response to Mommy's voice. When Mommy goes away, Naomi stops smiling and cooing. She is learning that she and Mommy are separate.

Since there is a universal human need to be connected, the realization that we are "separate" is accompanied by fear and distress. We see this in the "separation anxiety" that babies experience some time between six and nine months of age. When little Naomi has matured enough to develop the ability to "sort out and classify the world into me and not-me, inside and outside, human and non-human, mother and not-mother,"[10] she will suddenly show fear and distress when separated from her mother. Before this time, any good caretaker would suffice, but now she will cry inconsolably if mother is out of sight, and reject even the most loving attention from "not-mother." Of course, most children pass through this stage and gradually become relatively autonomous human beings, but the need and desire to feel connected remains throughout life.

Connection feels good; separation is painful. We feel

safe and secure when connected; we feel anxious and insecure when disconnected. Separation anxiety is so distressing that many psychologists think that it triggers fear of death. For example, Otto Rank talks about "birth fear" as a primal fear associated with the trauma of separation from the mother. "Birth fear" is made up of "fear of life and fear of death, since birth on the one hand means the end of life (former life) and on the other carries on the fear of a new life."[11] Lifton and Olson say that birth activates the child's innate potential for death imagery.[12] In their view, fear of death is simply part of living. Judith Viorst[13] expresses a similar view:

> For the presence of mother—our mother—stands for safety. Fear of her loss is the earliest terror we know . . . Separation anxiety derives from the literal truth that without a caretaking presence we would die.

Naomi seems to know instinctively that her life is in jeopardy if she is separated from "Mommy." If she hears a loud noise while she is alone in her crib, she will become startled and cry; when she is in Mommy's arms, the same noise will startle her, but she will not cry. Children seem to have an intuitive recognition of their absolute dependency, and so separation from their primary source of nurturance elicits terror. Reconnection brings comfort and tranquility.

We never lose this unconscious relation between separation and death, and between contact and safety. As adults, being alone may not bring the terror it brought us as children, but we may feel vaguely, inexplicably uneasy when we are alone. We may be startled and frightened by sounds that we don't even notice when another person is present.

Most of us just feel safer and more secure with someone else there.

Memory of early fears certainly contributes to our separation anxiety, but the deepest root of the edgy feeling we have when alone is the longing of the soul for connection with its Divine Source. Without another person present to give us the *feeling* of completeness, we experience our incompleteness. We sense our life and death need for connection with the Divine. We intuitively feel the spiritual danger of being cut off from God.

The soul uses our need for connection to help us make the journey back to the "King." What starts out in infancy as a life and death dependency on others for survival turns into a real psychological need for people. We feel the divine spark in others, and we develop a real need for human closeness. In *Bereishis*: (2:24), God tells Adam about oneness: "Therefore shall a man leave his father and mother, cleave unto his wife; and they shall be one flesh." So powerful is human love that the *Song of Songs*, which has been described as the "holiest of holies," uses human love as a metaphor for the love between God and the Jewish people. Human intimacy gives us a sense of the pleasure of oneness with God.

Ideally, then, our first connection to "Mommy" expands to include "Daddy" and others, and eventually it transfers to God. This transferral is just the opposite of the psychological notion that belief in God is nothing more than an introject of the all-powerful father (or, as Erich Fromm would have it, the all-powerful leader).[14] Relating to a seemingly omnipotent father is a necessary developmental stage in our later ability to relate to God. *God is not a substitute for father, father is a substitute for God.* Our entire mental and emotional structure was designed to help us to achieve our spiritual goal of reconnecting with our Source.

If handled correctly, the need for connection propels us up the ladder to love of others and, eventually, to love of God. In the Torah system, the ideal for interpersonal connection is to establish close relationships based on giving, and to strive to reach the lofty heights of being able to "love the other as you love yourself" because "you" and the "other" are actually one, both being sparks of the same Divine Root—God. Knowing this, it is easy to understand why disturbances in the ability to connect are so damaging. They interfere with satisfaction of a basic need and disrupt our movement toward God.

Let us follow the development and expansion of the need for connection as it is expressed at different levels of the soul. At the elemental level we are not aware that our souls yearn for connection with God. All we can experience is a desire for safety, security and relief from tension through some kind of contact or distraction. We yearn for the physical presence of another person, for belonging and being part of a group, or for a grown-up version of a "blankie" (for example, a pet or a blaring radio). At this stage, therefore, the need for connection is often expressed through sex, constant casual group companionship and curiosity about people (consider the fascination with gossip).

At the social level, the needs for connection, safety and security are expressed in terms of the need for identity. We don't feel safe unless we know who we are and where we belong. People with serious identity problems are often very insecure and anxious. They feel empty and panicky when left alone. They are excessively clingy and dependent on others, because they get their sense of self exclusively through others. For people who do achieve an adequate sense of self-identity, loving and being loved, meaning through membership in a group (community, society, country, etc.) and success become important at the social level.

When we reach the religious level, we begin to understand that our need for connection cannot be satisfied without a spiritual connection to God. By learning Torah, we come to see that the life-and-death feeling associated with separation is based on reality; we do die spiritually without a connection to God. We have to use our "separation anxiety" to motivate us to search for the only eternal connection, our connection with God. At the religious level, the needs for connection, safety and security are expressed as a need to give to others, to get closer to God, and to involve God in our love. Love at this level becomes the ultimate human connection. This is reflected in the saying of our Sages that there are three partners in the creation of a human being: man, woman and God.

We have seen that the need for connection is so central and so powerful that it affects our emotional, spiritual and physical health. Therefore, we have to be very careful in how we respond to this need. Only if connection has a spiritual component, only if it unites body and soul, can it give real satisfaction. The need, however, can be so urgent, we can feel so miserable and lonely when not connected that we are tempted to grab anything that will still the yearning. But settling for partial, substitute or temporary satisfaction boomerangs.

Not only do we end up lonely over and over again, but we slowly lose our sensitivity to the authentic need, the need for spiritual connection. We lose our ability to recognize the authentic need and to discriminate between it and its physical counterpart. As time goes on, the unrecognized, unfulfilled need becomes greater and greater and has less and less chance of being satisfied. Therefore, though the journey be long and hard, we must keep searching for real satisfaction of the need for spiritual connection.

THE MASCULINE/FEMININE DIMENSION

In the Torah view of human nature there are fundamentally masculine and fundamentally feminine responses to the universe. Both masculinity and femininity are considered essential, and neither is devalued or oppressed. I want to emphasize that there is absolutely no implication of good and bad associated with the terms masculine and feminine; the terms simply reflect characteristic response modes. Both modes are important to balanced personality development, to harmonious interpersonal relationships and to doing the many things that have to be done in the world.

This masculine/feminine dimension in human existence has long been acknowledged by conventional wisdom and has often been studied by psychologists. It has been referred to as yin/yang, active/passive, active/reactive, instrumental/expressive, agency/communion, allocentric/autocentric, anima/animus, instrumentality/expressiveness, rational/relational and assertive/gentle. Most languages are imprecise, however, and none of the rubrics, including the present one, seem quite complete. Nevertheless, all of us know that there is a difference between a forceful, externally focused approach to life and a more gentle, internally focused approach. I know that I might be touching on a sensitive issue here, but I venture to say that many of us tend to consider the more forceful approach to be "masculine," and the more gentle approach "feminine," regardless of whether they were manifested by a man or a woman.

All people have both masculine and feminine aspects to their personalities, but the proportions are different for different people. In general, obviously, men have more of the masculine end of the continuum and women have more of the feminine end. However, some women will have more of certain masculine traits than some men, and some men will have more of certain feminine traits than some women. Each of us, as individual men and women, needs to find the proper balance in order to achieve completion.

Depending on the proportion of masculine and feminine in our personalities, we will be more comfortable playing certain roles than others. For example, people who are predominantly masculine will find it very difficult to take submissive roles, and vice versa, people who are predominantly feminine find it very difficult to be assertive. The masculine person who works for a masculine boss may chafe at the limits imposed, while the feminine person in such a job would enjoy being told exactly what to do. The feminine person who takes on managerial responsibilities will cringe whenever a decision has to be made or a recalcitrant employee has to be dealt with, while the masculine person would find the challenges stimulating and exciting.

Why did God create us with essential masculinity and femininity? Why does it take two people, a man and a woman, to create a whole, rather than each individual being a complete entity? Let's look at the psychological implications. If we were complete in and of ourselves, we would be very independent, and we would have very little need or desire for closeness or cooperation. We would be competitive and focus our energies on insuring our own fulfillment and acquiring as much as possible for ourselves. But, if we were dependent on God and others, we would have to collaborate, cooperate and share. We would need to find many ways to accommodate differences, to grow close, to establish secure bonds, to foster each other's growth and to strengthen partnerships. We would want to try to unite all of our own powers with the powers of others to create the optimal harmonious society. It seems obvious that incompletion is exactly what we need to promote movement toward our ultimate destiny, which is building a harmonious society through unity within ourselves and among people. Being sufficient unto ourselves would impede such movement.

Now that we can understand why we were created incomplete, let's learn a little more about what we mean by masculine and feminine. In Torah, the masculine mode is to seek progress, while the feminine is to seek unity. In terms of the model we are developing in this book, then, men tend to work on what we will call elevation, or moving closer to God, and women tend to work on what we will call unification, or being more like God (see Chapter 5 for a discussion of elevation and unification). We all need both modes in order to achieve *sheleimus*, or completion. The masculine part drives us to elevate ourselves, and the feminine part drives us to integrate and harmonize ourselves. The two modes are complementary, and the Torah ideal is for the two to be combined in marriage, with the partnership benefiting from both styles.

Let's look at a few examples of typical masculine and feminine responses at various stages of development. At the elemental level we have the will to live. The masculine response to the will to live is to generate the means of survival, e.g., build homes, harness natural resources, earn a living, engage in medical research and application. The feminine response is to use the means of survival to create the best quality of life. At the social level, we have the quest for meaning. The masculine response to the quest for meaning is to generate different ideas and build society. The feminine response is to find meaning in family, community and society. At the religious level, we have the need for truth. The masculine response to the need for truth is to study Torah. The feminine response is to promote harmony in family, community, and society and build a Jewish identity.

We see that in Torah life the masculine and feminine modes can be expressed in meaningful ways at each and every stage of development. Therefore we can find fulfillment without violating our fundamental masculinity or femininity.

SUMMARY

RESOURCES

The body has three resources which the soul can use for spiritual growth: the life force, the senses, and the intellect. Each resource is portrayed in this book as a ladder.

STAGES

Each ladder has five stages of development: the elemental level, the social level, the religious level, the transcendent level, and the absolute level. Each stage is described as a rung of the ladder.

SPECIFIC MANIFESTATIONS

Each stage of the soul activates different needs and powers (see diagram), which in turn interact with the resources at each level to produce specific effects.

GENERAL MANIFESTATIONS

There are two general manifestations: The need for connection, safety and security, and the masculine/feminine dimension.

Only a Torah view of personality development can be comprehensive. While most secular personality theories deal with only the first two stages, the Torah-consistent model presented here covers all five (elemental, social, religious, transcendent and absolute). Torah teaches us that there is much more to life than most of us ever dreamed possible. Let's go on and learn more about the Torah model of the development of the soul.

Growth and Development of the Soul

CHAPTER 5

Persons are not their stage of development; persons are a creative motion.[1]

I n the last chapter we discussed the structure of the soul and its effects on the psyche. We delineated five stages of development: elemental, social, religious, transcendent and absolute. Lest all this talk about stages give you the impression that people can be neatly pigeonholed ("Sheila is at the elemental level; Michael is at the social level"), I want to emphasize that we are not static creatures. As the quote above says, we are a "creative motion," always yearning, always reaching, always striving. Stages are primarily resting points on the journey.

Depending on our goals, we are either moving up or moving down. For example, among people who appear to be comfortably settled at the social level, many are actually groping for spirituality, while others are toying with the idea of acting out more elemental desires. Among those who are moving up would be those who are involved in an internal process of preparation for becoming religious (future *baalei teshuvah*). Among those who are moving down would be the stable, successful "solid citizen" who gets involved with someone at the office and is seriously thinking about leaving his wife and children in order to have more time for other pursuits.

We transform our personalities as we move from one stage to another. The transformation can be generative or degenerative. If we move up we elevate ourselves, and if we move down we defile ourselves. When moving up, positive disintegration,[2] or *loosening* of existing structure, necessarily precedes integration at a higher level. We have to experience some conflict between "what is" and "what ought to be," some frustration and dissatisfaction with ourselves, before we are willing to take the next step. Change is unsettling, but the rewards of progress are well worth the temporary discomfort.

All orderly development follows certain principles. For example, a principle of fetal development is increasing complexity (from a single cell to a multi-cell organism); a principle of cognitive development is movement from concrete to abstract thinking; and a principle of personality development is a "progressive redefinition or reorganization of the self"[3] in relation to all that is non-self (others and the world). In this chapter we are going to discuss the principles of the development of the soul.

THE DEVELOPMENT OF THE SOUL

There are two principles in the development of the soul: elevation and unification (horizontal and vertical).

THE ELEVATION PRINCIPLE

The soul has the job of elevating us, of moving us up the ladders toward spiritual perfection. The elemental soul does this by activating or "turning on" the life force, the senses and emotions, and the intellect and then using these resources to raise our spiritual level. Just as a good driver starts a car and then skillfully maneuvers it through traffic, starting and stopping according to the lights, adjusting the speed to the flow of traffic, avoiding hazards and paying attention to monitors and warning signals, so the divine soul maneuvers us through life. If the lower *physical* soul is in control, there is power without direction. The car follows the curve of the road, and collision and damage are inevitable. If the social soul is in the driver's seat, we have only local, temporary goals for our trip. We might want to win a race, impress someone with our new car, or strengthen our identity by having the "in" car. We need the guidance and direction of the higher levels of the divine soul in order to steer safely through life and reach our desired destination.

We are all born with the elemental soul, or the body, in charge. The soul works at linking up with higher and higher levels and putting them in the driver's seat. For example, at the elemental stage of the ladder of the intellect we are curious about the world. A walk around the block with two-year-old Billy can take hours; he wants to watch the ants, pick the flowers, roll in the grass, chase the butterflies and pet the neighbor's dog. This is fine for little Billy, but in time the soul pushes him to start seeing some order in the world rather than just responding to whatever passes by.

When Billy is nine years old he writes a science report on the kinds of butterflies that live in his part of the country. His awareness of the world is more sophisticated now, but he is still at the elemental level in that he is collecting more information and sensation without reflecting on what it all means.

By the age of fifteen, Billy has become quite an expert on butterflies. He learned all about the anatomy of butterflies by studying specimens in biology lab. But he has begun to wonder whether it is right to kill in order to learn. He loves to sharpen his wits in heated philosophical debates about the rights of living things. Billy has now reached the social stage of the intellectual ladder, a stage which is characterized by the quest for meaning.

The soul keeps working on Billy, and when he is a twenty-three year old biology graduate student he is struck by the infinite mystery of the butterfly. How could such a gorgeous creature come into existence? How could such a delicate organism survive? Billy realizes that neither science nor philosophy can answer his questions. For Billy, the butterfly has become testimony to a higher power in the universe and he now has a desire for spiritual truth. At the urging of the soul, Billy has now elevated himself to the religious stage.

UNIFICATION: HORIZONTAL AND VERTICAL

The second developmental principle is *unification*. *Unification* is harmonious integration of all the needs and powers activated by the soul *at any given level of development* (horizontal) or *on any given ladder* (vertical).

Let's look at an example of *unification* in an area we are all familiar with: the desire for food. At the elemental stage we respond only to our lower needs, without acknowledging our higher needs. We treat the impulse of the moment as an isolated need. We eat whatever is on hand when we are hungry. At higher stages, higher level needs combine with lower needs. At the social stage we hold off eating in order to have the additional pleasure of eating with good friends and going to the right restaurant. At the religious stage we eat only if the food fulfills the requirements of the soul, i.e., if the food is kosher and we have said the correct blessing.

At the elemental level, the emphasis is on satisfying the physical appetite as quickly as possible; at the social level, interpersonal and status needs are combined with the need for food; and at the religious level, physical and social needs are integrated with spiritual needs. At the religious level we still get hungry, we still want to eat, we still enjoy eating, we still want good company and pleasant surroundings, but all of these needs are satisfied in a way that unifies them harmoniously with spiritual needs and thereby elevates them.

The above example demonstrates *vertical unification*, or the integration of the needs and powers activated as we climb one ladder, the ladder of the senses. For the personality to be balanced, however, *unification* has to proceed in two directions, vertical and horizontal. *Horizontal unification* is the integration of the needs and powers of all the ladders up to the current level of development.

Let's go back to Billy and the butterflies to try to get a clear picture of *vertical* and *horizontal unification*. Billy's story illustrated *vertical unification* on the ladder of the intellect. Billy successfully integrated the curiosity of the elemental stage, the quest for meaning of the social stage and the desire for truth of the religious stage into a unified intellect. That same curiosity that spurred him on intellectually as a child later lead him to search for absolute truth.

But there is more to Billy than his intellect. Let's suppose that in terms of his senses and his life force, Billy is still at the social level. Up to the point where the butterfly became testimony to God, Billy had successfully unified all of his needs and powers at the social level. He found pleasure within a committed relationship, and he used his life energy and intellect to study for a respected career. He felt a sense of balance and harmony in his life.

As soon as Billy became aware of God, however, his unity was disrupted. He rose one stage higher on the intellectual ladder than on the other two, putting himself in a state of imbalance. He will be uncomfortable until he is able to integrate his new awareness of the Divine into his life. Since Billy is Jewish, the ideal first step would be to start learning Torah. From Torah he could learn how to raise his senses and life force to the religious level, restoring unity, balance and harmony to his life. Step by step, Billy could bring himself closer to being the ideal Torah personality.

The ideal, or *fully* developed, Torah personality results from a balanced *integration* of all three of the resources at all five of the stages of development (horizontal and vertical unity). Our purpose in life is to strive toward the ultimate goal of complete unification at the highest levels of elevation by living according to Torah principles. We get our direction from Torah, but each of us grows toward our potential at our own rate. Torah tells us that when we get to Heaven we will not be asked why we weren't as great as Moses but why we weren't as great as we ourselves could have been.

The two principles of elevation and unification explain a very common problem, the problem of giving up when we "bite off more than we can chew" (elevating more than we can unify). For example, we read an article on fitness and then decide to eliminate all sweets from our diet and exercise an hour every day. After a couple of days we think, "With all the exercise I'm doing, one ice cream cone won't hurt me" or "I really am too busy to exercise today. I'll go back to my fitness program tomorrow." But tomorrow never comes, because we tried to do too much too soon.

Another all too common example occurs among Jews who are trying to return to Judaism. People who have never kept *Shabbos* before attend a *Shabbaton* (a special *Shabbos* program) and are deeply moved. The glow of the *Shabbos* candles, the taste of the *challah*, the stirring singing and the closeness of a shared experience touch their souls. They feel elevated, but alas, the "high" is temporary. They try to keep the next *Shabbos* alone but find the services uninspiring and the day long and boring. They can't wait for it to be over. Unless they realize that they need to find spiritual leadership and the companionship of like-minded people to help them keep *Shabbos*, they are in danger of giving up on *Shabbos* observance or becoming spiritual thrill-seekers, going from one program to another looking for a spiritual "high." If they make the mistake of thinking that spiritual pleasure is the criterion for the truth, they may even give up Judaism entirely.

If we jump to a level before we're ready to integrate it, we actually interfere with our development. We create cognitive dissonance (see discussion of cognitive dissonance in Appendix A) in ourselves and have to reduce the discomfort by denying the new information ("*Shabbos* was nice, but I can get the same warm feeling without the restrictions by having a party with good friends") and avoiding the experience that created the uncomfortable dissonance.

As a general rule, balanced growth can be accomplished by dedicating ourselves firmly to our goal and then taking measured steps (elevation) toward the Torah ideal. When we have integrated one, or a few, steps into the whole fabric of our lives (unification), we are ready to move forward again. The *process* of elevating and unifying ourselves is exciting and challenging, and the rewards are great. It is very important to know that no matter where we're starting from, it is never too late to start.

FREE WILL: THE PROCESS OF DEVELOPMENT

How do spiritual elevation and unification happen? Is there "spiritual DNA" containing a genetically encoded plan for the unfolding of the stages of the soul? The answer is a resounding "No!" That would defeat our purpose in life, which is to *unify* and *elevate* ourselves by our own *free will* choices. As explained in Chapter 2, the soul progresses *only* if we make the right choices. Free choice is a fundamental Torah principle. We are free to heed the urgings of our divine souls, or to deny them.

We feel a great sense of satisfaction and accomplishment when we use our powers for elevation. But, when we use our powers incorrectly, or fail to use them, we actually feel a sense of shame and embarrassment. These uncomfortable feelings are gifts from the divine soul, signals that we are mistreating ourselves (and perhaps others). Like the pain of a twisted muscle, the shame and embarrassment of twisted behavior warn us to change our ways. If we disregard or misinterpret the warnings, we are in danger of doing irreparable damage to ourselves. If we tell ourselves that no matter what we do we have nothing to be ashamed of, we risk letting our spiritual muscles atrophy and becoming spiritual cripples. If, on the other hand, we recognize and heed the warnings, we can use the energy generated by the discomfort as a propellant to change. The feelings can also serve as a "homing" device to help us stay on course: "I feel embarrassed. I had better examine what just happened and see what went wrong."

We have the choice of refining ourselves, enriching our lives and living with the deep joy that comes from dedication to higher goals, or of settling for short-term gratification and long-term despair.

Ideally, unification and elevation work hand in hand. When we make free will choices that *elevate* us, we add new needs and powers to our lives. We then have to *unify* by integrating those new needs and powers into our personalities. When we successfully elevate and unify ourselves, we feel great serenity and joy. But if we try to unify without elevation, or elevate without unification, we risk serious personality imbalances.

PERSONALITY IMBALANCES

DEVELOPMENT OF ONE RESOURCE AT THE EXPENSE OF OTHERS

I once gave a university extension course entitled, "Intimacy Skills for Successful Women." It was very well attended by physicians, lawyers, executives, and artists, all of whom were lonely and dissatisfied with their lives. Without exception, the women in the class had developed the resource of competence (the life force) at the expense of the resource of closeness (the senses). And without exception, they suffered psychologically from the imbalance.

One of the students, Kim, was an exceptionally attractive and brilliant physician. She had a very successful private practice as well as a faculty position at a prestigious medical school. She combined professional competence and dedication with a warm and cheerful "bedside manner" that made her beloved and respected by her patients. Unfortunately, her warmth, dedication and good cheer disappeared in intimate relationships. When she was not in control of a relationship, she became critical and demanding. The daughter of a prominent physician, her entire life had been focused on achievement. Her natural warmth and nurturance were used in the service of her career. She had to learn how to untangle her professional persona from her personal identity, and then learn how to satisfy her needs for intimacy and belonging. When she was able to put her need for love ahead of her need for control, she was a much happier woman.

GETTING STUCK AT ONE LEVEL

There are also other kinds of imbalances. One of my clients, Carl, had a history of poor relationships. His problem, according to his previous therapist, was that he didn't know how to assert his needs and feelings. The therapist believed that if Carl could be more assertive and more direct he would improve his relationships. So he taught Carl to "express himself." To Carl's dismay, things began to get worse instead of better. After a divorce and innumerable first dates that never progressed to a second, he sought my help.

Carl's problem was that he had gotten stuck at the elemental level. He was almost completely self-absorbed. Teaching him to express himself was like taking the muzzle off an angry dog. He demanded, criticized, blamed, confronted and complained. His expensive new skill of "expressing himself" offended people and brought him constant retaliation and rejection. Each interpersonal failure generated more and more negative feeling and this led to a vicious cycle of anger, expression, alienation, insecurity and lowered self-esteem.

Carl was helped by learning what his real needs were. When he realized that he *needed* to give as well as take; that he needed to act in a loving way rather than just fall in love; that he *needed* to be sensitive to the feelings of others rather than be preoccupied with how they were treating him, then his relationships improved, as did his general level of well-being. He progressed to the social level and learned how to live in a way that brought him genuine self-approval rather than an inflated sense of self.

We have looked at two kinds of personality imbalances. The first type, which we saw in Kim, was caused by emphasis on one resource over another (elevation without unification). Success was placed ahead of connectedness. This pattern produces people who are psychologically "muscle-bound." One set of overdeveloped muscles (competence) actually interferes with development of another set (intimacy).

The second type of imbalance, which we saw in Carl, was caused by mixing *levels* before he was ready. He tried to satisfy social level needs with elemental level skills. This is like trying to crochet lace with a hatchet.

Carl and Kim are examples of elevation and unification to the social level. Both were helped to become sensitive and realize more of their potential, but neither was yet at the religious level. From the point of view of Torah psychology, this is partial treatment. Complete treatment includes elevation and unification at the religious level.

PERSONALITY BALANCE

All of us can learn to lead balanced lives. There is, however, a very strong human tendency to keep doing what is familiar, whether it works or not. We always feel awkward doing something new, and great self-discipline is required to overcome our resistance to doing the unfamiliar.

At every step there are difficult challenges with unknown consequences. And at every stage there are pleasures which make it tempting to take the easy way out and avoid the challenges involved in moving up. For example, at the lowest level we live with a minimum of responsibility and pressure. By being self-oriented and focusing on satisfying our own needs without concern for others, we do simplify our lives, even if the ultimate consequences are not very pleasant.

But most of us can't settle for life at the lowest level because our souls won't let us. The soul beams its subliminal message to us, "There is more, there is more." We feel a vague discomfort, a restless stirring, a desire for more. More what? At the elemental level we think we want more of the pleasures of the world. "If I had a new car I would be happy." "If I had a new dress I would be happy." "If I could go to the latest movie, newest restaurant, etc., I would be happy." And yet, when we succeed in getting these things, we are still not happy. We feel a moment of pleasure and satisfaction and then we immediately want something else.

Freud observed this pattern of chronic yearning and saw it as evidence of a serious psychological conflict embedded in human nature. He came to the conclusion that we were "neurotic animals," doomed to live with deep psychic conflicts. His view of human nature was seriously distorted by the fact that he did not look at the human being as a creature with a soul. His theory fits a "soulless" creature quite well (or someone who oppresses his soul), but it debases a creature who is divine.

For a creature with a divine soul, it is not neurotic to be dissatisfied with a spiritually shallow life; it is normal. When our bodies are deprived of adequate physical nourishment we feel weak. When our souls are deprived of adequate spiritual nourishment we feel dissatisfied. *Dissatisfaction is the normal response to spiritual malnutrition*, whether it is malnutrition caused by complete starvation or from a diet of junk food. We have a need for God whether we know it or not. As Rabbi Eliyahu Lopian said, "Faith for the soul is as the air one breathes, and without air man cannot endure at all."[4]

Our souls work very hard at their jobs of trying to keep us on a spiritual path. They will not let us settle for trivial satisfaction. They exert unrelenting pressure on us to make us see that the pattern of wanting and getting does not lead to enduring satisfaction. But sometimes we try to resist the responsibility inherent in the message from our souls. There are four possible ways to evade the pressure we feel from our souls.

RESISTING PRESSURE FROM OUR SOULS

SUBSTITUTE GRATIFICATION

We stay tuned in to the pressure from the soul but we try to mollify it with substitute forms of spiritual gratification. For example, we get a spiritual pleasure from listening to music or seeking religious "highs." We feel uplifted, but the experience does nothing to build our character or elevate us spiritually.

Margaret is an example of spiritual substitution. She considers herself to be a "spiritual" person. She is not satisfied with a materialistic life, and she seeks out all kinds of spiritual experiences. She has traveled to the Himalayas in pursuit of Nirvana; she has tried meditation; and most recently, she has tried "channeling." She gets a spiritual "high" from many of her experiences, but ends up feeling empty and unsatisfied because she is reaching for unification without elevation. She never admits to herself that after all the years of searching, she still does not have a firm, meaningful foundation for her life.

PARTIAL FULFILLMENT

We stay "tuned in" to the pressure from the soul but we settle for partial fulfillment. Occasionally, *when we feel like it,* we pray or attend religious services, but we don't make a commitment to our spiritual progress. By placating the soul when the pressure builds up, we risk damaging our capacity for wholeness and integrity, which are essential parts of spirituality.

GIVING UP THE SEARCH FOR THE TRUTH

We stay "tuned in" to the divine channel but fail to take any constructive action. We say, "I believe that Torah is true and I want spirituality in my life, but it just doesn't come. I've tried praying and going to services, but it doesn't work. I just don't feel anything. What can I do? Maybe a beautiful sunset or something will inspire me." We equate spirituality with some kind of pleasurable experience, rather than with pursuing spiritual truth. We don't feel obligated or motivated by the truth and we risk losing our sensitivity to the truth.

DESTROYING THE SOUL'S SENSITIVITY

We are annoyed by the pressure from the soul so we "tune out." We "fix" ourselves by switching over to other channels which bring us satisfaction *at the expense of our higher selves.* Some of these other channels are career, entertainment, drugs and promiscuity. By constantly stimulating ourselves, we distract ourselves from our deeper needs and eventually we destroy our sensitivity to these needs. By turning a deaf ear to the soul, eventually we silence the soul.

How is the soul silenced? What is the mechanism that cuts us off from divine influence? Rabbi Aharon Feldman (in his elaboration of the insights of the Vilna Gaon) explains that we were created for the purpose of arriving at:

> a clear recognition of God's sovereignty and to live a life which reflects this recognition. "Good" is anything which moves us toward this end. Conversely, "evil" is that which thwarts our progress toward it.[5]

We all struggle with the conflict between the the inclination towards evil (the *yetzer hora*) and the inclination toward good (the *yetzer tov*). According to Rabbi Yisrael Salanter,[6] there are two forms of the *yetzer hora,* and each creates a different spiritual/psychological conflict in us. One is the conflict between the *yetzer tov* and the *yetzer hora* of unrestrained lust, "to desire that which is momentarily sweet—without taking heed of the future, though the end will be a bitter one." The other is the conflict betweeen the *yetzer tov* and the *yetzer hora* of *ruach hatumah* (a spirit of defilement) "which surrounds the individual, so as to cause him to sin," even though there is no passion or benefit to the transgressor.

If we indulge these two forms of the *yetzer hora* we create spiritual defilement (*tumah*) and our souls are dulled (*metamtem hanefesh*). *Tumah* is like a veil drawn over the higher soul which darkens it and prevents its light from illuminating our lives. "Once man becomes involved in his self, his drive to come close to God—his *yetzer tov*—weakens and eventually falls silent."[7] When this happens, we can no longer recognize the truth and actually think that the bad is good and the good is bad.

Torah teaches us that what is true in the spiritual world has its counterpart in the physical world, and science has provided us with the physical analogue of *ruach hatumah.* Immunologist Ted Steele[8] has shown that every organism contains blank DNA (unprogrammed genetic material) whose function is to be programmed by life experiences. This blank DNA can be programmed in different ways: by damage to the RNA (the messenger of DNA) from infections and radiation, by the formation of new behavior patterns and by introduction into the organism by injection or ingestion of the RNA of another organism. Scientists have actually demonstrated memory transfer from one organism to another. In a series of experiments with different species, they found that if one organism is trained to complete a maze, an untrained organism who eats or is injected with the RNA of the trained organism will learn the maze much more quickly than untreated, untrained organisms.

The spiritual counterpart is that just as the DNA can be modified, the soul can be modified. We are affected spiritually by noxious environmental influences, our own deeds and what we introduce into ourselves by injection and ingestion (we truly are what we eat). If we are exposed to spiritual toxins (things forbidden by Torah), we damage our spiritual DNA and create *ruach hatumah*. The effect of this spirit of defilement is that we desire certain things not because of an inherent drive for them, but because past events have distorted our spiritual DNA and made us desire unwholesome things.

The damage to the soul is a purely metaphysical phenomenon which we cannot see by observation. We need the Torah to teach us to discern between healthy and unhealthy soul food. Could we ever figure out on our own that indulging in things forbidden by Torah (for example, eating non-kosher food) could cause *spiritual* damage and distort our personalities by strengthening the *yetzer hora*, darkening our souls and impairing our ability to tell bad from good?

Secular psychology has absolutely no way to understand, explain, prevent or remediate the personality damage caused by violating the soul. Only *teshuvah* (repairing our relationship with God) can remove the veil from the soul and psyche.

RESPONDING TO PRESSURE FROM THE SOUL

The correct way of responding to pressure from the soul is to stay connected to the "divine channel" and go through the difficult but very rewarding process of self-evaluation and change.

What do we have to do to make the correct response? How can we learn to recognize the message from our souls? And what can we do about it when we hear it? The rest of this book is devoted to answering these questions.

SUMMARY

DEVELOPMENTAL PRINCIPLES OF THE SOUL

Elevation: upward movement towards greater spiritual perfection.

Unification: harmonious integration of the needs and powers activated by the soul.

a. vertical unification is integration of the needs and powers of any one ladder.

b. horizontal unification is integration of the needs and powers of all the ladders up to one's current level of development.

PERSONALITY IMBALANCES

Development of one resource at the expense of others, e.g., professional competence (life force ladder) at the expense of personal relationships (sensory/emotional ladder).

Getting stuck at one level because of ignorance, lack of skills, or a lack of motivation.

WAYS OF RESISTING PRESSURE FROM OUR SOULS

The four ways are: substitute gratification; partial fulfillment; equate spirituality with pleasure, rather than with truth; and oppression of the soul by destroying sensitivity.

THE

LEVELS

OF THE

SOUL

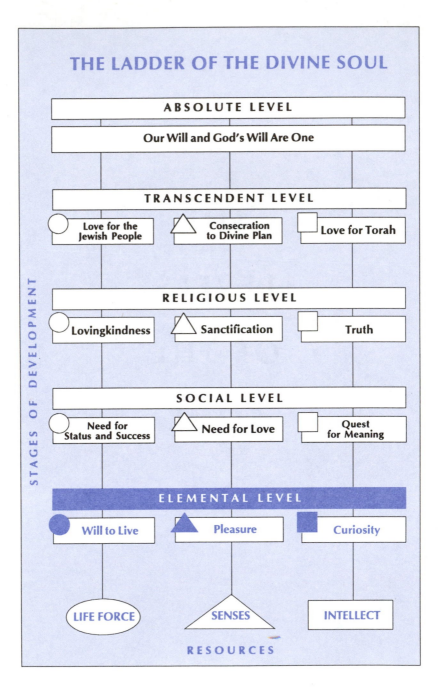

THE LADDER OF THE DIVINE SOUL

ABSOLUTE LEVEL

Our Will and God's Will Are One

TRANSCENDENT LEVEL

Love for the Jewish People | Consecration to Divine Plan | Love for Torah

RELIGIOUS LEVEL

Lovingkindness | Sanctification | Truth

SOCIAL LEVEL

Need for Status and Success | Need for Love | Quest for Meaning

ELEMENTAL LEVEL

Will to Live | Pleasure | Curiosity

LIFE FORCE | SENSES | INTELLECT

RESOURCES

STAGES OF DEVELOPMENT

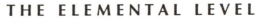

CHAPTER 6

Will Power and the Need for Satisfaction

We can't will what we will.[1]

Here we are at the elemental level, which is the bottom level of the soul. It is here that we start our extended journey upwards.

It would be worthwhile to study this diagram of the ladders of the soul (opposite page) for a few moments before continuing.

The very essence of the elemental soul is a focus on self-survival and gratification. The elemental soul activates the will power and the need for satisfaction, and these two driving forces are the themes of the elemental level. We feel a compelling need for life, pleasure and information.

WILL POWER

The will is the feeling behind the statement, "I want. . ." The will is the primary energy source in our personalities. Sometimes it is conscious, sometimes not. Sometimes we don't know what we want, but our behavior reveals our will. The will itself is very primitive; it is raw energy. It can be used for very base pursuits, but it can also be used for elevated pursuits. In fact, the will is crucial for spiritual growth and development. Without will, we would stay forever infantile, and we would never make any progress. We have to will ourselves to move beyond the elemental level, beyond creature comfort. We have to will ourselves to curb our impulses, to transcend narrow self-interest, to refine our personalities.

The undisciplined will, however, can get us into a lot of trouble. When the full energy of the will is attached to elemental drives, it overrides higher concerns. We often seem to be at the mercy of the will. "It" is in power, and the intellect seems powerless to interfere with "it." For example, when trying to diet, we stuff a piece of candy in our mouths while telling ourselves, "You really must control yourself."

And yet, we have all experienced moments when "we" are in control, when suddenly we are able to bend the will to our advantage. Many successful dieters have told me that after years of struggling in vain to lose weight, they simply woke up one day and knew that they were ready to restrict their eating. "It" was no longer in control of them, they were in control of "it." Unfortunately, at some later date, many of them found that "it" was again in control, and they gained back all the weight they had lost.

The problem is that we don't seem able to determine when that moment of control will arrive or how long it will last. We know how to use the will once it is sparked, but we can't seem to spark it ourselves. And while we wait for that moment, we may be killing ourselves physically and spiritually.

In psychology, the problem is often discussed in terms of motivation. Everyone knows that motivated people perform much better than unmotivated people. When little Shmuel doesn't do well in school in spite of the fact that he seems very bright, we say that the problem is that he's not motivated. But that raises the question: how do we motivate him? How can we develop the power to evoke and harness the will?

Five factors affect the level of will power: self-esteem, difficulties, the real, the ideal and meaning. If we want to strengthen the will power, we have to do one or more of the following: raise self-esteem, increase the difference between the ideal and the real, give meaning to the ideal, decrease the difficulties and give meaning to the difficulties.

Before going on to give examples of how these factors relate to will power, let us explain the second factor. When we talk about increasing the size of the difference between the real and the ideal, we don't mean just quantitative size, say the difference between earning $20,000 a year and $1,000,000 a year. We're also referring to qualitative difference, measured by how much the ideal means to us.

Qualitatively, a large difference between the real and the ideal means that the ideal is very important to us. For example, we might not be very motivated to take a new job with more responsibilities just to raise our salary from $30,000 to $32,000 a year (small quantitative difference), but we might be very motivated to do it if we desperately needed the money for special education for a disabled child (small quantitative difference, large qualitative difference).

We sometimes have to increase the difference between the real and the ideal (quantitatively or qualitatively) because our goals have to be way beyond our immediate reach to really inspire us. To really evoke the will, the ultimate goal has to be worth struggling for. We don't need a lot of motivation to do something that is easy.

Now we'll look at some examples of how these factors operate.

Let's say that Barbara wants to become a teacher so she can do meaningful work (the ideal). Since she now works as a saleswoman, which she considers meaningless (the real), there is a big discrepancy between the real and the ideal. Also, there are many difficulties, because her family is very poor and they prefer that she continue to work and bring in an extra income. But Barbara believes that if she applies herself she can get a teaching credential (high self-esteem) and then she will be able to help her family even more. Thus, even though there are many difficulties, the high self-esteem and the big difference between the real and the ideal mitigate the effect of the difficulties and produce strong will.

Let's look at another case to see what happens when we change just one variable. This time it is Carol who wants to be a teacher (the ideal). Carol is also a saleswoman (the real), and she too faces many financial difficulties with little support. But, alas, poor Carol has low self-esteem. She tells herself that it's not worth bothering to try to get a teaching credential because she'll never make it anyway. She figures that she may as well keep working as a saleswoman, even though she hates it.

Which girl will have more will power? Which girl is more likely to become a teacher? Barbara, of course, because her high self-esteem will reduce the effect of the difficulties. Carol, on the other hand, has no such mitigating factor and she will be stopped by the difficulties.

Now we will turn to Deborah who is also a saleswoman (the real) who wants to be a teacher (the ideal). Like Barbara, Deborah has great confidence in her ability to learn to be a teacher (high self-esteem), but unlike Barbara, she has few difficulties. Her parents support her desire to be a teacher and are willing to help her complete her studies. Deborah will have the strongest will of all, because all of the variables are in the right direction to promote the will.

We need one more example to explain the role of meaning in motivation. Obviously, the more the ideal means to us, and the more meaning we can find in the difficulties, the higher our will power. There is a wonderful story told about a sick, old man whose son became a *baal teshuvah* and in due course a learned rabbi. The man, who used to be a wrestler, had many discussions with his son, and he too became a *baal teshuvah*. He went to a *shiur* (class) and heard about the delight of learning the wisdom of the Torah. With great regret, he realized that his life had been completely devoid of this delight. He spoke to his teacher, who told him that there was great merit in learning at least one page of *Gemara*. He made up his mind not to leave this world without learning his page of *Gemara*. In order to do this he first had to learn Hebrew. He went to school with children and painstakingly learned the *aleph beis* (the Hebrew alphabet). Then he learned to read Hebrew. Next he found someone to teach him his page of *Gemara*. When he completed the page he called Rabbi Moshe Feinstein to ask if he could have a *siyum* (celebration of completing a unit of Torah). Rabbi Feinstein said yes, and agreed to come to the celebration. The *siyum* was a joyous and uplifting event. The man went to bed that night with a deep sense of fulfillment. He did not get up the next morning. It seems that he managed to push his tired, sick body until he fulfilled his will.

This story exemplifies the crucial role of meaning in evoking the will power. If someone had told this man before he was religious that he first had to learn a new language in order to learn a single page of a book, he would have said, "Who needs it? I'm old, I've worked hard, and I deserve to take it easy." But when he became a *baal teshuvah*, learning the page of *Gemara* (the ideal) became a way to grow closer to God (the meaning), and his will power was highly evoked. Knowing that God would appreciate and give him credit for every step along the way gave meaning to the difficulties, and added enormously to his motivation.

Now we can state a few principles based on our examples:

1. The higher the self-esteem, the stronger the will.

2. The greater the difference between the ideal and the real, the stronger the will.

3. The fewer the difficulties, the stronger the will.

4. The more meaningful the ideal and the difficulties, the stronger the will power.

In summary, if we want to strengthen the will in any given situation, we have to: raise self-esteem, increase the difference between the ideal and the real, give meaning to the ideal, decrease the difficulties and give meaning to the difficulties. Now that we know how the equation works, we can explore how to apply it to our lives.

In this section we will present a psychological view of self-esteem. This view has general applicability to Jew and non-Jew alike. In Chapters 12 and 16, we will raise questions about self-esteem that cannot be dealt with by secular psychology, for example, how is *bitzelem Elokim* (being in the image of God) related to self-esteem at the social and religious levels? Also, in this chapter, we will discuss uniquely Jewish contributions to developing self-esteem.

SELF-ESTEEM

First, let's look at the relationship between self-esteem and will power.

Many psychologists consider self-evaluation to be a central component of personality that affects every aspect of life. Psychologist Jerome Frank states[2] that low self-esteem is a nearly universal ingredient in clients seeking psychotherapy. He considers improvement in self-esteem as the primary ingredient in successful treatment.

According to psychologist Albert Bandura,[3] there is a clear-cut relationship between self-evaluation of efficacy (an aspect of self-esteem) and motivation.

> People's self-efficacy beliefs determine their level of motivation, as reflected in how much effort they will exert in an endeavor and how long they will persevere in the face of obstacles. The stronger the belief in their capabilities, the greater and more persistent are their efforts.

Bandura marshals impressive evidence from laboratory studies and the records of human triumphs to show that self-efficacy beliefs play a key role in motivation. How we feel about ourselves affects our effort and persistence in the face of obstacles, and it also affects how clearly we think, how much distress we feel and how quickly we recover from criticism and self-doubt. The more efficacious we judge ourselves to be, the wider the range of career options we consider and the better we prepare ourselves. Evidence suggests that perceived self-inefficacy, on the other hand, is related to phobic behavior, depression and even impairment of immune system functioning.

We see that self-evaluation has a very powerful effect on the will. How can we facilitate positive self-evaluation in ourselves and others?

We can find some answers in a recent book on the development and maintenance of self-esteem.[4] Self-esteem, which is a more general and comprehensive self-evaluation than self-efficacy, is defined as "a subjective and enduring sense of realistic self-approval." The authors emphasize that self-approval is not hedonistic self-indulgence. It is the result of conducting our lives in a manner congruent with our most deeply held personal views and values regardless of the difficulty in doing so. Self-approval is having a realistic belief in the adequacy of the self, based on prior life experiences.

According to the authors of this book, self-esteem is a dynamic, changeable state rather than a static one. Our level of self-esteem will be affected by external feedback from family and society; internal feedback, or our constant process of self-evaluation; and our emotional, cognitive and behavioral reactions to the feedback. If we get so hurt and discouraged by negative feedback that we tend to avoid difficult, threatening situations, our self-esteem decreases. But if we respond to negative feedback by coping with the challenge, our self-esteem increases.

When does the self-concept start to develop? Developmental evidence suggests that children can't conceptualize a separate sense of self until the age of eight or older.[5] Long before we are able to evaluate ourselves, however, we are getting a sense of our worth from the environment. We translate our early experiences into feelings about ourselves and the world. In order to develop a solid foundation for self-esteem, or what psychiatrist Erik Erikson called "basic trust" (the feeling that "the world is a safe place, people are kind and loving, and I am a valued, cherished person"), we need unconditional love from our earliest caretakers.

But unconditional love alone is not enough; in fact, by itself it is hazardous to our development. Eventually, standards and limits have to be imposed on us. If not, we are in danger of becoming vain, self-indulgent, inconsiderate, incompetent people who have no source of *authentic* positive self-evaluation or positive evaluation from others. Unconditional love has to change to what psychologist Diana Baumrind calls *unconditional commitment.*[6]

> The parent continues to care for the child because it is her child and not because of the child's merits—her interest in his welfare does not depend upon his actions and is abiding. This abiding interest is expressed not in gratifying the child's whims, nor in being kind with him, not in approval of his actions, nor even in approving of what he is as a person. Unconditional commitment means the child's interests are perceived among the parent's most important interests.

Baumrind studied competence in children and found that children who were high in self-reliance, self-control, happiness and ability to respond appropriately to peers and adults had parents who could be described as *authoritative* (as opposed to *authoritarian* and *permissive*). Authoritative parents balanced warmth with control, were attentive to the child's expressed needs and made high demands with clear communication about what was required of the child. Similar findings are reported by psychologist Stanley Coopersmith,[7] who found that parents of children with high self-esteem clearly communicate their *acceptance* of the children; communicate *well-defined* limits and *high expectations for performance*; and *respect* the children's individuality, allowing them to be different and unique within the general boundaries established.

In summary, we can see that the development of self-esteem is a multifaceted developmental process. Its roots go all the way back to infancy, and although it involves every aspect of the social environment, parents (and/or their surrogates) are clearly central figures. Self-esteem is also affected by the individual's own temperament and reactions. How we respond to the people and events in our lives is also a major factor in our self-esteem. Our internal responses (how we talk to ourselves) and our external responses (how we relate to others and how we act) both play a big part in how we feel about and assess ourselves.

We turn now to a discussion of the problems that can develop from the three factors that make up self-esteem.

PROBLEMS IN SELF-ESTEEM

External feedback has tremendous power to shape the self-concept. In my work as a school consultant, I see children literally shrink in the face of sarcasm and criticism, or blossom in the face of support and praise.

Because we are so dependent on external feedback we

try very hard to maintain the values of parents and, to a lesser extent, society, even if we decide that the values are wrong. For example, many of us come from materialistic, success-oriented families. When we begin to feel spiritual stirrings and start pursuing spiritual goals, we often begin to question our former exclusive emphasis on acquisitions and status. When our shift in values begins to be reflected in our lives (we start keeping *Shabbos*), we are often subjected to intense negative feedback ("You've gone off the deep end with this religious stuff"). The rebukes threaten our self-esteem and make it very difficult for us to stay on our spiritual path. Unless we can transfer our need for positive external feedback to sources supportive of our spiritual goals, we may turn away from spirituality or find less demanding versions.

We are also deeply affected by the way we talk to ourselves (our internal monologue). Negative "self-talk" produces and reinforces depression and withdrawal. Positive "self-talk" facilitates optimism and constructive activity. Changing "self-talk" from negative to positive has been shown to have powerful therapeutic effects.

The potency of internal feedback can create two kinds of problems. The first problem is that our "self-talk" may be unrelated to objective measures of achievement and success. Some of us can never be good enough, no matter how well we do, because we have deeply entrenched negative self-concepts, or because we are measuring ourselves against unrealistic standards of excellence. The second kind of problem, creating an inflated sense of self-competence by exaggerating our successes ("I'm the greatest") or focusing only on successful areas, will be discussed later in this chapter.

If we develop avoidance or withdrawal response styles, we leave ourselves few opportunities to develop self-esteem. We exaggerate our difficulties in order to preserve a fragile illusion of self-worth ("I was doing a great job, but I quit because the boss was paranoid; he criticized everything I did"). In extreme cases, people with avoidant response styles will dodge difficulties by settling for work far below their potential (the college student who drops out and becomes a clerk). In less severe cases, people will use their skills and talents in limited capacity to assure themselves success (the accomplished pianist who becomes a rehearsal accompanist).

IMPROVING SELF-ESTEEM

First, we will discuss general psychological approaches to improving self-esteem, and then we will discuss the Jewish approach.

THE PSYCHOLOGICAL APPROACH

External feedback can be changed in many ways. To name just a few, parents can learn more effective parenting skills, children can be given new sources of support (a "big brother," a kind teacher or a therapist), or expectations can be made more realistic so that praise can be earned.

Internal feedback can also be changed in many ways. We can learn to focus on our strengths instead of our weaknesses. And we can become "process-oriented" rather than outcome-oriented. We can learn to endorse ourselves for effort rather than success, to treasure every small step of progress we make rather than to focus on and criticize ourselves harshly for every misstep we make. "Process-orientation" is a key concept, because it has the power to make every step count. When we are process-oriented, every moment becomes an opportunity to make a choice of which we can approve. Every moment becomes an opportunity to experience success and to build self-esteem. From countless tiny steps we can build an enduring sense of self-approval.

(A caveat is needed here. It is crucial that self-evaluation be based on realistic self appraisal. Therapeutic approaches such as "affirmations" in which positive, but not necessarily true, self-statements are repeated over and over again ("I will pass that test with flying colors" or "I will get that job") can be dangerous to an enduring sense of self-worth. Cognitive reframing to eliminate negative self-statements is fine if the statements are true; positive self-feedback is certainly better than negative. But if the self-statements are false they are very dangerous because they can *artificially* and *temporarily* raise self-esteem. If we exaggerate our capabilities, we won't do the work needed to achieve the ideal, and we will probably fail, causing our self-esteem to plunge. Thus, the long-term effect of the ego-inflation is ego-deflation.)

Our style of response to feedback can also be improved. We can work on all the three components of response style: cognition, emotion and behavior. If we tend to get discouraged and immobilized by criticism and the possibility of failure, we can gradually learn to redefine difficulties as exciting challenges. This can help us confront the challenges and take the steps necessary to accomplish our goals. Then, rather than destroying our self-esteem through withdrawal and avoidance, which leave us no opportunity for success, we can raise our self-esteem by giving ourselves credit for competent, persistent coping and realistic facing up to threatening situations. This is obviously not an overnight process, but there is a great deal of anecdotal, clinical and research evidence that it can be accomplished.

JUDAISM'S SECRET INGREDIENT FOR SELF-ESTEEM

The discussion of self-esteem above applies equally well to Torah life and non-Torah life. For all people, religious and non-religious, Jew and non-Jew, self-esteem is a central feature of the personality. The self-esteem of all people is shaped by external and internal feedback and by their own response styles. All people can benefit from self-affirming external and internal feedback and by an active, optimistic response to risks and challenges.

But Judaism offers a unique and special contribution to the development of self-esteem. Torah life adds a dynamic ingredient which can change self-esteem immediately: our relationship with God.

In Judaism, we see God as the source of our external feedback. Just as He is infinite, His positive feedback can be infinite. When we learn Torah, when we pray, when we read Psalms, we get constant external feedback. In society there is a limit to the amount of positive feedback we can get because when we succeed in competitive situations we threaten others. Spiritual progress, however, is not competitive. We are striving to fulfill our own potential, not to surpass others, and hence our progress is not threatening to others. Therefore we can get great *kavod* (honor) for learning Torah and living according to Torah principles.

Torah also gives us a way to improve our internal

feedback through our relationship with God. In Judaism we are taught that each of us was created by God with a special mission to fulfill in the world. Each of us, with our individual endowment, has a unique mission. And every mission is precious to God. It doesn't really matter what abilities, characteristics and talents we have or don't have. What really matters is that we learn to recognize, appreciate and fulfill our own God-given individual potential, rather than always comparing ourselves with others.

In Judaism we develop *internal*, absolute standards that free us from dependence on values adopted from family and society (if those values contradict Torah values). Judaism even gives us a way to make our failures meaningful. In spite of the fact that process orientation is a major psychological tool, it has its limits as compared with the Jewish process orientation. As we saw in the story about the man who learned a page of *Gemara*, putting God in the picture enables us to give enormous meaning to every sub-goal. This increases the discrepancy between the real and the ideal and will power is enhanced proportionately.

In secular terms, the ideal can have meaning, but never the kind of meaning we get from wanting to get closer to and be more like God. When it comes to giving meaning to the difficulties, we see another difference between the secular and Torah approaches. In Torah life we have very lofty goals. But when we have very high goals, we tend to be afraid of the difficulties. In order not to be overwhelmed by the difficulties, we have to break the goals down into meaningful, achievable sub-goals. What makes the sub-goals meaningful is that we know that God realizes exactly how difficult the climb is for us: He tailors the challenges to our abilities and circumstances. He judges us according to our efforts, not our success. He gives us credit for every *alef* and *beis*. *Every step is meaningful in and of itself, whether we achieve the final goal or not.* Even if the former wrestler had died before learning his page of *Gemara*, he would have been elevated by his intention and his struggles. Every difficulty we overcome brings us closer to Him.

Secular psychology can teach us how to break the difficulties down into achievable increments and reinforce each sub-goal (either by external or self-reinforcement). This makes our tasks more manageable, but it doesn't give each step meaning in and of itself. And it can't make the steps meaningful, *whether or not the final goal is ever achieved.* Let's take the example of a secular person whose ideal is to be a doctor. Suppose the admissions committee tells him, "You can go to medical school, take all the courses, labs, etc., but you can never get your M.D. and practice medicine." Would there be any way to make the steps meaningful to him? No. But if his final goal were a spiritual one, such as having a better appreciation of God's wisdom and more detailed evidence of design and purpose in the world, then each step could be tremendously meaningful in and of itself.

We get something else from our relationship with God that helps us develop self-esteem. As we said, unconditional love is essential for the development of self-esteem. We are badly damaged if we grow up without unconditional love. The damage is almost impossible to repair by any secular approach. But Judaism has a way to heal the wounds inflicted by the lack of unconditional love. *The one place we can really get absolutely unconditional love is from God.* Jews who have faith and trust in a living, omnipotent, omniscient, loving God have the most solid foundation for self-esteem. If God loves us with all our human foibles, surely we can love ourselves. If God cares enough to watch over us and correct us, surely we are capable of growing and making progress. If God created us in His image, surely we have potential beyond our wildest dreams. And if we are sparks of the Divine, we have divine souls which ennoble us and give us a sense of sanctity.

If we take these ideas into our hearts and make them part of the fiber of our being, we have an unshakeable foundation for self-esteem. We also have a way to repair any cracks in the foundation for self-esteem created by negative external and internal feedback and self-defeating response styles.

THE REAL AND THE IDEAL: A PSYCHOLOGICAL APPROACH

Let us look at the difference between the real and the ideal from a psychological approach. According to Bandura,[8] human self-motivation relies on *discrepancy production.* We motivate ourselves by setting challenging standards and goals. We create a discrepancy between the ideal and the real which results in a state of disequilibrium. If we have a positive sense of our efficacy, we then mobilize ourselves on the basis of an estimate of what we have to do to accomplish our goals and restore equilibrium. If we don't feel efficacious, we tend to withdraw from the challenge, settling for the status quo and immediately reinstating equilibrium.

Those of us with enough self-efficacy to be able to tolerate discrepancy and disequilibrium usually accomplish one goal and then set even higher standards for ourselves. Therefore we create a long and continuous cycle of discrepancy/disequilibrium, motivation, sustained effort and restoration of equilibrium. We achieve one goal and then move on to the next. This cycle insures us a lifetime of growth.

Those who can't tolerate discrepancy and disequilibrium kill motivation by avoiding all risk or by falsely reducing the discrepancy between the real and the ideal. If we have an exaggerated view of the real ("Being a saleswoman is very meaningful. I make people happy selling them the things they want.") or if we minimize the ideal ("Teaching isn't so meaningful. Kids hate school."), we reduce the difference between the ideal and the real and thus destroy will power. If we believe that what we already have is very close to the ideal, or if we discredit the ideal, we have no impetus to make progress.

Psychology acknowledges the importance of discrepancy and disequilibrium, but secular values create a vicious cycle that forces many secular people to keep the discrepancy between the real and the ideal so small that it shrinks will power. Let's see how this works. In secular life self-esteem is defined largely in terms of success. Thus, in order to ensure success and maintain self-esteem, the difference between the real and the ideal has to be kept small. Since setting high goals in weak areas (large difference) threatens our self-esteem, we tend to keep doing what we are good at (small difference) rather than taking on challenges to develop ourselves in areas where there are a lot of difficulties. But, by keeping the difference small, we lose the motivational benefits of a large difference. We thus maintain self-esteem at the expense of will power in areas that need improvement. For example, we have the aggressive, high-level executive who pours all his energy and time into furthering his career, but refuses to see how his family suffers from his detachment and callousness. It is true that if he were to evaluate himself on the basis of his success as a parent and husband, his self-esteem would temporarily plummet, but he would at least give himself a chance to correct his mistakes and balance his life.

When we are caught up in this vicious cycle, how do we avoid the drop in self-esteem that accompanies awareness of weakness or failure? We simply erase it from our minds or reduce the ideal in our weak areas to make it seem closer to the real ("It's true I don't spend much time with my children, but I'm providing them with the means to have a good life"). This vicious cycle of maintaining self-esteem by artificially reducing the discrepancy between the real and the ideal and thereby killing will power is the main reason so many people have such unbalanced development.

JUDAISM'S APPROACH TO THE REAL AND THE IDEAL

In the area of discrepancies between the ideal and the real we find another way that living a Torah life gives us an advantage far beyond any secular approach. Torah tells us that God is perfect, that His essence is lovingkindness, that His power and wisdom are infinite. The ideal is for us to "walk in His ways," to make our behavior more and more like His. In practical terms, this might mean controlling our anger, using the gift of speech only for the good or doing more acts of kindness. The real is how we actually behave. Fortunately, God has implanted in us the desire and the ability to become more and more like Him. The divine soul implores us to sanctify and elevate ourselves, to make ourselves as God-like as possible. The discrepancy between the ideal and the real is enormous, but we reduce the difficulties by breaking it down into small steps with great meaning. The knowledge that God appreciates every step and gives it ultimate importance keeps the discrepancy from damaging our self-esteem. With a *Jewish process orientation*, the enormity of the discrepancy and the disequilibrium it produces can give us the will power to take the steps needed to refine and elevate ourselves.

Without the divine ideal, our concept of our potential is shrunken by the limits of our human perception. Secular thinking is finite and temporal rather than infinite and eternal. It is earthly, rather than heavenly. As we see in even the most positive psychological views of human nature (e.g., Maslow, see Chapter 4), the concept of the ideal can soar no higher than the best of what *is*, rather than what *should be* and *can be*. For secular psychology, actualization and transcendence are defined in human terms, not divine terms.

Thus, Judaism gives us another way to strengthen the will power by teaching us that our potential is unlimited. As the Rambam writes in *Pirkei Hatzlachah*, "Every person who seeks perfection can become like Moshe Rabbeinu (our teacher Moses)". The difference between the real and the ideal is enormous, but every ounce of struggle has great meaning.

We turn now to the second theme of the elemental soul, the need for satisfaction.

THE NEED FOR SATISFACTION

Once upon a time there was a beautiful princess who lived in a magnificent castle. Her bed was made of gold, her sheets were silk, and her quilt was filled with the finest goose down. She had gowns of velvet and lace, shoes of satin and jewelry made of precious stones. The princess ate the finest food from a table set with linen, china, crystal and silver. She rode in a cushioned carriage and had servants to fill her every need. Of all her pleasures, however, the greatest was the sublimely beautiful music played in the King's court.

The princess was kidnapped and thereafter lived the life of a poor commoner. She married a very kind man, but even though he gave her the best he had, nothing he gave her could satisfy her. The princess lived like a commoner, but deep inside she yearned to be back in the magnificent castle. One day, far off in the distance, she heard the King's music, and for the first time since she had been kidnapped, she felt joy. She was rejuvenated by a glimmer of what was missing and she set out in search of the source of the music.

This sense of something missing, of longing for something just beyond our grasp, is a universal human experience. It has been expressed by Torah Sages ("Everyone has this nameless inner yearning"[9]), by poets ("On every stage from youth to age, still discontent attends"[10]) and by philosophers ("a yearning that knows no satisfaction"[11]).

This longing arises from the divine soul within us. The soul seeks satisfaction, but nothing on this earth can satisfy it. King Solomon tells us that "if the soul were to be brought all the delights of the world, they would be as nothing to it,"[12] since the soul desires higher things. The divine soul was united with God before being placed in the human body, and it retains a memory of the ultimate pleasure of that union. The divine soul longs for the true joy that comes solely from union with God.

Why, then, is the soul placed in the human body? Isn't it cruel for God to have imprisoned within us an entity which is doomed to dissatisfaction? It does seem cruel, but in reality it is a great gift. If we can understand this, we will have a profound insight into the intricacies of human nature and behavior.

The soul is separated from God because it has the goal of elevating and perfecting itself through its connection to the body. This was the theme of the parable about the lowly peasant and the king (see Introduction). The king showed the peasant the splendor of the palace and then sent him back to the world. The memory of the ultimate pleasure of being with the king gave the peasant the strength to overcome obstacles in his efforts to return to the palace of his memory. The soul is placed within us to bind us to our divine roots. It is through the conduit of the soul that divine influence is transmitted to us.[13] *The soul is the divine channel, our channel to God.*

The yearning of the soul has powerful psychological implications. Torah gives us the deep insight that the inner "longing of the soul for its state of perfection"[14] provides the primary motivation for the development of the human personality. We feel the yearning of the soul as an insatiable drive for "more." Like the naive husband of the princess of our parable, we try to satisfy the longing with ever more clothes, more cars, more food, more money, more honors, etc. But still, we are not satisfied. As Rabbi Mordechai Gifter said:

> Therein lies the tragedy of modern man. The *neshamah* (soul) seeks completion and fulfillment and man feeds these burning desires with ever more *guf* (material). Modern man is disillusioned. With all his success, with all his achievement, he lacks peace and knows not why.[15]

If we don't acknowledge the existence and true nature of

the soul we have no way to understand this relentless force within us.

A comparison with animals will help us to understand this driving need for more. Animals eat when they are hungry, but once their needs are met and their hunger is satisfied, they stop eating. Pleasure reinforces, but is not the goal of, their eating. Therefore, they consume only what they need.

We, on the other hand, eat not only to satisfy our physical hunger but also to get pleasure. And so we eat even when we are not hungry. We even stimulate ourselves to enhance our appetites for erotic pleasure and material acquisitions as well as food. We create needs artificially and become obsessed with obtaining and consuming. But like the princess, we are not fulfilled because we are really searching for spiritual pleasure.

The soul is a constant reminder that we are sparks of the Divine, that we are much, much more than intelligent animals. The soul keeps us from degrading ourselves and settling for shallow satisfaction. It is a great kindness to us that the soul keeps searching for the spiritual "magnificent castle" it once knew.

A LIVING EXAMPLE OF SEARCH FOR THE SUBLIME

The life of Uri Zohar[16] is a good example of this "nameless yearning." Uri was the top comedian, talk-show host, social satirist, actor and film-producer in Israel. He was wealthy, famous and greatly admired. He seemed to "have it all," and yet he found himself strangely moved by a meeting with a former acquaintance who had become religious.

Uri was invited to attend a celebration in honor of the birth of his friend's baby girl. While at the celebration, he struck up a conversation with a "Yerushalmi" (a Torah-observant Jew of the historic Orthodox community of Jerusalem). They discussed issues such as whether or not there is a Creator of the world and, if so, whether we are under His direction and care, etc. Uri took the position that it was absurd to propose that God, if He did exist, would want anything from us.

The Yerushalmi disagreed and said that the Creator revealed Himself to the Jewish people at Mount Sinai for the express purpose of giving them the Torah as a system by which to live.

Uri was confident that he was right because he was convinced of the intellectual superiority of modern man over old-fashioned religious man. He was also convinced of

> my own superiority over the Yerushalmi, simply because I was wearing designer jeans and he wore a hopelessly out-of-date frockcoat ... After an entire evening of probing and searching in the hopes of finding even the tiniest flaw in his psychological or intellectual armor, I had to admit that I had found none.

Uri was very unsettled by the encounter. He spent the next few months studying Torah in an effort to prove to himself that the Yerushalmi was wrong. But he had to admit that he had failed to refute the truth of Torah. He found himself engaged in a frantic struggle to defuse the personal implications of what he was learning.

> As I looked down the path which my defeat indicated

that I must take, I felt I was living through one of the darkest days of my life. I pictured myself living the life . . . [of] a religious Jew, and I wanted to barf .

Judaism was the greatest threat I had ever encountered. It threatened . . . my freedom to do whatever I felt like doing, provided I didn't hurt anyone, break any enforceable laws and had the money to actualize my desires. In short, it threatened much of what I considered to be the essence of life itself.

Even after being convinced of the truth of Torah, Uri continued to look for a way that required the minimum effort and change. As reluctant as he was to give up the comforting and familiar life he had been living, he became a Torah Jew because his yearning for the truth was so strong that he could not ignore it once he found it. Uri is now a respected Torah scholar and all the members of his family have also become Torah Jews.

We have all found, each in his or her own way, our lives as Torah-observant Jews to be the source of the greatest satisfaction and happiness of our lives.

The yearning of Uri Zohar's soul was almost completely stifled by the distractions of the slick, trendy, fashionable, successful life he was living. But fortunately for Uri, his longing for the truth pressed him to meet with the Yerushalmi who touched his soul and opened his "divine channel." Only after living as a Torah Jew did Uri realize how much he needed the truth and how barren his life had been without it.

So we see that the activation of the personality by the divine soul has profound effects on the psyche. If these effects are recognized and heeded, our lives are enriched and we feel deep joy. On the other hand, if the effects are ignored, denied or trivialized, the personality becomes distorted and the result is misery. Therefore it is crucially important for us to know how the soul affects us and to learn to decode the messages of the soul.

SUMMARY

Themes of the elemental soul: Will power and the need for satisfaction.

In order to strengthen the will we have to raise self-esteem; increase the difference between the ideal and the real; and give meaning to the difficulties.

Self-esteem is the basis of good mental health. It is a dynamic, changeable state that is affected by external feedback from family and society; internal feedback, or self-evaluation; our emotional, cognitive, and behavioral reactions to the feedback.

THE SECRET INGREDIENT IN SELF-ESTEEM

God is the ultimate source of positive internal and external feedback and of unconditional love. Putting God in the picture raises our will power by increasing the difference between the real and the ideal and by giving meaning to every step toward the ideal goal.

THE NEED FOR SATISFACTION

Everyone has a "nameless inner yearning," a relentless

longing for satisfaction. This yearning is the psychological manifestation of the soul's desire to be reunited with God. The need is spiritual and cannot be satisfied by physical, emotional or social pleasure.

CHAPTER 7

Love of Life
and
Fear of Death

I shall cling to this clod of earth,
The deepest longing for life,
Cries out in me.
Now I feel . . . oh, let me . . . that I can live!
Why, Death,
Must you be the one to teach me to see life?[1]

This poem expresses the two main themes that will be discussed in this chapter, the will to live and the unwillingness to die. These two corresponding forces arise out of the two main themes of the elemental soul, the power of the will and need for satisfaction. The elemental soul activates within us the life force producing the desire to live and its corresponding dread of death.

THE WILL TO LIVE

Our powerful desire to live has been implanted deeply within us to ensure the survival of the species. However, when our lives are moving smoothly, we tend to get out of touch with our lust for life. We take for granted the wondrous fact that we are alive. After all, we don't have to long for or fight for what we already have.

In the midst of our complacency, however, events remind us how precious life is. We pick up a newborn infant and thrill to the tender new life in our arms. We watch little children run, jump, skip and explore, fascinated by everything in sight. They are in love with life. The experience of living is so exciting to them that they fight to stay awake even when their eyelids are closing. We walk along a city street with tall skyscrapers towering all around us and suddenly notice a single blade of grass poking up between two concrete slabs of sidewalk, a tiny green victory for life. Or we hear of someone deathly ill and are shocked into a renewed appreciation of our own vitality.

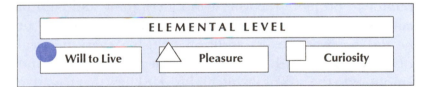

We may not think about it, but if we observe our behavior, we'll realize that our will to live is a basic, underlying principle in our everyday lives. Otherwise, why exercise? Why follow a healthy diet? Why drive carefully? Why look both ways while crossing the street? We do these things because we want to stay alive. Rabbi Tucazinsky[2]

relates a story that shows just how fundamental the desire for self-preservation is:

> It happened once that a man was sentenced to be hanged. He tried to commit suicide by taking poison or by stabbing himself to death but did not succeed. As he was being led to his execution, a large stone fell off a roof. Instinctively, he moved his head aside to avoid being hit!

Rabbi Tucazinsky* points out that the condemned man did not do this deliberately. It was automatic. The protective response shows that man has an inherent drive for self-preservation. Here at the elemental level of the life force ladder, the desire to stay alive is instinctive; it is not mediated by elevated concepts such as life being a bridge to a higher form of existence. Therefore, the body is all-important and the instinct to preserve the life of the body operates reflexively.

The will to live is so strong that it can affect the course of life-threatening disease. Norman Cousins, a prominent journalist, editor and medical writer, purposefully used humor to promote recovery from a crippling and painful collagen disease. Doctors told him he was likely to die, but he did not want to. In addition to using every medical resource available, he decided to harness his mind and emotions to the task of saving his life. He knew that negative thoughts and feelings could produce negative reactions in the body, so he reasoned that positive thoughts and feelings could cause positive reactions. While in the hospital fighting for his life, he made himself laugh by watching his favorite comedians on tape and film and observed that "ten minutes

* for more information on Rabbi Tucazinsky see biographical notes (p.421).

of belly laughter produced an anesthetic effect lasting at least two hours."[3] Mr. Cousins recovered from his illness.

The will to live also has the power to prolong life. Folk wisdom has long held that people could postpone death until after a special occasion that they were determined to live for. For example, it was believed that a sick person could will himself to "live until my daughter's wedding" and then die soon after the event. This effect has now been demonstrated in statistical studies.[4] Two sociologists looked at the relationship between birthdays and dates of death for forty-four "notable Americans" and found a "statistically significant death-dip in the month before the birth-month" and a "death-peak," in the four months following the birthday. In other words, it seems that these notables somehow kept themselves alive until after their birthdays.

A similar effect has been found with important religious occasions. For example, there was a death-dip before *Yom Kippur* (the Day of Atonement) for Jews, but not for non-Jews; and there was a death-dip in September and October of presidential election years.

From this personal, anecdotal and scientific evidence we can see that the activation of the life force by the elemental soul creates a powerful will to live, a will so strong that it can promote healing and prolong life.

LOSING THE WILL TO LIVE

Strangely enough, the incredibly strong will to live can be disrupted. Under certain circumstances, the primitive power of the will can be withdrawn from the desire to live or (God forbid) even be turned against it. For example, there are documented cases of patients who seemed to be disposed toward death. "Without open conflict, suicidal intention, profound depression or extreme panic,"[5] these patients predicted their own deaths. One man was hospitalized for a duodenal ulcer after twenty years of stewing over a fight with a friend and an unsuccessful court battle over the issue. He was determined to avenge his cause by outliving all who had opposed him, and finally, when his last enemy died, the man said that it was time for him to die. Three days after what seemed to be successful surgery for his ulcer, he suddenly developed complications and died.

Psychiatric reports indicated that since the pathology of patients such as these was no greater than that of other patients who lived longer, their mental states must have contributed to their deaths. "Death held more appeal . . . than did life because it promised either reunion with lost love, resolution of long conflict or respite from anguish."

Another phenomenon which indicates loss of the will to live is called the "giving-up reaction."[6] "Giving-up" means feeling that one is helpless and has no control. Typical expressions of this feeling are: "I had the feeling life wasn't worth living anymore." Or: "How much can I take? There's never any end." Or: "My whole world came apart when she died."

The giving-up factor has been shown to operate under conditions as diverse as terminal cancer, concentration camp internment, unbearable loss and voodoo curses. Research suggests that giving-up triggers profound effects in the autonomic nervous system and the pituitary-adrenal cortical system.[7] In general, it is hypothesized that the giving-up factor leads to excessive levels of stress hormones, which may impair immune defenses, damage arteries and disrupt other bodily functions. Our will produces real physical effects.

Suicide is the most extreme example of the weakening of the will to live. In fact, it is the use of the power of the will for self-destruction. In order to understand violence against the self, we have to remember that the themes of the elemental soul are the power of the will and the need for satisfaction, and the themes of the social soul are the power of awareness and the need for identity.

At the elemental level, if we suffer from a very negative outlook (or certain chemical imbalances) we may experience such mental anguish that we cannot find satisfaction. Life then becomes unbearable. At the social level, if we lose our identity (for example, the rich man who loses his money in the stock market or the brilliant student who is no longer at the top of his class), we may feel that life is not worth living.

If what we mean when we say "I" no longer exists (rich man or top student), we may then "depress" the will to live. If life is utterly devoid of satisfaction and meaning, and we feel helpless and hopeless, we may begin to turn our life energy against ourselves. Suicide may seem like a way to find relief from an intolerable state of interminable dissatisfaction and profound loss of identity.

Thus we see that the elemental will is a two-edged sword. It gives us the will to live, but it also gives us the drive for satisfaction. If we can't find satisfaction or meaning in life, we may withdraw the life energy from the will to live and passively welcome death, or in more extreme cases, we may actively use the power of the will against ourselves. In other words, we can use the power of the elemental will for living fully and promoting health and healing, or we can use it for self-destruction.

FEAR OF DEATH

A corollary of the will to live is the unwillingness to die, the resolute refusal to yield one's life to the Angel of Death. This is especially strong at the elemental level, because at this level, "I" am my body. "I" fear death because it is the end of me. The Torah teaching that physical life and death are only stages of eternal life cannot yet be understood. Death is therefore a frightening and terrifying prospect because we are looking into an abyss of complete nothingness; when our body disappears, we disappear. This is why the fear of death is as deeply implanted in the elemental soul as is the will for life.

In a study of death and the creative life,[8] people were asked what it was they feared about death. The answers fell roughly into three categories: religiously-conditioned fears, separation-abandonment fears and existential fears. In addition to the fears associated with death itself, there was the fear of the process of dying.

Fear of non-existence, or existential fear, was the most frightening of all the death fears. The most common defense against this fear was repression. In interviews with almost seven hundred people, the vast majority stated that they "hardly ever" think about their own deaths.

Another method of defense against the fear of non-existence is to try to live forever. This approach is exemplified by an article in the *New York Times* (Sept. 24, 1974) entitled "Sorry, we're here for eternity":

> Soon it will be possible to extend human life indefinitely. After thousands of years of desperate struggle against death and deepest anguish at its inevitability there is a last hope of

winning that struggle. In research centers around the world, efforts are now accelerating to overcome aging and, in time, death itself.

Another death-related fear that was expressed over and over again was the fear of dying before having lived fully. Life review studies of old or terminally ill patients show that if people look on the past with despair and with a feeling that their lives have been wasted, they cannot come to terms with death.[9]

Many studies (e.g., Tobacyk,[10] Smith et al,[11] and Danielsen[12]) have shown that religious conviction helps people deal with concerns about death. The studies suggest that while religious commitment is not a guarantee against death anxiety, it can be a stabilizing factor and a protection against the threatening loss of identity that dying people usually suffer.

People today are more apt to turn to psychology and psychiatry than to religion to help them cope with death. But since most secular psychological thinking is at the elemental and social levels of development, they often don't get the spiritual help they need.

For example, how much spiritual solace can come from Freud's elemental death theory? Freud believed that the idea of immortality was supreme among civilization's false hopes.[13] He thought that by pinning its hopes on the illusion of immortality, civilization undermined its only real hope, which is the rational pursuit of truth through science. According to Freud, the rational truth was that "the goal of all life is death."[14] To be alive is to be in a state of tension, conflict and desire. We seek death because it is the only way that we can achieve our goal of "Nirvana," of being perfectly

happy and satisfied.* "Psychoanalysis comes to remind us
that we are bodies . . . and that perfection would be the realm
of Absolute Body; eternity is the mode of unrepressed
bodies."[15] Freud's understanding of death was frozen at the
elemental level.**

Most other psychiatrists' and psychologists' conceptions
of death are at what we call the social level in our Torah
model. Theories at the social level at least give credence to
the spiritual element in human life. For example, although
Carl Jung[16] was unwilling to state categorically that there

---

*Freud's theory of death instincts is a good example of how the denial
of God and the Torah leads to a misinterpretation of the facts. Freud
correctly identified the primacy of the human yearning for pleasure and
understood that there is a memory of pleasure embedded in us. However,
he traced the origins of that memory back to the womb, rather than to
the much more elevated pleasure of the soul's union with God. Freud
realized that the ultimate pleasure could not be achieved by the body, but
since he did not believe in the soul, he resorted to the death of the body
as the final solution to the futility of human yearning. For religious
people, life, not pleasure, has supreme value, because it is the opportunity
to achieve the ultimate pleasure of the soul's connection with God.

**How can we explain the fact that people do sometimes put
themselves in life-threatening situations? In our culture, death is a trauma
rather than a crucial part of the life cycle. Therefore, we detach ourselves
from the fact that death is awaiting us. This knowledge is pushed to the
back of our minds, where it creates pressure for expression. We then do
dangerous things to remind ourselves of the reality of death. This is
similar to the behavior of people who suffer from amnesia after traumatic
events. The tension of their repressed memories compels them to search
for the missing parts of their lives. If death were treated as a meaningful
part of life, giving purpose to every moment, we would not feel this
pressure to remind ourselves of it by putting ourselves in dangerous
situations.

was life after death, he was nevertheless

> convinced that it is hygienic . . . to discover in death a goal
> towards which one can strive . . . I, therefore, consider the
> religious teaching of a life hereafter consonant with the
> standpoint of psychic hygiene . . . From the standpoint of
> psychotherapy, it would therefore be desirable to think of
> death as only a transition . . . one part of a life-process.

In other words, Jung believed that there was a mental health advantage to believing in an afterlife. Psychiatrist Robert Jay Lifton basically agreed with Jung on this point. However, the most he could bring himself to do was speak of a sense of immortality. According to Lifton, this sense of immortality was not a mere denial of death; it was a corollary of the knowledge of death itself. Lifton thought that the sense of immortality reflected a universal quest for continuity with what has gone before and what will continue after us.[17]

Both Jung and Lifton acknowledged the human yearning for perpetuity, but neither of them were willing to state that they actually believed in the eternity of the soul.

Without Torah, we are dependent on weighing the evidence of our senses to tell us whether there is a soul that is independent of the body and can survive the death of the body. Volumes have been published on the subject (e.g., Osis,[18] Moody,[19] Kastenbaum[20] and Noyes[21]), some believing that the evidence proves that there is an independent soul, and others believing that the evidence is inconclusive.

Dr. Raymond Moody, who wrote the classic text on near-death experiences[22] (an experience that occurs after a person has been pronounced clinically dead), writes in his most recent book[23] that near-death experience (NDE) re-search has convinced him that NDEs are evidence of life after life. What is an NDE? There are ten elements that make up an NDE: a sense of being dead; peace and painlessness; an out-of-body experience; passing through a dark tunnel toward a light; encountering "beings of light," often rela-tives who have died; encountering a supreme "Being of Light" who radiates total love and understanding; a life review; rising upwards; reluctance to return; and a different sense of time and space. Not all NDEs have all the elements.

The NDE seems to be a transformative experience. Dr Moody states that in twenty years of experience he has yet to find one person who has not had a very deep and positive transformation as a result of an NDE. He spoke to many scholars and clinicians who had interviewed NDEers and they all came to same conclusion: NDEers are better people because of their experience. They have more concern for others than before the NDE; they grapple with the unpleas-ant aspects of reality in an unemotional and clear-thinking way; they have an increased belief in God, an afterlife and a greatly decreased fear of death. In general, they are happier and more hopeful than those around them.

Dr. Moody and other researchers believe that NDEs are a glimpse of life after life, but as scientists they realize that they have not found "scientific proof" that we continue to live after our bodies die. For them, the most compelling evidence is the fact that in their "out-of-body" state, NDEers can report on accurate details of their own death scene in abundance and from the perspective of someone looking down on the scene.

People who have been resuscitated after being declared clinically dead can often recount the medical procedures used to try to save them, including precise readings from monitoring devices they could not possibly have seen while alive (not to mention that they were unconscious at the time.) They are often able to repeat comments the doctors and nurses made, like "Oh, she's gone." They can see equipment being brought in to save them, and they can see their loved ones in the hall praying for them. A particularly impressive case is the one in which a blind woman "saw" details of her death scene and was again blind when revived.

On the basis of such data, Dr. Moody said:

> What greater proof is needed that persons survive the death of their physical bodies than many examples of individuals leaving their bodies and witnessing attempts to save it?

Dr. Moody writes that the NDE occurs much more frequently than most of us realize. A Gallup poll showed that eight million adults in the United States reported NDEs. Dr. Moody was amazed when he began lecturing and asking people if they ever had an NDE or knew someone who did. He found that many people had been reluctant to talk about such experiences because they feared being considered crazy or because the experience was very hard to put into words. Many people told of having been referred for psychiatric evaluation after telling their doctors about an NDE.

There are, however, many physicians and scientists who believe that the NDE is nothing more than a physical or mental phenomenon that has more to do with brain dysfunction than with an adventure of the spirit. Charles Garfield, a psychologist who has both counseling and research experience with cancer patients, points out that the near-death experiences reported in the medical and psychological literature are not proof of life after death.[24] They are merely "altered state experiences" which are not specific to the dying process. He reports similar experiences by women during natural childbirth.

He doesn't dismiss these experiences as unimportant or unworthy of attention and study, but he denies their validity as proof of survival of the self after death. But the fact that they are not specific to the dying experience does not necessarily make them any less metaphysical. They may be out-of-the body experiences (OBEs), or the soul leaving the body. OBEs need not be linked to a brush with death. In fact, some experimenters believe that OBEs can occur spontaneously and may even be induced at will. Dr. Garfield is correct in concluding that this type of experience is not proof of life after death, but he fails to explain how people declared clinically dead were able to give accurate details of events happening in other rooms.

In his book *Is There Life After Death?*,[25] the respected clinical psychologist Robert Kastenbaum wrote about research that was conducted on a variety of metaphysical phenomena. He gives special emphasis to the work of professor of psychology Kenneth Ring because Ring's research on NDEs meets the highest scientific standards. Kastenbaum tells us that on the basis of his findings Ring interprets the NDE

> as a direct perception of reality that has been granted to the individual because of his temporary freedom from dependence on the physical body. In this condition, one escapes the routine perception of the world forced on us by

our experiences and bodily limitations and can appreciate the basic structure of the universe.

In interpreting his data, Ring refers to a new theory by neurologist Karl Pribram which suggests that we are "biologically equipped to register and interpret the complex frequencies which comprise the universe and 'translate' these into usable sensory experience." On the basis of Ring's work, Kastenbaum concludes:

> One does not have to dismiss the NDE as a peculiar, much less faulty, view of reality. Rather, the NDE offers a strikingly realistic view of reality that eludes our usual perceptions.

Kastenbaum gives us a critical review of additional research on NDEs and other psychic phenomena. While there were undoubtedly fraudulent cases, and others with inadequate data to form any conclusions, there are many that survive rigorous scrutiny. Among them are cases of people who were able to give detailed descriptions of what went on around them after they were clinically dead, and whose claims were carefully investigated with no falsification being found.

Among the most impressive evidence presented by Kastenbaum is the work of the eminent professor of psychiatry Ian Stevenson. Stevenson is a very careful researcher. He introduces cases, gives the exact names and full dates of everybody interviewed, sets forth all the details in tables that may run on for many pages, gives the names of informants, describes his method and does ample cross-checking of details. Based on his painstaking research, in his first book alone, Stevenson has shown twenty cases of reincarnation, each replete with verified detail. Kastenbaum concludes that

> cases of the reincarnation type are not limited to any one nation or cultural group, and are not as rare as might be thought . . . They cannot be dismissed as vague or unverified, nor is there any basis for challenging Stevenson's skill and integrity.

Most of the critic's "concerns" about reincarnation do not touch on the data themselves, only on his difficulty in opening his mind to a different view of the world.

Kastenbaum is very careful to spell out the basis on which critics dismiss this research. For example, they claim that we have no direct evidence for a surviving entity, only for an act of communication. And we all know how communication is fraught with error and distortion. Memory fades with time, some details disappear, others are added. But Kastenbaum also presents the other side:

> For our generation, belief in survival [of the soul] seems to require some kind of "certificate of approval" from science. This is the reason why we have given so much attention to empirical evidence as well as to the rules of good thinking. We have found varied and abundant evidences in favor of the survival hypothesis and have turned back the determined negativism of the critic.

As Kastenbaum points out, although many reports of survival phenomena remain untouched by responsible criticism, many scientists and laymen do not accept the reality of survival. No matter how abundant, how detailed, how validated the evidence, the facts do not seem to accord well with the established view of the universe and hence must be discarded. Kastenbaum makes an eloquent plea for us to have the courage to accept the facts no matter what damage they may do to our assumptions.

> Curious, is it not? . . . how some hesitate before the prospect of survival . . . how some hesitate and turn their intellects into weapons . . . and curious also how these weapons are then employed to inflict injuries on one's own frightened self! . . . Some scientists and intellectuals favor a highly abstract god-principle. It is the intellectual refuge for those who must acknowledge the abundant evidence of lawfulness and organization in the universe but who fear to commit themselves to a definite belief. In plain truth, there is little left of God in such abstractions. Others divest themselves of God and gods in every recognizable form.
>
> Survival can but dazzle and dismay such people. Identifying themselves more with man-made systems than with God . . . they see death primarily as the failure of physical apparatus. There is no clear sense of a transcendent purpose in life and—of even greater moment—there is no sense of worthiness for continued existence. "I am but a machine . . . and I must eventually fail and be scrapped." With this low self-esteem, the thoroughly modern person cannot imagine why the universe should care about him. Despite the brave noises he makes from time to time, fundamentally he does not care all that much for himself.
>
> And so we have a peculiar psychology at work; people . . . must arm themselves against any possibility that life might have a larger purpose. The universe must be as limited and purposeless as their own concepts of self.

In an earlier book,[26] Kastenbaum pointed out that the

question of whether or not there is survival beyond death has profound moral implications. He said that even the most atheistic of behavior modifiers could see the reinforcement possibilities of believing in an afterlife:

> Reinforcements could be associated either with immediate, intermediate or remote (afterlife) time frameworks. Still another way of putting it: Should we live for today? For the day after tomorrow? Or for eternity?

It is true that there are "reinforcement possibilities" in believing in and living as if life is eternal: There is more pleasure and meaning in life when it is seen as a passageway to eternity. But rather than saying that afterlife is a cultural invention designed to satisfy our psychological needs, we say that our psychological needs were designed by our Creator to fit our purpose. In other words, the yearning for perpetuity was embedded in us by our Creator to give us the motivation for the spiritual growth that leads to eternal life.

THE SECULAR VIEWS OF DEATH

What are the consequences of denying the eternity of the soul or waiting for science to provide definitive proof of life after death? At the elemental level death is seen as a great tragedy. Therefore, we try to keep the body youthful, fit, healthy and eternally alive in order to ward off the terror of nothingness. This leads to a "youth culture," or a society that venerates and imitates the young and has contempt and disdain for the old. Such a society is obsessed with physical fitness and attractiveness. This is a no-win situation. The flesh is temporary and subject to the ravages of time. Even among the most fit, the skin sags and wrinkles, the muscles weaken, the bones shrink, the eyes dim, the energy wanes.

At the social level, the difficulty lies in sensing that there is something more to life than the physical, but not knowing quite what it is. From this level come all the philosophers who try to give meaning to life by aggrandizing death. They say that death teaches us how to live better. While it is true that a brush with death can temporarily make us appreciate life and bring us to new depths of feeling, at the elemental and social levels we still don't really know what to do with our lives. We cannot put life and death in perspective until we elevate our souls to the religious level and recognize ourselves as eternal. As Rabbi Tucazinsky[27] says:

> To the person whose life is merely a "transition to the limbo of the past" . . . life is a prolonged dying . . . For the person . . . to whom life is a transition to a bright and enduring future, it constitutes the corridor leading to the palace . . . Hence this life has great and significant meaning for him . . . The first lives for the sake of his body, so when his body reverts to dust, he has nothing more to live for. The second lives for his soul, which endures, and so his life has no end.

What makes the difference between emptiness and fullness is the feeling that we're going somewhere, that our lives have meaning and purpose. When we know this, death does give meaning to life.

As Rabbi Meir said, "I saw death and found it to be *tov meod* (very good)." Rabbi Meir is telling us that death is one of the most important parts of God's Creation because it gives us a finite time on this earth to grow, achieve, make progress and prepare ourselves for the next world. In that sense, awareness of death can impart meaning to every moment of life. At the religious level, every moment becomes a splendid opportunity to do our share in perfecting the world through perfecting ourselves.

Rabbi Tucazinsky's[28] twin parable sums up the differences between a religious and non-religious view of life. Suppose there were twin brothers in the womb who could think and talk. They were discussing what would happen to them after they left the womb. One of them believed, according to the tradition that had been transmitted to him, that there was a future life beyond the womb. The other, being a "rational" creature who could only accept what his intelligence and senses could experience, denied the existence of anything but their intrauterine world. The "believing" brother told him that:

> with their emergence from the womb they would enter a new and more spacious realm, that they would eat through their mouths, see distant objects with their eyes and hear with their ears, that their legs would straighten, that they would stand erect and traverse vast distances on a gigantic nurturing earth, replete with oceans and rivers, while above them would stretch a sky with its starry hosts.

The "rational" brother jeered at his brother's naivete and mocked him for indulging in such fantasies. He kicked and punched at the womb in defiance. His "believing" brother told him that he was damaging himself and the womb and that instead of fighting he should be using his time in the womb to grow and prepare himself for the next world. But the "rational" brother said that there was no afterlife and he might as well indulge himself now. He believed that once they left the womb they would fall into an abyss from which there was no return, that they might as well never have existed at all.

In the heat of their argument, the womb opens and the "believing" brother falls out. The "rational" one is shattered by the "tragedy."

> As he moans the misfortune, his ears catch the cry of his brother, and he trembles. To him this spells the end, the last gasp of his expiring brother. Outside, at that very moment, joy and celebration fill the home of the newly born baby: "*Mazel tov, mazel tov*, a baby—we have a son!"

Rabbi Tucazinsky points out that however great the difference between life in the womb and our present life may be, the difference between life in this world and life in the world-to-come is immeasurably greater. As we can see with the "rational" brother, denial of the eternity of the soul and the splendor of the world-to-come leads to anxiety, despair, hopelessness and self-destruction. Without a clear sense of continuity beyond life as we know it, we have to confront the terror of non-existence. The whole world is like a womb and the gestation period is for the elevation of the personality. If we don't use our time on earth to exalt ourselves, we are committing spiritual abortion.

THE LIFE FORCE AT THE ELEMENTAL LEVEL

It is impossible for anyone living a Torah life to be a

complete life force primitive, but it is possible for Torah-observant people to have problems which keep them in patterns that are more appropriate to the elemental level of life force development. We can see this in Rachel, a fifty-year old married woman. Rachel was born in England. Her early years were spent in the bosom of a very close family. Her parents and brother and sister lived next door to her maternal grandparents, and she had an aunt and uncle and cousins in the neighborhood. The family got together for *Shabbos* and holidays and Rachel felt almost as comfortable in her grandparents' homes as in her own.

During the Second World War, Rachel's father went off to war. She missed her father, but life went on pretty much as usual. There were food shortages, but Rachel never went hungry and she was too young to notice or care about the menu changes. The air raids were frightening, but as long as she was with Mommy, who always calmed and comforted her, everything seemed all right. One day, however, everything changed. The bombs came whistling and crashing down, and there was a lot of confusion and screaming. When the air cleared, Rachel could not find her Mommy— or the rest of her family. She was picked up by a very kind man who took her to a shelter where she got very good care. Rachel waited and waited, but her Mommy never came back. And neither did her Daddy. In a few days, she was reunited with her grandparents and her sister and brother.

Rachel seemed very depressed when she first went to live with her grandparents. She kept hoping that Mommy and Daddy would come back, and she kept watching for them. So many times she thought she saw them coming, but alas, it was always someone who resembled them from a distance. She eventually stopped hoping and waiting and watching because she couldn't stand the disappointment when the figure in the distance turned out to be a stranger.

After many months had gone by, Rachel gave up her lonely vigil and started playing again. She laughed and talked and seemed to be her old self. Except that if Grandma had to go out, Rachel got very quiet and didn't feel much like playing. Her vigil was less obvious, but her life was "on hold" until Grandma returned.

Rachel grew up and got married and had two children of her own, Meyer and Donna. She now has a lovely home, makes wonderful meals and dresses stylishly. To the casual observer, she seems like a happy, normal person. But every time her husband goes to work a panic rises in her throat. She wants to hold onto him and say, "Please don't leave me." But she knows that she has to let him go. He sees the stricken look in her eyes, but he knows that he must go.

Rachel goes about her daily life, but her lonely vigil never ends. Her feelings of peace and joy are "on hold" until her husband returns. She never goes too far from home alone, because if she loses sight of familiar places and faces, the panic rises up into her head and she feels sick and faint. The horror of the early loss is triggered over and over again by the reality that something could happen to her husband and children. They might never return.

Rachel's happiest times were when her children were infants. They were completely dependent on her and were with her all the time. She was the most devoted mother and never left them with baby-sitters. When they got old enough to go to school, she had great difficulty letting them go. They saw the stricken look in her eyes, and they each reacted in their own way. Meyer didn't want to come back home because he couldn't stand to see that look in Momma's eyes.

Donna didn't want to go to school, because she couldn't stand to see that look either. Meyer became very independent and aloof: "If I get too close I'll get trapped." Donna became very dependent and had separation anxiety whenever she left home: "What will happen to Momma/me if I go away?"

Rachel fights a courageous battle with her terror, but the emotional wounds of her broken connection have never healed completely. She still reacts emotionally like the helpless child she was when the traumatic severance from her parents occurred. If Rachel could develop a very strong feeling of connection to God, she might be able to overcome her terror and find the peace and comfort so violently torn away from her years ago.

THE RIGHT WAY TO USE THE WILL TO LIVE

What is the correct use of the will to live and the knowledge of death? These two factors together should arouse in us an urgent quest for eternal life. The will to live inspires the search for immortality, and the knowledge of death provokes the urgency. It tells us that our time is limited. God implants these intense feelings, needs and powers in us so that we will be propelled toward Him. If we use them to progress toward God, we can reach great spiritual heights, but if they get detached from their root, our energy gets diverted into self-destructive paths.

In this chapter we have seen that the will to live and the fear of death can be twisted into a will to die and a fear of life. We have seen that the power of the will can be used to heal and prolong life, or it can be used to destroy life. We can depress the will to live and just "give up" on life, or we can live joyfully and purposefully. We can have a view of life limited to this body in this world, or an elevated view of life which includes the divine soul in the world to come. The limited view leads to anxiety, hopelessness and despair because of the inevitability of death; the elevated view leads to joy, hope and meaning because of the possibility of eternal connection with God.

Thus we see that it is vital that we use our life energy appropriately; *it is truly a matter of life and death.*

As Rabbi Tucazinsky says:[29]

> Human existence—as man passes through this world from birth to death—is either all or nothing. Either life constitutes a passage to nothing, without any substance at all, or else it endures for eternity, retaining all its original good and happiness. Either one's days are a bridge to death or a bridge to life.

If we live our lives for the survival of our bodies, we are on a bridge to death. If, however, we live for the survival of our souls, we are on a bridge to life. A good life on this earth is a life used to get closer to God. We are, of course, human, and our bodies are important to us. Our bodies are part of the raw materials we were given to use in the development of our spiritual potential. Thus, we have to take care of our bodies and keep them healthy and strong so that we can use them for spiritual growth. But it is crucial to remember that we are the riders, not the horses. We must treat our horses lovingly while we guide them ever upward. And we must know that even though the ride in this world is temporary it is very important. Every moment of life is a precious gift.

But the time will come when we must separate from our horses; we must die in order to live. The temporary separation (death) and ultimate reunion of body and soul (eternal life in the world-to-come) is a fundamental principle of Judaism. For all but the most elevated, the separation is poignant and painful. After all, we have had a very intimate partnership with our horses and we have grown very close. "Dear horse, you have served me well, but you are old and tired. Now we have to part, but we will be united again—happier and younger then ever."

Let us go on to the next step in the quest to elevate our souls.

SUMMARY

The life force at the elemental level instills in us a powerful will to live and a corresponding dread of death.

THE WILL TO LIVE

The will to live is so powerful that it can promote healing and prolong life. Under extreme conditions, however, it can be so weakened that people sometimes "give up" on life or even take their own lives.

FEAR OF DEATH

The fear of death is particularly strong at the elemental level because at this level "I" am my body and the death of my body is the death of "me." The fear of death can be diminished by belief in the eternity of the soul and life in the world-to-come. In the Torah view, death is a great gift because it gives us a finite time to progress spiritually and prepare ourselves for life in the next world. In that sense, awareness of death can give meaning to every moment of life.

The Need for Physical Sensation, Feeling and Pleasure

The art of the living is an art of dealing with needs, and man's character is shaped and revealed by the way in which he shapes his passions and desires.[1]

H ere we are at the base of the ladder of the senses and emotions, ready to start our climb upward. This climb is very important, because the issues that arise in relation to our senses—the way we deal with our emotions and the kind of pleasures we seek—are at the very core of our being. The choices we make in these areas profoundly affect the quality of our inner lives and our relationships to others and to the world. It is crucial to choose wisely.

The connection between our senses

180

and our psychological and spiritual development may not be clear at first. What does the ability to see, hear, taste, smell and touch have to do with our psychological and spiritual well-being? The answer to this question comes from an enriching insight into the beauty of the Torah system: All of our God-given abilities can be used for elevation; every sense, every muscle, every bone, every organ can be an instrument of fulfillment or an instrument of degradation.

How can we use our senses and emotions for elevation and unification? Before we can answer that question we have to know what forces the soul stirs up inside us at the elemental level.

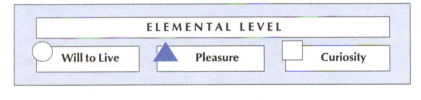

WHEN THE SOUL ACTIVATES THE SENSES

The elemental soul activates the senses by producing the need and desire for sensation, feeling and pleasure. (These needs are modified as we elevate ourselves and interact with the higher levels of the soul. These changes will be discussed in subsequent chapters.)

THE NEED FOR SENSATION AND FEELING

The power of the will interacting with the elemental soul gives us a relentless drive for sensory stimulation. From the moment we're born our senses are turned on and we need them and want to use them. We need excitement and we're always looking for something new.

The need for excitement is a special case of the need for sensation and emotion. What is at the root of the need for excitement?

THE NEED FOR EXCITEMENT

People spend precious time and money to go to the movies. In rain and snow, they wait in long lines to see the latest film. And what do they have left at the end? Nothing. And yet the film industry is extremely successful. Film stars are idolized. Why? Because movies fill a deep need—the need for excitement.

Sports events fill the same need. If the competitors are well matched and a fierce struggle for victory ensues, there is great excitement. If, however, the score is lopsided and victory is assured, people walk out before the end. There is no excitement.

We might think that watching a game between highly skilled professional teams would be more appealing than a game between amateur university teams. But more people attend college games than professional games. Why? Because we can identify with the players. Most of us can't identify with the pros, but we can identify with a team made up of people who are in the same class as us and who represent our school. When we elicit the power of identification, we get even more excited. The same thing happens when we go to the movies. The more we can identify with the hero and heroine, the more excited we get. Why should we be more excited when we can identify with the players or stars? Because more parts of our personalities are involved. When the pros play, we are curious about the outcome and we are stimulated by the battle. When the home team plays we add the thrill of identifying with the players. Think of how excited Little League fathers get when their sons play ball. Love and pride are added to the mixture. The more parts of our personalities involved, the more excited we are.

The root of our need for excitement is the religious level need for unity. Unity, or the harmonious expression of all our needs, is the ultimate pleasure and excitement. From partial unity, we get partial excitement. Why do people get so excited when they get married? Because somehow they feel that it is a religious moment. If it were just a social contract, as some people claim, it wouldn't be any more exciting than signing a lease. But for most people it is very thrilling because it is a contract with elemental, social and religious meaning. It combines the needs for pleasure, love and elevation. Whenever two or more parts are united, there is a flow, like an electric system. The ultimate excitement occurs when all the parts are united.

We like varied stimulation best because we adapt rapidly to all but the most extreme levels of steady stimulation. For example, when you first put the tip of your big toe into a hot bath it seems impossible to get in, but if you slowly immerse yourself in the water, you begin to get used to the sensation of heat. After soaking a few minutes, the water no longer feels hot; it feels comfortably warm even though it may have cooled just a few degrees.

Sensory deprivation studies have demonstrated the deleterious effects of restricted or monotonous stimulation. These studies include the effects of limited sensory and cognitive stimulation. Performance on motor (speed and quality of handwriting) and complex intellectual (verbal fluency and creativity) tests declines, and susceptibility to influence increases.[2] Emotional and behavioral breakdown is common in people who spend prolonged periods of time in monotonous environments such as the North Pole. The need for variety in stimulation is so strong that people in such settings have been known to endanger their lives exploring hazardous restricted areas. When we are exposed to monotonous stimulation or sensory deprivation, we get bored. Monotony and boredom are among the most noxious feelings. We do everything in our power to escape boredom and monotony, and when we can't, our behavior deteriorates. For example, bored children misbehave in school and bored workers on assembly lines are more likely to make mistakes and have accidents.

THE DESIRE FOR PLEASURE

The elemental soul also drives us to pursue physical and emotional satisfaction and pleasure. We not only want to feel, we want to feel good. We have strong sensory preferences and tastes: "I hate modern art, but I love the Impressionists." "I'd love some chocolate ice cream. If all you have is vanilla I'll skip it." Certain tactile sensations make us feel "cozy" and others make our "skin crawl." Certain odors make us sick, and others make us feel secure. I know a real estate agent who instructs clients who are trying to sell their homes to bake an apple in the oven whenever a prospective buyer is coming. The results are amazing. The "homey" smell makes more sales than any list of structural features.

We actively seek experiences that give us pleasure and

we avoid experiences that give us "unpleasure." If this sounds like Freud's pleasure-principle, it is because Freud had a shred of the truth when he said, "Our entire psychical activity is bent upon procuring pleasure and avoiding pain."[3] Freud was right when he concluded that pleasure was a powerful force in human affairs, but he was wrong when he further concluded that "it is simply the pleasure-principle which draws up the program of life's purpose." Erich Fromm[4] acknowledged Freud's insight into the intensity and passion of human pleasure seeking, but he went on to say that

> brilliant as his assumptions were, they are not convincing in their denial of the fact that a large part of man's passionate strivings cannot be explained by the force of his instincts.

Like a man who looks through a peephole and sees a pen moving and then concludes that the pen moves by its own will, Freud's constricted view of human existence excluded the real cause of human behavior. There is a greater power than pleasure drawing up "the program of life's purpose." That power is the spark of the Divine—the soul.

Pleasure does have a very significant and positive role in human existence. As discussed in Chapter Six, our Sages tell us that our souls were united with God before being placed in our bodies. This union is the *ultimate spiritual pleasure*, and we are born with a faint recollection of it. It lingers within us like a subliminal message indelibly imprinted on our minds. All our lives we seek that pleasure. Our capacity for pleasure, then, is a beacon leading us toward God. Of course, at early stages of our souls' development, we are not aware that there is anything beyond physical pleasure.

So we see that two powerful drives are set in motion when the elemental level of the soul interacts with the senses: the drive for sensation and feeling, and the drive for physical pleasure. These two drives are not independent. When they are pursued in combination, they produce positive excitement. Separating the two creates problems. Children who are neglected and emotionally disturbed people will often seek non-pleasurable stimulation. They will hurt themselves or misbehave just for stimulation and reaction. Something is better than nothing.

Healthy people want to explore the world of sensation and to feel good. Knowing this, the relationship between our senses and our psychological, spiritual, social and moral growth becomes clear. The drives for sensation, feeling and pleasure can be dynamic forces for advancement. They can stimulate and motivate us to search for spiritual pleasures— or they can mire us in compulsive pursuit of stimulation and pleasure.

What is the difference between elemental physical pleasure and more elevated spiritual pleasure? We all know what physical pleasure is. It is immediately apparent through our senses. Spiritual pleasure is more subtle and delicate. It has two components: unity of all our parts and the embedded memory of the ultimate pleasure.

How are physical and spiritual pleasure related to each other? And how can we discriminate between the two? It is crucially important for us to know that they are different and to be able to tell the difference between them. Those who say, "I enjoy nightclubs, you enjoy prayer, it's all the same," make us and the cows and the angels the same. The key to developing spiritual awareness is to differentiate between these two kinds of pleasure. The union of the two is the ultimate spiritual pleasure we can experience in this life.

PHYSICAL AND SPIRITUAL PLEASURE

Here are the outlines of the vast contrast between these two primary forms of pleasure we can enjoy.

PHYSICAL PLEASURE IS NOT CUMULATIVE

If I'm hungry or tired, it doesn't help me at all to remember my last meal or my last night's sleep. In fact, thinking about a luscious, moist piece of chocolate cake or a warm, cozy bed tends to make my hunger and weariness all the more unbearable.

SPIRITUAL PLEASURE IS CUMULATIVE

An uplifting experience changes me; it raises my spiritual level. Spiritual stimulation is not just a temporary arousal; it is not just consumed, digested and passed out of the body. It becomes part of me. The great party I had last year does nothing for me now, but the *chessed* (act of kindness) I did last year still gives me pleasure. So, too, the glow of *Shabbos* illuminates my life long after *Shabbos* is over.

SENSITIVITY TO PHYSICAL PLEASURE DECREASES

We adapt to any level of stimulation and we need ever increasing, ever changing doses to get the same high. To keep us from being bored, music has to be louder, the beat more insistent; visual effects have to be more startling; violence has to be more graphic.

SENSITIVITY TO SPIRITUAL PLEASURE INCREASES

I get much more spiritual pleasure from the same twenty-five hours of *Shabbos* than I used to. In fact, at first *Shabbos* seemed endless to me. "What? Are they going to say another prayer? Do they have to sing so many songs? Why all this ritual? Can't we just eat?" Now that my spiritual sensitivity has increased, now that I've learned how to turn on my spiritual motor, I feel uplifted by the same things that used to bore me. I don't need more and more just to get the same reaction. *I get more and more* out of the same twenty-five hours of *Shabbos.*

IN THE WORLD OF PHYSICAL PLEASURE, AGING IS DREADED

In the realm of physical pleasure, aging is dreaded because of the inevitable decline in agility, beauty, strength and endurance. Here is a quote from a review of a dance performance by a sixty-two-year-old Bolshoi ballerina. She was dancing the *Dying Swan* and relied on wriggling, snake-like arm movement to make up for what her body could no longer do. The reviewer said, "This was merely a circus trick and one that backfired, the hyper-fluency in her arms calling attention to the fact that age has deprived the rest of her body of its earlier phenomenal flexibility and fire. In the end, the dance was an inadvertent demonstration of the death of physical prowess—a fate to which we must all succumb."

IN THE WORLD OF SPIRITUAL PLEASURE, AGING IS AN ASSET

In the realm of spiritual pleasure, aging is an asset. Because spiritual pleasure cumulates and sensitivity increases, spiritual powers are deepened and refined with age (*if they are used*). Among religious people, age is revered. In very religious families, older people are respected and admired. And in religious societies, older leaders and advisors are sought.

SUBSTITUTING PHYSICAL PLEASURE FOR SPIRITUAL

Because we don't know how to build and express spiritual pleasure, we substitute physical pleasure for spiritual pleasure. If I don't know how to show my wife that she is dear to me, I'll buy her a ring. If I don't know how to relate to my children, I'll get them new toys. If I don't know how to elevate myself, I'll buy a bigger house.

Also, because of the lack of cumulative effect and decreasing sensitivity in physical pleasure, we are driven to substitute one physical pleasure for another in our search for satisfaction. Each time we hope that the next one will do it for us. And it does, for the moment. If my BMW seems ordinary, I'll buy a Jaguar. If Beverly Hills is *passe*, I'll find a condo in Bel-air.

COMMITMENT IS NATURAL TO SPIRITUAL PLEASURE

It's just the opposite in the spiritual realm. We need and want commitment for our spiritual elevation. Without commitments, we can't develop our personalities; we can't learn how to work things out and see things through. Also, because spiritual pleasure cumulates and sensitivity increases, we are not always driven to look for something better. We can make commitments because we are confident that as we progress spiritually, we can get more and more out of what we already have. Our pleasure grows qualitatively, not quantitatively.

FRUSTRATION AND ALIENATION FROM PHYSICAL PLEASURE

From all that I've said above, it is obvious that the usual outcomes of a life focused on physical pleasure are frustration and alienation. We see an example of this in drug use. As we said earlier, physical pleasure decreases, driving us to increasing doses to get the same "high." Because of this, many drug users die from overdoses. Suppose we tried to counsel them by saying, "Look, you're going to kill yourself. Why don't you settle for a lower dose? You'll still have twenty percent of the pleasure and you won't hurt yourself." Would they accept this suggestion? No! Because they compare this twenty percent with the memory of the original pleasure. What they are left with is an eighty percent deficit, and therefore they feel terrible. This is one of the main problems in many modern marriages. The memory of the early excitement makes the present level of excitement very frustrating. But terminating relationships, or violating them in search of excitement, leads to loneliness and alienation. We see that memory of physical pleasure is a very destructive force.

HAPPINESS AND WELL-BEING FROM SPIRITUAL PLEASURE

Because spiritual pleasure accumulates and sensitivity

increases, spiritual memory is a very constructive force. We can look back at earlier periods and see how much we have grown spiritually. We have a deep sense of belonging when we realize how much more our spouses, family and friends mean to us with each passing year.

Why is happiness the outcome of a life based on spiritual pleasure? We find an answer in the structure of the Hebrew language. Words that have the same root are related conceptually. The Hebrew word for happiness is *osher*. It comes from the word *eeshur*, which means confirmation. The wisdom of the Hebrew language is telling us that we are happy when we feel confirmed, and when we give priority to spiritual pleasure we feel confirmed by our relationships, our learning and our progress.

From the analysis of physical and spiritual pleasure above, we can see that giving primacy to physical enjoyment eventually destroys pleasure and excitement. In accordance with our principle of unity, combining physical and spiritual pleasure greatly enriches life.

PLEASURE IN MODERN SOCIETY

Unfortunately, we live in a culture which treats the most elemental forms of pleasure as though they were the most important part of the personality. This produces many people who are "sensual/emotional primitives." There have, of course, always been "sensual/emotional primitives," people who live only for the pursuit of pleasure. The problem today is that secular society teaches and endorses values that keep many of its citizens locked at the elemental level of the ladder of the senses. The values of the secular world are insidious—they have even infiltrated the Torah world. Many religious Jews today have absorbed secular beliefs and attitudes that are antithetical to Torah.

In many cases, the secular values are so completely internalized that they are not recognized as being inconsistent with Torah. They are heralded as modern psychological insights which shed light on Torah and improve Torah life. For example, it is taken as a truism that it is good for the individual to express feelings, that it is damaging to hold them in. This belief contains a nugget of truth, but it leaves out the possibility that there are more constructive ways to deal with feelings than always expressing them or swallowing them, and it leaves out the effect of emotional expression on the recipient. In the words of Rabbi A. H. Lapin *zatzal*, "If holding in feelings hurts me, and expressing them hurts you, is it really better to hurt you?" I have seen Jewish marriages and families destroyed by the effects of living by the slogan "It's good to express yourself."

Please understand that I am not advocating that we deny or ignore our feelings. I am, however, advocating that we learn to deal with feelings (and every other aspect of life) within Torah guidelines. Torah most certainly acknowledges the power of emotion in human personality and behavior. But we are told that we have to work on making the heart feel what the mind knows. The heart, or seat of emotions, has to follow the mind, not vice versa. We have to work very hard on ourselves to accomplish this, but the rewards are well worth the effort.

Psychologist Jerome Frank[5] has pointed out that American society and "all psychotherapies . . . share a value system that accords primacy to individual self-fulfillment . . . maximum self-awareness, unlimited access to one's own feelings." This value system does not produce the Torah personality. As Alfred Adler[6] saw many years ago, it produces the vain, pampered, egocentric personality of modern psychological man.

Modern man's insistence on being unfettered and feeling good is reinforced constantly by the media. Without absolute values to guide us, we are programmed by the values and norms implicit in the media. Consider what we and our children learn when we see the following commercials:

Mother comes home to find a trail of half-eaten food indicating that her child, who was home alone, has tasted everything in sight. She finds him sitting on the couch feeling ill. But, have no fear, a famous stomach remedy will save the day.

Beautiful scenes of nature bathed in golden light. The narrator saying words like "life," "grain," "nourishing," "clean, fresh, taste." How do you get all those wonderful things? From a popular "light beer" which puts the "light in life."

A picture of a sleek car—"looks like a BMW." The car zooms away into the fading sunset in the distance—"feels like an expensive sports car." The punch line—"Built for the human race."

What do these "messages" teach us? They tell us that it's okay for Mom to leave the kids alone as long as she has healing medication nearby. They make subtle but powerful associations between beer and the beauty of nature, between the right car and being human.

What makes these messages so insidious and so dangerous? Because the media is stirring up our deepest human
needs—the needs for pleasure, for status, for connection, for
love—and associating them with the many different prod-
ucts they want to sell. According to psychologist Philip
Cushman:[7]

> Ads sell by convincing the public that a certain product
> is indispensable to their well-being or by implicity addressing
> or exacerbating a personal fear in the customer that could
> be reassured or soothed by purchasing the product.

Cushman says that the significant absence of community, tradition and shared meaning in modern society is
experienced as a lack of personal conviction and worth—an
empty self. In a society where there are no absolute values,
a society where people feel alienated and empty, these
"messages" seem to fill a vacuum. The empty self is desperate to be filled. It

> must consume in order to be soothed and integrated; it
> must "take in" and merge with a self-object celebrity, an
> ideology or a drug, or it will be in danger of fragmenting
> into a feeling of worthlessness and confusion. (p. 606)

No one else seems able to tell us how to find happiness,
so we might as well try the newest car (beer, drug, etc.). Our
growth is stunted as we settle for these simple-minded
solutions.

These "messages," written for no purpose other than to
sell us something, shape our minds and the minds of our
children. The media are a commercial enterprise, and they

need a large audience in order to survive. Therefore, they appeal to the lowest common denominator. They present very intense, extreme images in order to elicit excitement. But inevitably, we adapt to that level of intensity. Murder and mayhem begin to seem normal. If the extreme no longer generates excitement, the media will give us the bizarre. And eventually, that too will seem normal.

The media affect us another way, too. They set norms for us. Most, if not all, of the material produced and distributed via the commercial media today is vulgar by Torah standards. Movies and television programs show us simulated violence, but in case we're inured to that, we can see the real thing on the news. Real blood, real corpses, and real grief become standard fare. Vulgarity and violence begin to seem like normal life.

The tragedy is that this material, by way of television, radio, movies, magazines, newspapers, etc., enters many an otherwise Torah-observant home. Exposure to this material has a corrosive effect on spiritual growth. We become desensitized to horror. We become numb and calloused. We get used to the coarse and obscene, and we fail to recognize its degrading effect on us. We lose our ability to distinguish between the sacred and the profane.

I saw this effect very clearly in a *shiur* (class) on Torah marriage that I presented to a group of women in a Torah community. The class was composed of three different groups of women: Those who had been raised in Orthodox homes and had always maintained their Orthodox identities; those who were returning to Jewish life after turning away; and those who had been raised in completely secular homes. All of the women were now committed to living Torah lives.

I felt it necessary to do some consciousness-raising, and therefore, in the first session I presented material from a wide range of "women's" magazines which I knew could be found in some of their homes. Most of the women were shocked to realize that while they were very careful to screen their children's reading material, their homes still contained objectionable material in the seemingly innocent magazines purchased for recipes and homemaking hints. These women had become so accustomed to seeing this type of material that they tended to underestimate its pernicious influence on them and their families.

As they learned more about the role of the woman in a Torah marriage they came to realize that the images of women and relationships in such magazines were not only potentially damaging to their children, but in some cases were actually interfering with their own development of a "Torah consciousness." For example, their taste in clothes and cosmetics were being shaped by what they saw in the advertisements, with the result that most modest attire seemed unfashionable. Some of them felt unattractive and dowdy when they dressed themselves in even the finest clothes.

One result of their consciousness-raising was that they became much more careful about what kind of reading materials they allowed to be brought into their homes. They saw more clearly that the media played a major role in shaping their attitudes and preferences even when they were making a conscious effort to internalize a different value system.

These women were certainly not sensual primitives. They were, in fact, all working hard to elevate themselves and to provide sanctified Jewish homes for their families.

They were all trying to develop identities as Torah women, and for most of them this required, first of all, learning what it meant to be a Torah woman and then struggling to integrate that knowledge into their personalities. Almost all of them had to painstakingly weed out remnants of secular thinking about what it meant to be a woman, and in order to do this they had to stop exposing themselves to aggrandized, glorified images of secular women.

One woman said that she had always loved to read "love stories" until she realized that her completely unrealistic romantic expectations were keeping her from being satisfied with her truly wonderful husband and family. This woman had been dissatisfied because her romantic fantasies were at the elemental level while she was trying to live at a much higher level. She brought harmony into her life by making *kedushah* (sanctity), rather than elemental pleasure, her goal.

It is virtually impossible for a Jew living in complete accord with the Torah to be a sensual primitive, but as we have seen, it is possible for growth to be hindered and for personality imbalances to occur because of the extremely powerful downward pull of the sensual stimulation from society. If we expose ourselves to this stimulation we augment the elemental soul's desire for stimulation, pleasure and connection and therefore throw ourselves out of balance. Like every level on the ladder of the senses, the elemental level is important, but only as an early stage of a grand developmental scheme. If we overemphasize any one part of the scheme, we hinder growth and make it impossible to achieve unification with more elevated parts of the personality.

ELEMENTAL IMBALANCE

The destructive effects of overemphasizing the senses can be seen in Michelle, a young woman who had been a *baalas teshuvah* for about a year. She was very serious about her commitment to Torah, had started to learn Hebrew, attended *shiurim* twice a week and was *shomer Shabbos*. Michelle ate only kosher food—*most of the time*. Occasionally, however, when she drove past a certain "fast food" restaurant that she used to frequent, she felt an irresistible impulse to drive in and eat. She struggled with herself, but to no avail. Whenever she was in the presence of that stimulus, she succumbed and then felt terrible afterwards.

She was so upset by her inability to control herself that she was beginning to doubt the sincerity of her commitment to Torah: "If eating this food is more important to me than keeping the *mitzvah* of *kashrus*, maybe I'm not up to living a Torah life. Maybe I'd better quit for a while." Michelle was actually being pulled down by giving in to her lust for food. Fortunately, she worked up enough courage to talk to her rabbi about the problem, and she was able to see that her problem was not that she was insincere or inadequate, but that she was out of balance in her spiritual development. She realized that in order to correct the imbalance she had to continue to learn and live a Torah life, not give it up.

In a man named Reuven we see another kind of imbalance, this one caused by substituting lower sensory/emotional pleasures for inaccessible higher ones. Reuven had been an outstanding student and had gotten along quite well with the other students in his *yeshivah*. Everything seemed to be fine until he was old enough to think about getting married. After many unsuccessful attempts at starting a relationship, it became clear that he had difficulty with closeness and intimacy. He became very anxious and self-conscious in unstructured social situations, worrying about whether he was liked and what kind of an impression he was making. He was so uncomfortable and self-absorbed that he was completely unable to make contact with the other person.

As the years went on, his marriage possibilities declined, and Reuven became lonelier and lonelier. He suppressed his need for connection and withdrew more and more into a private world. He continued to make superficial contact with others, but he felt close to no one. He filled his spare time with food and television, where he was stimulated by defiled images of women and life in general. Reuven was using the most elemental forms of sensory stimulation and pleasure to blot out his misery and mitigate the emptiness of his life. Reuven was out of balance, because although he was functioning at higher levels on the intellectual and life force ladders, he was at the lowest level on the ladder of the senses. In order to restore balance and harmony to his life he needed to give up his sensual crutches and face his painful feelings and social deficiencies. Substituting one sensory need for another doesn't solve problems, though it may provide short-term relief.

From the examples above we see that it takes vigilance and courage to repel the flood of sensual stimulation that threatens to engulf us and prevent us from climbing the ladder of the senses. We have to know that our senses and emotions are raw materials that have to be refined to be useful. Like a garden that requires digging, irrigation, planting, fertilizing, weeding, pruning and pest control in order to be beautiful, our sensory systems and the emotions and desires they generate need cultivating. If we let every weed "do its own thing" and give all pests equal rights, we end up with an ugly tangle of misshapen growth, flowers choked off by weeds and damaged by disease. Similarly, if we follow every impulse and give every feeling equal importance, we end up with a tangled, misshapen, damaged emotional/spiritual and social life.

▲ USING THE SENSES AND EMOTIONS

The Torah tells us that if we want to use our senses and feelings correctly, we have to use them in the context of our overall purpose in life: elevation and unification. We must look at the sensory/emotional ladder and see that there are five levels, not one. We have to know that at the first, or elemental level, our senses and emotions are raw materials which have to be refined. Unrefined and undisciplined, they are dangerous.

Remember our horse and rider—the body and the soul. Just as an untamed horse is dangerous, untamed passions are dangerous. The skillful rider must lovingly but firmly train the horse, gently placing the saddle on its back and teaching it to respond to commands. If the rider is afraid of the horse and doesn't exert assured control, the horse will run wild and trample everything in its path. If we are afraid to tame our feelings, they will run wild and trample our higher selves. In order to elevate ourselves we have to train our "horses" to take orders that emanate from the soul.

While writing this, my "horse" has wanted to go shopping, eat chocolate cake, call a friend and take a nap, all of which *it* can do, but not while *I* am writing if *I* want to finish this book. I have had to tug at the reins and say "A little more, a little more." *It* will get its sugar cube, but not until *I* have accomplished my goals.

So we see that we *do* have elemental souls and senses. We *do* desire stimulation and enjoy pleasure and long to be connected. Good, we're normal healthy human beings. The question is, will we choose to use these desires in ways that will ultimately be elevating and fulfilling, or in ways that turn us into "sensual primitives"?

In the Torah system, elemental needs are combined and integrated with higher needs. As we climb the sensory/emotional ladder, we are able to have sensual pleasure, but we have it in the context of a stable family life. We can go beyond narrow self-absorption and develop loving relationships. We are able to serve our communities and our God. Climbing the ladder is a great challenge, but the reward is the abiding sense of well-being and peace-of-mind that come with living in accord with our deepest needs.

SUMMARY

The elemental soul activates the senses and emotions and produces the need and desire for sensation, feeling and pleasure.

THE NEED FOR EXCITEMENT

Excitement increases as more parts of our personalities are involved. The greatest excitement occurs when all the parts are combined.

THE PLEASURE PRINCIPLE

The desire for pleasure is a powerful force in our lives. We want to feel good. The root of the desire for pleasure is the yearning of the soul to re-experience the ultimate pleasure of union with God.

THE DIFFERENCE BETWEEN PHYSICAL AND SPIRITUAL PLEASURE

It is crucial to know that there are two kinds of pleasure: physical and spiritual, and to be able to recognize the difference between them. The union of physical and spiritual pleasure is the ultimate pleasure that we can achieve in this life.

The media reinforces elemental sensory and emotional expression and thus has a corrosive effect on our sensitivity. We become desensitized to horror, vulgarity and obscenity.

Actually, our senses and emotions are precious raw materials which need refinement and discipline.

Curiosity and the Drive to Explore

CHAPTER 9

Curiosity is a powerful motivating force in human behavior. It has a developmental line, from a state of alert wakefulness in the infant to active investigation of the environment—and then includes a wide range of interests in the outer world as well as in the inner psychological world.[1]

Here we are on the first rung of the ladder of the intellect. At this level of development, the intellect is activated by the elemental soul. As we learned in Chapter 6, the elemental soul brings us the need for satisfaction and the power of the will. Remember that at this level, we are like engines without wheels or a steering mechanism. We are revved up and full of

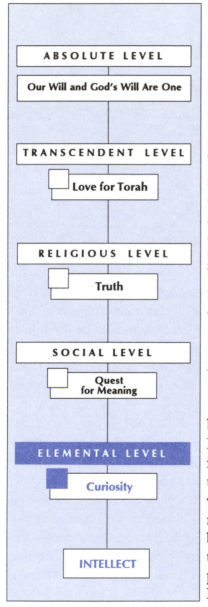

ABSOLUTE LEVEL

Our Will and God's Will Are One

TRANSCENDENT LEVEL

Love for Torah

RELIGIOUS LEVEL

Truth

SOCIAL LEVEL

Quest
for Meaning

ELEMENTAL LEVEL

Curiosity

INTELLECT

raw energy and determination, but we don't know where we're going or how to get there.

What happens when this primitive energy source connects with the intellect? The main effect of the interaction between the elemental soul and the intellect is curiosity, or the desire for intellectual stimulation and the desire to explore. We see this raw, primitive curiosity in young babies, who are even fascinated by the discovery of their own hands and feet.

CURIOSITY

Curiosity is a powerful and basic drive. Psychologists (e.g., Berlyne[2] and Harlow[3]) have found that animals will work to solve problems and puzzles without receiving any external reward. They seemed to be motivated by some satisfaction that is inherent in completing the tasks themselves. Based on this type of data from research with different animals, and on clinical and historical evidence from human behavior, Abraham H. Maslow[4] concluded that "... man *does* have a need to know, and more than that, a need to understand ..." Maslow said that curiosity has

> an element of desire, drive or need, of a yearning, a longing, demanding satisfaction for the fullest growth of the person, a satisfaction that could be avoided only under peril of pathology and of diminution of the person.

According to Maslow then, healthy development is dependent on curiosity. However, Maslow also tells us that in the hierarchy of needs, curiosity plays second fiddle to safety. The "need to feel safe, secure, unanxious, unafraid is prepotent, stronger than curiosity." Even children, who tend to be irrepressibly curious, explore most confidently from a safe harbor. Put young children and their mothers in a strange and new environment, and the children will become clingy and shy, only gradually and cautiously venturing away from mother to explore. If the mother disappears or if the children are frightened, exploration ceases. McReynolds[5] found that school children who were rated maladjusted were less curious than those rated better adjusted. Research has shown that psychologically healthy people are indeed curious, and psychologically sick people tend to be threatened by the unfamiliar and the unknown.

Anxiety and fear can kill curiosity, creating a vicious cycle. Out of fear, we may avoid new experiences; as a result of impoverished experience, we become less competent to take on challenges successfully. Sensing our own inadequacy, we become more fearful and restrict ourselves even more. Once curiosity is inhibited, growth and development are stunted.

Just as anxiety stunts our curiosity about the outer world, it can also stunt our curiosity about the inner world. Our curiosity can become so dulled that we end up fearing knowledge itself. We sometimes shut out knowledge that may threaten the integrity of our self-concept or decrease our self-esteem:

> the great cause of much psychological illness is the fear of knowledge of oneself—of one's emotions, impulses, memories, capacities, potentialities, of one's destiny. We have discovered that fear of knowledge of oneself is very often isomorphic with, and parallel with, fear of the outside world.[6]

There is another kind of knowledge that we may defend ourselves against—knowledge that compels us to take on responsibilities which repel or frighten us. What do many Germans answer when asked why they didn't actively protest the horrors being perpetrated by their government during the Second World War? "I didn't know what was happening." Ignorance is presented as an acceptable excuse for inaction. Knowledge brings responsibility, and so we shut out knowledge (see discussion of cognitive dissonance in Appendix).

As valuable as curiosity is, it also has a negative side. Greek legend has it that Pandora's curiosity caused her to lift the lid on the box of evil and unleash enormous suffering on the world.

Because of this tendency for curiosity to lead us onto dangerous paths, we are cautioned to "let well enough alone," and to "let sleeping dogs lie." In other words, we shouldn't be too curious. It will get us in trouble.

How much curiosity is "too much"? When is curiosity beneficial, and when is it destructive? In order to answer this we have to make the distinction between curiosity for varied experiences and curiosity for knowledge.

SEARCHING FOR VARIED EXPERIENCES

Curiosity for varied experiences is beneficial when it motivates us to explore and learn about the world around us—within the limits of Torah. By definition, we are not permitted to indulge our own curiosity for things that are physically or spiritually dangerous: these things are outside the limits of Torah. We can try any cuisine—French, Italian, Chinese—as long as it is kosher. We cannot eat pork no matter how curious we are.

It is easy to understand why we are not allowed to do things that are physically dangerous. Spiritual danger, however, is much harder to explain. In Chapter 5, we discussed *metamtem hanefesh*, or damaging the soul by doing things not permitted by Torah. We can see how this mechanism works from analyzing drug usage. Many people have used drugs with no evidence of physical harm. Should we then say that drug usage is permitted by Torah? No, because it is spiritually harmful.

In contemporary society, many young people have opened a "Pandora's box" of troubles for themselves because they were curious about drugs. They found out the hard way that long after their curiosity had been satisfied, they were still dependent on drugs. They were damaged spiritually, if not physically, because no pleasure could compete with the memory of the drugged state and because they damaged their spiritual sensitivity. Their lust for immediate, intense pleasure was increased and their sensitivity to the message of the soul was destroyed. Why take on responsibilities, concentrate on studies, or struggle to grow, when pleasure can just be inhaled? Using our horse-and-rider metaphor, we can say that the horse had found an easy way to escape the reins.

Even within the limits of Torah, curiosity can be destructive when it is so strong that we can't curb it in the face of danger, when we can't stop exploring even though we know that we are on the edge of a precipice (physically, spiritually or emotionally). The curiosity of infants and children can be dangerous because they lack adequate information about the world to guide their explorations. They have no idea what will happen if they poke a little finger into a light socket or drink the pretty pink liquid in the bottle in the medicine cabinet.

We can see that curiosity for experience within the limits of Torah is beneficial if it is expressed within a framework formed by knowledge, experience and preparation. Columbus had good reason to think that the world was round when he set sail, and the Wright brothers worked long and hard on the first flying machine before they attempted to fly. The legendary Dedalus, on the other hand, suffered the fate of those whose curiosity pushes them beyond the limits of their knowledge and experience when his wax wings melted as he made a futile attempt to fly to the sun.

All breakthroughs come about as a result of taking informed risks. But if we find that in spite of all of our hard planning, we have reached the edge of an unexpected precipice, we have to stop, regroup, reevaluate our information, redeploy our resources and find another way to proceed besides plunging straight ahead. We might have to take another route, drop a ladder or say, "This is as far as we go." We can do this if our hierarchy of needs has not gotten disordered, if our safety needs are still prepotent. But if we are compulsively curious, and our curiosity for experience need overrides other needs, we may not be able to tolerate the delays inherent in using good sense. We may not be able to accept the idea that there are limits on what we can explore.

Curiosity is an essential part of all discovery, but the primitive energy behind it has to be harnessed in order for curiosity to serve us well.

THE SEARCH FOR KNOWLEDGE

In the area of curiosity for knowledge, almost all areas of study are allowed and recommended because they can help us to learn Torah (Vilna Gaon). The only proviso is that we remember that secular learning is of secondary importance. Secular studies are permitted *if* they leave ample time for Torah, and *if* they help us to learn Torah. For example, if learning about the incredible complexity of the transmission of nerve impulses makes us marvel at the wonders of the Divine Creation, the study has served a useful purpose. If the knowledge makes us marvel at the wonders of evolution or our own cleverness, the study has been counterproductive.

There is one type of intellectual inquiry which is not permitted by Torah. Questions regarding God which do not have their answers within the realm of logic, for example, why God made the world the way He did, should not be pursued. If we want to understand the world, fine. But, if we want to understand God, we are in trouble. Trying to know the unknowable is destructive because it distracts us from learning what we can know and because it leads to a sense of futility or falsehood. Whether we like or not, we do have intellectual limits. Our thoughts are not His thoughts. We can learn about God from His Torah and His Creation, but we cannot know His essence. As Rabbi Saadia Gaon said, "If I were to know Him, I would be Him."

Many people find it repugnant to think that the human intellect is finite, that there is an infinite divine intellect that they simply cannot understand. Some say that they cannot relate to something that they do not understand. But will they walk out of a sixth floor window, refusing to obey the law of gravity until they can understand it? Scientists do not claim to understand the electron. The only thing they can know is how the electron acts, the laws governing its behavior. Should they refuse to use electricity until they can understand it? Even those of us who are not scientists can learn the rules of using electricity that relate to us (for example, don't plug a radio into a socket while you are in the bathtub). We can relate to God in a similar way. We can learn about Him by studying the rules of His behavior (from the Torah and history) and we can follow His rules for us, even though we cannot know Him.

HOW CURIOSITY DEVELOPS

Healthy curiosity is crucial to intellectual and emotional development. How does normal curiosity develop? And how does it change from healthy curiosity to compulsive curiosity? We see inquisitive behavior in tiny infants. Brazelton,[7] the eminent developmental pediatrician, describes the quiet, awake infant as a baby alertly interested in the environment, and the active, awake infant as a baby who is exploring the environment, first with its eyes then, as it matures, with all of its sensory-motor equipment.

The curiosity drive begins to be shaped by experience from the day of birth. If the caretakers provide a stimulating environment, respond positively to signs of curiosity, react with interest, encourage safe exploration and regulate dangerous exploration by limits and diversions, the drive develops in a healthy direction. But if the environment is sterile, or if curious exploration is harshly punished or completely ignored, curiosity can be squelched, producing a very passive, timid child. In extreme cases this treatment can produce retardation.[8] As Maslow said:[9]

> primitive curiosity is not *just* within the individual . . . curiosity is an interest in the environment, which pulls, which is fascinating and attractive—curiosity is transactional, a relationship between a primed organism and an interesting environment . . . (p.202)

Overcontrol of the environment or lack of reinforcement of curiosity can have another effect: it can turn the curiosity drive into a battleground between caretaker and child, with the child exploring provocatively as a way to defy or antagonize the caretaker. When this happens, the normal curiosity drive is deformed and becomes something of a psychological monster.

Ideally, we hope to provide our children with a safe,

appropriately stimulating environment in which exploration can be encouraged and guided, promoting ever-expanding skills and interests. In this way, primitive curiosity
can be raised to social and religious levels of striving for
meaning and truth.

ENTERTAINMENT

Psychologists have shown that we need intellectual stimulation as well as sensory stimulation. When we are
understimulated, we suffer from "stimulus hunger."[10] Psychologists theorize[11] that low stimulation leads to low cortical
arousal levels, which we find unpleasant. That is, monotonous environments don't provide enough brain stimulation
to keep us satisfied. The discomfort of this understimulation
motivates us to restore "sensoristasis," an optimal level of
cortical arousal by increasing our stimulation. In truly
deprived circumstances, people will do almost anything to
entertain themselves. Subjects in REST (restricted environmental stimulation) studies have been known to request
repetitive presentations of extremely boring material, such
as old stock market reports. Anything was better than nothing!

This helps us to understand the obsession with television
and other forms of instant entertainment today. Thanks to
technology, we have more free time to fill, but we have less
skills for filling it in active ways. Before the advent of radio,
movies, television and the VCR, entertainment was much
harder to find. We actually had to be active and at least
somewhat skilled in order to entertain ourselves. We gathered around the piano and sang (someone had to learn to

play the piano); we sang in choirs; we formed chamber groups; we read; or else we listened attentively to stories, vividly imagining what the characters looked like, how they were dressed and where the story took place. We could see the fog roll in, feel the sun on our shoulders and thrill with excitement when the hero appeared on the scene. On special occasions, we might go to a concert or to the theater, but in order to really enjoy the music or the play, we had to develop and refine our tastes. Now we can flip a switch and just sit back and let ourselves be washed over by a flood of meaningless, trivial and often vulgar stimulation.

Entertainment-seeking is the more passive side of the curiosity drive. Elemental intellectuals prefer to satisfy their desire for brain stimulation without effort, either because they are lazy or because they are running away from themselves. Some of them become "couch potatoes," sitting in front of the TV for hours on end. The most passive people watch any program on the air, while the more discriminating watch videotaped reruns of their favorite programs or videotapes of movies. Others seek more varied forms of entertainment, always listening to the radio or tapes in their cars, or to headsets when they shop or exercise.

Elemental intellectuals can't stand the absence of external stimulation, because they don't stimulate themselves by exercising their minds. Either they don't know how to, or they don't want to make the effort to use their imagination, think through problems, contemplate ideas or introspect. No wonder entertainers are the idols of our society. They are labor-saving devices, keeping us from doing the hard work of thinking and facing ourselves.

If we subject ourselves and our children to TV, we are manipulated by market researchers who use their findings to determine just how much variation and novelty to pro-gram in order to keep us from getting bored and either going to sleep or turning off the set. We become condi-tioned to rapidly changing images, carefully timed to hold our interest. Since we no longer have much reason to concentrate on anything, we become less and less able to sustain concentration for long periods of time.

The greatest victims of the "sound bite" mentality are our children. Because of the short attention span in school-age children, it was recently suggested by an educator that school textbooks be written in magazine format: banner headlines, lots of pictures, short text. This was considered necessary in order to get children to read. The most shocking finding is that "educational" TV has been a major cause of lowering children's intellectual level and ability to concentrate.

Educational programs have conditioned children to pay attention to thirty-second units of highly entertaining mate-rial. This conditioning makes it very difficult for them to apply themselves for longer periods of time to more com-plex material. Tragically, many children have been turned from curious, active learners into people who need to be entertained. These are children who may never take on the active quest of becoming doctors, lawyers, musicians, scien-tists or Torah scholars.

SCIENCE IS THE ULTIMATE CURIOSITY

We tend to think of science as the pinnacle of human intellectual achievement. However, in this Torah model, science is on the lowest rung of the intellectual ladder. Let's try to understand why science, which is so revered in the secular world, is here considered to be just an expression of the primitive curiosity drive.

To many scientists, science is more than mere curiosity. They are not just seeking intellectual stimulation, but rather trying to find some meaning or ultimate truth about the universe. Albert Einstein wrote[12] that "science can only be created by those who are thoroughly imbued with the aspiration toward truth and understanding." It is easy to see the link between curiosity and scientific inquiry. Our need to know motivates us to seek answers to the intriguing mysteries which surround us and the painful problems which beset us; science helps us to answer many of these questions.

And what questions scientists deal with! When does life begin and end? Is there life on other planets? Scientists are currently trying to untangle the mystery of how information gets transferred from the surface of a cell to the nucleus of the cell. They know that a hormone comes and attaches itself to the cell and tells it what to do—but they have no idea *how* the information is communicated, how it is transported from the membrane through the cell tissue to the nucleus. This knowledge is extremely important, because when things go wrong it may be because of a miscommunication between the messenger and the cell nucleus. When the scientists can figure this one out they may be able to solve problems such as the pathological proliferation of cancer cells by correcting the communication between the messenger and the nucleus of the cell.

The fact that scientists delve into these kinds of questions is awe-inspiring to most of us, and makes science seem like a very elevated pursuit. As Professor Chernievsky[13] said:

The tremendous success of technological applications

and the exaggerated faith of widely diverse sectors of the population in the omnipotence of science had implanted a certainty in the mind of 19th century man that there was no problem that science was incapable of explaining and that everything which was not scientific was, at best, expendable.

Faith in the omnipotence of the natural sciences gave rise likewise to the certainty that they were capable of replacing all other achievements of the human spirit, and among them the place of religion. In the place of religious theology, a theology of natural science was formulated.

It is certainly true that science has had a tremendous impact on our lives; it has doubled our life expectancy, freed us from backbreaking toil, put us in instant communication with the far reaches of the universe and enabled us to walk on the moon. It seems rather audacious in the face of such spectacular success to relegate science to the elemental level of the ladder of the intellect. Yet this is where we put it. Why? Because the astonishing scientific progress of the last century has shed absolutely no light on the fundamental questions of humanity—individual morality and social harmony. Science cannot answer questions of purpose and meaning. As physicist Aaron Katzir[14] said:

> Who is better, a man or a microbe? It is clear that this question simply lacks meaning in the realm of pure science. The tuberculosis-microbe (bacteria) is not better or worse than human life . . . according to science which by its very nature cannot inquire into concepts such as "good" and "bad."

Science can tell us how to kill germs and on the other hand how to use them in germ warfare to kill human beings.

It cannot tell us which is better from a moral point of view.

Science teaches us how to change the world. The Torah teaches us how to change ourselves. In the contemporary world where the strength of the society is the goal and the person is just raw material, science is a religion because it is the origin of the power of society. But in a world where the well-being of human beings is the goal, Torah is the religion and science is just a tool.

Scientists do not deserve to be our high priests. Because of the prestige of science, however, we tend to attribute wisdom to scientists in areas far beyond their fields of competence, including political, moral and ethical wisdom.

The fact is that scientific progress often brings new ethical dilemmas in its wake. Scientific advances in an ethical vacuum often cause undreamed-of human heartache. Now that we know how to determine whether an unborn child has certain defects, what do we do if we discover that the child will be born with Down's syndrome? When do we "pull the plug" on our comatose loved one? What are the rights of the surrogate "birth mother"? Who gets custody of frozen embryos? Should we implant a baboon heart in a baby? In the absence of absolute standards of good and evil based on a divine system of morality, questions like these cannot be answered authoritatively.

Fortunately, Torah Jews do not live in an ethical vacuum. They see the world as God's creation. There are no independent "laws of nature"; there are only God's laws. As Rabbi Dessler[15] said:

> We call God's acts "nature" when He wills that certain events should occur in a recognizable pattern with which we become familiar—Nature has no objective existence; it is

merely an illusion which gives man a choice to exercise his free will: to err, or to choose the truth.

By exposing the workings of the "natural world," science reveals God's will. It can help us to appreciate God's greatness, power and wisdom. It can even help to answer *halachic* questions. (For example, a computer scanning system called STaM has been developed to check for textual flaws in Torahs, *tefillin* and *mezuzos* much more quickly and accurately than human proofreaders can.) But science cannot tell us how to live. Like the computer, it analyzes data but doesn't tell us what to do with it. In our example above, the computer can identify errors in sacred writings, but it cannot know the spiritual significance of the errors.

Torah Jews do not deify science or any other intellectual pursuit. The Torah attitude toward human wisdom can be seen in the fact that there are different blessings for the two kinds of *chachmah* (wisdom), Torah wisdom and secular wisdom. Upon seeing a sage of Israel one says, "Blessed be He Who *shared* His wisdom with those who revere Him." For non-Torah sages, the blessing is: "Blessed be He Who *gave* of His wisdom to His creatures." God's wisdom is given to the non-Torah scholar, but it is shared with the Torah scholar, because the wisdom of Torah is never totally disassociated from its Source and because the Torah scholar is never disassociated from God.[16]

Rabbi Carmell asks which blessing is appropriate for a Jewish secular scholar such as Albert Einstein? His answer is that neither is appropriate, for Einstein was a Jew and his mind was prepared for Torah. As it says in *Psalms* (111:10), "The beginning of wisdom is the fear of God." A Jewish mind without fear of God, no matter how brilliant, gets no blessing. Although Einstein made statements like; "God doesn't play dice with the universe," I have found no evidence that he believed in God as a source of moral imperatives. Had Einstein also been a Torah scholar, he would have received the blessing of shared divine wisdom.

Rabbi Mordechai Gifter[17] tells us that

> all aspects of wisdom in this world are sparks from the great Source of Perfect Wisdom, Blessed is He. If someone attaches himself to the spark without recognizing the Source, his wisdom is empty, without soul or content.

As long as it is a handmaiden of Torah, recognized as revelation of God's will, science is an integral part of Judaism. It is a link between the elemental level of curiosity and the higher-level pursuit of the Truth. But when science is disassociated from its Divine Source and heralded as the ultimate source of truth, it is nothing more than a very elegant and sophisticated expression of the elemental curiosity drive combined with the will for power. And we all know that power without values is dangerous.

THE ELEMENTAL INTELLECTUAL

It is difficult to imagine that anyone living a Torah life could be an "elemental intellectual," but it is possible that someone could go through the motions of Torah observance without struggling with the meaning (social level) of what he is doing and without understanding the truth (religious level) which underlies and makes sense of all the rules he follows. A person like this could use intellectual stimulation as a way to avoid grappling with the real issues in life. This would make him an elemental intellectual.

Bob is an example of a very sophisticated elemental intellectual. Bob is a very clever twenty-eight year old man. He was raised in a religious home, went to Jewish schools and then went on to college and graduate school. He has a Master's degree in Business and manages the family real-estate business. Throughout college Bob always observed *Shabbos* and ate kosher food, even though special arrangements with professors and administrators were often needed to avoid taking exams on *Shabbos*, etc. No matter how inconvenient, Bob always kept these *mitzvos*.

But lately, Bob has begun to wonder if it is really necessary to be *shomer mitzvos* (to keep the commandments of the Torah). He is a very cultured and well-informed man. He has an active, inquiring mind, reads the newspapers from cover to cover and knows what is going on in the worlds of art, entertainment, business and finance. He works very hard and has a lot of responsibility. Naturally, he enjoys relaxing whenever he can by going to the theater, concerts, lectures, museums and movies.

More and more lately, Bob has been tempted to go to an interesting lecture on a Friday night or to the Philharmonic on Saturday afternoon. Why should he miss stimulating programs? Surely they enrich his life and give him a much-needed break from his rigorous daily routine.

Until recently, Bob had never really thought about why he was *shomer mitzvos*. He was raised that way and he grew up expecting to live that way for the rest of his life. But he is beginning to feel hemmed in by rules which keep him from doing some of the things he loves to do when he wants to do them. And he isn't sure what good the rules are doing him.

His life seems very full and satisfying. But as far as he can tell, the people he sees at concerts and museums also seem to have good lives *without all the restrictions.*

Bob is in a very dangerous position spiritually. His curiosity drive, coupled with his intelligence, have motivated him to become a very accomplished and successful man. He feels comfortable as long as he can keep himself busy and entertained. When he is cut off from worldly pursuits, however, Bob feels quite desolate. He suffers from very limited spiritual resources. For some reason, Bob's Jewish observance never gave his life meaning and purpose. Being Jewish became a strong habit, but it never became an integral part of his identity or a way to bring him closer to God. If Bob doesn't learn how to "turn on his spiritual motor" so he can be elevated by Judaism, if he can't raise his curiosity drive to the social and religious levels, he may turn away from Judaism and find himself cut off from his roots and very far from his real potential.

THE PROPER USE OF THE CURIOSITY DRIVE

The development of the intellect is pivotal to the Torah personality. According to Rabbi Moshe Chaim Luzzatto:[18]

> God granted us one particular means which can bring man close to God more than anything else. This is the study of His revealed Torah . . . These words have the unique property of causing one who reads them to incorporate in himself the highest excellence and greatest perfection . . . when one strives to understand these works, either through his own intellect or through the explanations provided in

their commentaries, he can earn even greater perfection, according to his effort.

In addition to Torah study, Rabbi Luzzatto[19] teaches us that we have to use our intellect to examine the Creation:

> Examination of the wisdom manifested in the universe . . . is the most direct and surest road to a realization of His existence and reality . . .

Rabbi Luzzatto points out that we are worse than dumb brutes if we don't use our minds to "perceive, understand and acquire knowledge of the mysteries of the Supernal Wisdom."

How do we conduct this examination of the Creation? Rabbi Luzzatto continues:

> Examination of created things means a close study of the original elements of which the universe is composed; the products that result from the combination of these elements; the character of the constituents of each compound; its various uses; the marks of wisdom exhibited in its production, form and shape, and in the purpose for which it was created; the beautiful spirituality of this world, its causes and effects; and the complete perfection for which it was created . . . and to realize that the Creator created the universe in a perfect and orderly combination . . . so that it indicates and points to the Creator, as clearly as a piece of work points to the workman or a house indicates the builder.

Thus we see that in order to fulfill our purpose in life, we have to develop our intellect past the elemental level of mere curiosity. We need to progress intellectually to the social level, in which we seek meaning and ultimately reach the religious level in which we seek the truth. If we get stuck at the level of elemental curiosity, we are wasting a precious gift and are lower than the beasts. It is supremely important to nurture the curiosity drive in children and foster in them love of learning and discipline of intellect. God, in His wisdom and kindness, has given us the means to grow closer to Him. He has given us the curiosity drive and the need for intellectual stimulation. If these gifts are properly developed and applied to learning Torah and examining the Creation, they have the power to bring us closer to God.

SUMMARY

Curiosity is a basic and powerful human drive. There are two kinds of curiosity, curiosity for varied experiences and curiosity for knowledge:

1. Curiosity for varied experiences is beneficial if we explore within the limits of Torah and a framework formed by knowledge, experience and preparation. Beyond these limits we risk spiritual and physical damage.

2. Curiosity for knowledge is permitted and recommended if we remember that secular knowledge is secondary and if it reveals God in the world. Scientific inquiry is at the elemental level unless it is pursued as revelation of God's will. Disconnected from its Divine source, science is nothing more than an elegant and sophisticated expression of the elemental curiosity drive.

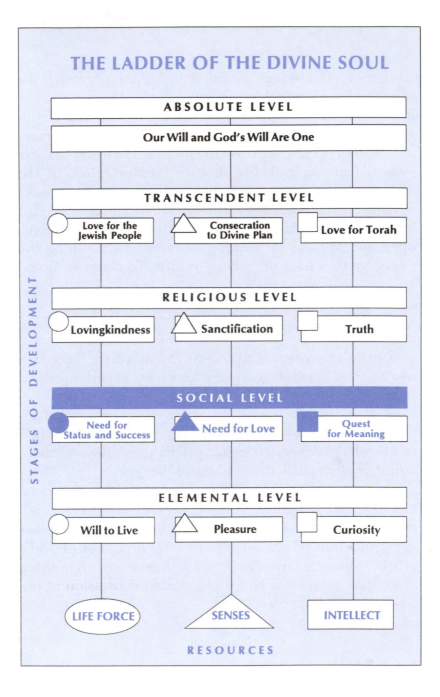

CHAPTER 10

Forming a Stable Identity in an Ever-Changing World

What we call our sense of identity is our sense that our truest, strongest, deepest self persists over time in spite of constant change. It is a sense of self sameness that is deeper than any differences, a true self on which all our other selves converge. This steadying sameness includes both what we are and what we are not . . . And it also includes both our private, inner "I am I" experiences and the recognition by others that "Yes, you are you."[1]

The very essence of the social soul is a sense of movement, a desire for progress. We are driven to push forward, to ask questions about ourselves and the world and to search for meaningful answers. We become aware of ourselves and ask, "Who am I?" The search for ever-expanding self-awareness and stable self-identity are the themes of the social level. They set the tone for all of the challenges we face at the social level: our quests for success and status ("How do I compare with others?"), love and belonging ("Who do I love and who loves me?"), and meaning ("What is my life all about?"). Once we are aware of ourselves and have established a stable self-identity, we have the tools we need to raise ourselves beyond enslavement to elemental drives and needs.

Let us look at how our senses of self-awareness and self-identity are formed. Then we'll see how the Torah enables us to use these senses for our maximum good.

SELF-AWARENESS

The very first step in the formation of a stable identity is the development of a subjective sense of self, the "I" of self-awareness. In infancy, each of us has come to realize that we are separate from other persons, that we are individuals and that we can cause things to happen: Mommy goes away but "I" am still here; "I" cry and Mommy comes back; "I" coo and Daddy smiles and coos back at me.

Once we have a subjective sense of self, we can go on to develop a sense of ourselves as objects, the "me" of self-awareness: "I" am a girl; "I" have blue eyes like my mommy; "I" am not as big and strong as my brother.

Our awareness of ourselves as subjects ("I") is usually accomplished by about fifteen months of age, and our sense of ourselves as objects ("me") is usually well under way by the end of the second year of life. From that point on we continue to form an increasingly complex and abstract "self-theory": "I like candy"; "I do better in spelling than I do in arithmetic"; "I am an honest person."

At about the age of eight a new facet is added to the "I." We develop a "Super-I" who can step back and observe both the "I" and the "me."[2] Emerging out of this "Super-I" is the capacity for self-criticism. This does not imply that younger children do not experience self-evaluative feelings such as shame and pride, but until middle childhood they do not have the ability to judge themselves objectively. For example, when asked to define the emotion "ashamed," a typical four-to-five-year-old reply is, "Ashamed is a bad feeling." A typical five-to-seven-year-old reply is, "My Mom was ashamed of me for hitting my sister." A typical eight-to-nine year-old response is, "I was ashamed of myself when I failed the test."

During adolescence self-awareness is further enhanced and refined by the appearance of the potential for introspection. The ability to reflect on one's own thoughts, feelings and motives adds depth to the self-theory: "It makes me happy to help people. I think I'll study to be a physician." "I've been very sad lately, but I'm not sure what's bothering me;" "Even though I love my friend Michael I felt a little jealous when he was picked for the choir and I wasn't."

Throughout our lives, we are involved in the process of revising our self-theory according to our observations of ourselves interacting with the world. ("I thought I wanted to be a physician but I can't stand the sight of blood. Maybe I had better become a psychologist instead.")

In general, developmental progression of self-awareness goes from concrete, observable characteristics such as physical attributes, material possessions and behavior, to

more abstract self-definitions based on psychological processes such as inner thoughts, emotions, attitudes and
motives.

Many psychologists agree that the evolving self-theory
or self-structure is centrally important in the personality.[3] It
is creative and dynamic, organizes our interpretation of the
world, serves as a framework for our lives and determines
how we respond to events. Getting a "C" on a music
appreciation test will affect me one way if I see myself as a
potential music teacher and another way if I see myself as
someone who has to get through some "artsy" courses in
order to graduate and get on with my engineering career.

SELF-IDENTITY

How do we synthesize a unified sense of self out of the
varied roles we play? How do we learn to sustain a stable
identity in the face of our ever-changing experiences and
perceptions? How can we ever answer the question "Who
am I?" when we are all so many things? Now I am a writer.
Fifteen minutes ago I was a wife making breakfast; one hour
ago I was a woman praying to God; any minute now I may
be a mother reassuring my daughter, who is pregnant for
the first time. Later today I will be a psychotherapist, and
later still I will be a student in a *shiur*. Each of these roles
utilizes a different aspect of my personality, and sometimes
the speed with which I have to switch aspects is difficult to
handle.

Ideally, a stable sense of identity will emerge gradually
out of our concept of self. For we all theorize, consciously
or subconsciously, about our selves and our roles in life. In

order to form an identity we sometimes have to deal with inconsistent self-observations ("I am an honest person, but I just let the clerk charge me for one bunch of parsley even though there were two in the bag"), and inconsistencies between self-perceptions and others' perceptions of us ("I think I'm an even-tempered person, but my husband just told me I'm moody"). Unlike some psychological approaches, Torah does not require us to get rid of the discomfort caused by inconsistencies by learning to live with them ("Inconsistencies are normal; after all, I'm only human") or by distorting the truth to make it more palatable ("My husband doesn't know what he's talking about"). From a Torah point of view, the proper way to deal with personality inconsistencies is to strive to bring the real ("I'm moody") into line with the ideal ("I would like to be an even-tempered person"). We can be aware of inconsistencies without a loss of self-esteem if we take a process orientation and focus on our progress and effort as we work toward our goal. (See Chapter 6 for a fuller explanation of these principles.)

Identity formation can be a painful and difficult process because while we're doing it we don't quite know who we are. This uncertainty throws us off balance. However, it is well worth the effort to have a stable and accurate sense of self.

To help us understand the process of identity formation we will use the developmental model of psychiatrist Erik Erikson[4] which is a useful model of identity formation through the social level. While limited in its range, it is not inconsistent with Torah thought. Erikson proposes a fixed series of developmental stages. At each stage we face a different developmental task, and each task precipitates a different *psychosocial crisis* in us. For example, in the infancy stage, the main developmental task is *basic trust* versus *mistrust*; in the early childhood stage, the task is *autonomy* versus *shame* and *doubt*.

Each stage of development rests on the foundation laid by the preceding stages. The developing personality reveals the strengths and weaknesses of all the previous crisis resolutions, but the final identity is more than the sum of all the previous resolutions. For example, if we fail to develop basic trust in infancy, all the succeeding stages will be affected by the feeling of mistrust that we bring to every situation. Lest this sound like we are doomed by our early experiences, we need to know that there is always the possibility that we will be able to resolve the "psychosocial crisis" of an earlier stage in a more positive way at a later time.

It is in adolescence, with a surge in the capacity for introspection, that we reach the task of creating an identity. The crisis we face at this stage is identity versus role confusion. If we have been able to resolve past crises in constructive ways, we are now ready for the major task of synthesizing our many selves into one harmonious self. We will still play many roles with many different requirements, but we will develop a unifying self which integrates and organizes all the roles.

We will develop a central core of selfhood which will allow us to behave consistently and with integrity in a wide range of situations. If we succeed, we will have an "I" directing traffic who has the same standards and values in all situations. This "I" has to be firm enough to maintain standards in the face of temptations that would violate the sense of self, but flexible enough to know that different behaviors are appropriate in different situations. For example, as parents, we have to be patient with our children and allow them to get messy as they struggle to learn to feed themselves, but we have to be firm and unyielding when it comes to getting antibiotics down the throat of a struggling, sick child.

For various reasons, we are sometimes unable to form a flexible unifying identity. Obstacles may come from society, and they may also come from our families or our own personalities.

Erikson focused on how a society affects identity formation. He believed that people need commanding ideals and ideas by which to live in order to build an identity. In societies that are heterogeneous, disorganized and changing, children do not get the consistent values and support needed for the development of a viable identity. In such societies, many people grow up without a clear sense of identity. We see this in America today where young people struggle well past their mid-twenties with what used to be called adolescent issues.

When society was stable, getting our identity from society did not create the kind of identity crises it creates today. But from a Torah point of view, getting our identity from secular society is in itself a fundamental problem. The values of secular society are relative and time-bound. They change according to fad and fashion. They may reflect real values, but only because they seem right at the time, not because they are absolute. Many of the "truths" that were held to be self-evident by our founding fathers are no longer held to be true.

Whether societal values change rapidly or slowly, they do change. And when they change, those of us who get our identity from dominant social values lose part of our identity. This is, of course, a major problem in American society today. American society changes constantly, leaving us without a firm base for our identity. We constantly have to create new relative truths to match society's new values. For example, five or six decades ago the societal value was that family and home were of primary importance. Men were the breadwinners, and women were the homemakers. Therefore, we believed that married women *should* stay home to take care of their children.

A few decades ago there was a shift in societal values. Anatomy *should not* be destiny. Women *should* have the same options as men. Marriage, family and homemaking are options, but they are not nearly as fulfilling as having a career. So we had to create new "truths": children need to be taken care of, but not necessarily by their mothers. Any good day care will do. It's quality time that counts, not quantity time. Recently, values have shifted again. Women *should* have the same options as men, but for those women who experience "baby hunger" there *should* be a corporate "baby track." Good day care is hard to find, and so family and home *should* be a respected option for men and women. Once again, we have had to create new "truths" to fit these values. Some women need to be mothers. It is not necessarily pathological for men and women to choose to be a homemaker.

How can we develop a steadying sense of self-sameness in such a fluctuating society? How can we know what is true? We may make major life decisions based on one set of values and truths, only to find ourselves out of sync with the next set of values and truths. Or we may find that our biological clocks have wound down and left us truly choiceless.

Absolute truth is eternal. Therefore, an identity based on absolute truth is stable and sustaining. An upbringing based on absolute truth would *ideally* preclude the problems discussed above.

The Torah community is the perfect setting for the development of a strong identity. Torah endows us with an ethical and behavioral framework for our climb up the developmental ladders. It keeps us from swinging too far in any direction as we struggle with the psycho/social/spiritual issues at each stage. Torah gives us an overarching identity—Jew—which unifies all the crises. It gives us consistent standards, values and goals against which to measure ourselves as we strive for self-definition. Optimally, the Torah home provides a nurturant, stable, supportive environment, giving us the security we need to face the challenges of growth. And the Torah educational system uses the home, the school and the synagogue to teach and reinforce the message of Torah.

However, we live in a real, not an ideal, world, and even in Torah communities, identity problems can develop. There are general identity problems and problems that are specific to Torah life. General identity problems can emerge out of overly rigid or inappropriate demands ("No matter that you are learning disabled, you *will* be a scholar"). In such cases the child may form a negative, rebellious identity ("I will *not* be what you want me to be"). If conflicting demands are imposed ("Entertain me with your pranks, but be a good boy"), the child may suffer identity confusion ("I don't know whether I'm a good boy or a mischievous boy"). If there are not enough demands made ("I won't impose many limits on you so you will be happy"), the child may have difficulty establishing a firm sense of identity.

There is one kind of identity problem that is specific to Jews. In Jewish communities where Judaism is just a loose framework for living what is basically a secular life according to secular values, it is very difficult to internalize the identity of a Torah Jew. The individual *may* develop a stable identity, but it is a secular identity, rather than a Torah identity. With a secular identity, it is very difficult to take on the yoke of Torah ("In general, I can see the benefits of Torah life, but some of the *mitzvos* just don't fit into modern life"). Such people straddle the fence between Torah life and secular life and miss the benefits of full participation. In a sense, Judaism is like marriage.

In marriage, there are borders and fences to protect and strengthen the relationship. But a marriage that is all borders and fences, without love and pleasure, is a joyless marriage. Many such marriages end in divorce. A joyful marriage combines restrictions with positive feeling and actions into a harmonious whole. The same is true for Judaism. Picking and choosing *mitzvos*, or having only fences and borders without love of God and Torah, leads to a joyless, unsatisfying Judaism. As the Psalmist said, "The laws of God are truth. They are right in unison." (*Psalms*, 19:10) As Erikson points out, "identity formation goes beyond *identifying oneself with* . . . It is a process of *letting oneself be identified* as a circumscribed individual in a relation to a predictable universe."[5] If we are afraid to act and look "too Jewish" we may never experience the fulfillment of Jewish life.

DIFFERENT LEVELS OF IDENTITY

We are all aware of different parts of ourselves. We say, "One part of me knows that I ought to go to class tonight, but another part of me wants to stay home and go to bed early." To which part do we attach the word "I"?

Rabbi Dessler[6] teaches us that this is a very crucial question. He shows us that there are three different levels of self. Thoughts which arise from our desires (elemental level) tend to present themselves in the first person: "*I* want ..." Thoughts which contain spiritual stirrings (social level) present themselves in the second person: "*You* ought to ..." Thoughts which represent pure spirituality (religious level) tend to present themselves in the third person: "He wants me to. . ." Thoughts from this higher source are not perceived as present in our consciousness; they seem to come from outside ourselves.

Rabbi Dessler explains that before we have elevated ourselves we identify with the "I" of the elemental soul. We perceive the voices of the higher levels as alien forces which make unpleasant demands on us. Of course, just the opposite is true. The "I" of the elemental soul is unrelenting in its demands, and its demands are unreasonable. It demands that *I* be the best, that *I* have the most, that *my* needs be gratified immediately. When we succeed in elevating ourselves to the religious level, our reference for "I" changes. What used to be perceived as "he" becomes "I." In other words, we begin to identify with our religious soul. The promptings of the elemental "I" are still experienced, but they become much less central. We experience them in a more detached way. We feel them, but we don't allow them to determine our thoughts and actions.

If we want to advance spiritually, we must learn to internalize and identify with the voice of our divine soul. And each of us must "treat the demands coming from his higher self with mercy and compassion." Only then will we realize that the forces which we thought were alien were *in reality our own true needs.*

In the next three chapters we will see how the themes of the social soul—self-awareness and self-identity—produce the needs for success, love and meaning.

SUMMARY

1. The essence of the social soul is a sense of movement, a desire for progress. At this level, we search for self-awareness and a stable self-identity.

2. Out of our elemental self-awareness we eventually develop a stable self-identity, a central core of selfhood that allows us to behave consistently in a wide range of situations and to integrate and organize all the roles we play.

3. In order to develop a self-identity we need to live in a stable society that teaches commanding ideals and values.

4. The Torah ideal is to get our identity from eternal, absolute truth, independent of the influence of fluctuating, relative social values.

CHAPTER 11

How to be a Real Success

Jonah the Prophet boarded a ship in flight from the Almighty. In time, the attention of the sailors was drawn to him, and they asked him a flock of questions about his origin, his occupation and his nationality. His automatic response was not, as some of us might have answered, "a Brooklyn lawyer," "a Long Island doctor," "a midtown manufacturer of cloaks and suits," it was rather, "I am a Hebrew, and the Lord, the God of Heaven, do I fear." Torah, the voice of Divinity speaking to man, is the concern, the career and occupation of the knowing, authentic Jew.[1]

H ere we are on the second rung of the life force ladder. At this level, the life force is activated by the social soul. The

237

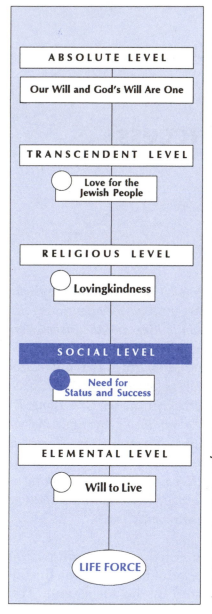

social soul introduces the power of awareness and the need for identity and progress into our lives. It adds a more spiritual quality to our elemental will to live. It is no longer enough *just* to be alive and secure. We now feel that we have to have our identity confirmed by being successful in the game of life. Questions like "How do I compare with others?", "Am I a success?" and "What is my status?" become vitally important.

STATUS AND SUCCESS

The needs for status and success are an impetus to growth. If we were content just to survive, we would not be willing to invest time and energy in elevating ourselves. However, these needs can be extremely dangerous. They can become an obstacle to growth if they become central to our definition of who we are. Take, for example, the person who tries to fulfill his need for identity only by his profession. There is the story of the proud surgeon who acts with the same crisp life-and-death authority at home as he does in the operating room. He relates to everyone, even his wife and children, as a surgeon to his staff, because that is the only role he can tolerate. His limited identity does not permit intimacy and closeness, and his definition of success does not include being a good parent and husband.

Such a person can only partially fulfill his need for identity because his entire sense of self comes from only two rungs of the social level, on the life force ladder—the need for success and on the ladder of the intellect—the quest for meaning. He is lacking the emotional ladder. He gets some meaning from his work, but he neglects love and leaves out the religious level entirely. This kind of person almost inevitably faces an identity crisis at some point in his life. He may "burn out" on work, feel overwhelmed and threatened by younger competition with more up-to-date training or feel despairing loneliness.

If any or all of these things happen, he has to confront the emptiness of his existence and try to forge a new identity. He may regress and settle for a life of more primitive pleasures (divorce, travel, golf), or he may elevate himself by adding relationships and religion to his life.

According to psychiatrist Erik Erikson,[2] vocation *is* one important aspect of identity. It becomes a problem when it is identity's *only* foundation. As Addison Steele says:

> It comes down to this: The more a person invests his ego in his professional identity, the more vulnerable he becomes to the vicissitudes of corporate [hospital, university, etc.] life. People who would never in a million years willingly give

anyone else power over where they live or what they eat give others power over the most important single thing in their life—their identity.[3]

As suggested above, people who base their identity solely on their professional or vocational success are actually very vulnerable. Since they do not have an inner sense of identity, their well-being is in the hands of an impersonal power structure. There is always the chance that someone even more driven than themselves will come along and usurp their position. They have all their ego eggs in one basket, the basket of worldly achievement, status, success, recognition and material acquisitions. They must fight very hard to protect that basket in a very competitive, ruthless world. Think what a strain it must be to try to succeed in a society where

> the word "combat" as an image nicely combines the concern for achievement and power characteristic of American businessmen.[4]

Now let's take a closer look at the needs for status and success which can cause so much trouble. In extreme cases, these needs can become so strong that they may actually supersede the will to live. We have all heard the stories of men who ended their lives during the Depression when they heard that they had lost their fortunes in the stock market crash. For these men, the loss of their money meant the loss of their identity and self-esteem. For them, the answer to the question "Who am I?" was so bound up with their financial success that "I" no longer existed when their money was gone. The survival of the body was an unbearable burden:

"It" remained when "I" (the "I" of social status) was already dead. The only thing to do was to get rid of "it" by throwing it out of a twentieth-story window.

The needs activated by the social level of the soul can be very powerful, so powerful that they can override the elemental will to live. How can it be that a spiritual need can take precedence over something as basic as the need to live? Psychologist Abraham Maslow[5] explained this by saying that when our basic needs (the physiological needs and the safety needs) are satisfied, other higher needs emerge and demand satisfaction. These higher needs now take center stage in the psyche and become so important that life is not worth living unless we can fill them. He referred to this as a hierarchy of needs which he believed was "to be found in the very essence of human nature itself." (p.xiii)

I find these psychological ideas of an inner need for self-improvement very consistent with Torah ideas, although as I will explain later, they represent only a pale shadow of the complete Torah perspective.

In this chapter we are talking about what Maslow called the esteem needs. He believed that all people have a need or desire for self-esteem, self-respect, esteem and respect from others, achievement, mastery and competence, prestige, status and recognition. According to Maslow, when these needs are filled, we feel self-confident, capable, adequate, useful and necessary in the world. When these needs are unfulfilled, we feel inferior, weak and helpless.

According to psychologist Alfred Adler[6], feelings of inferiority are the major motivations to growth in the human personality. Adler theorized that all human striving is organized around overcoming feelings of inferiority. In Adler's theory, children inevitably feel inferior because they *are* inferior; they *are* small, weak, helpless, incompetent and dependent. Adler believed that the child's objective inferiority produced the need for a feeling of superiority as a compensation.

> We all strive to reach a goal by the attainment of which we shall feel strong, superior and complete. We shall always find in human beings this great line of activity—this struggle to rise from an inferior to a superior position, from defeat to victory, from below to above. It begins in earliest childhood and continues to the end of our lives. [7]

Adler did not see this striving for superiority as a negative need to dominate or control others. He saw it more as a positive, innate striving to overcome one's own inferiority and achieve self-actualization.

The Torah gives us a different slant on children's inferiority. Torah teaches us that the helplessness and immaturity of children is crucial to their *spiritual* development. From their position of inferiority and dependence, children develop intense feelings of fear and love for their seemingly all-powerful and all-knowing parents. However, as children mature and become more aware of themselves and the people around them, they begin to realize that their parents don't know everything and can't do everything. How disappointing it is to find out that our parents have human frailties! Some of us are so devastated that we never forgive our parents for being human.

Why did God set up a system that was bound to produce frustration and disappointment for parents and children alike? The answer lies in the basic principle that all human capacities are tools for spiritual development. The early formative experience of relating to parents with fear and love gives us an internal reference point for the proper attitude of awe and love for God. From their position of inferiority and dependence, children are learning the correct attitude toward the Almighty.

The path from dependency on parents to an attitude of dependence on the Almighty is not a direct one. First a child must pass through a stage of adolescence, when peer groups partially replace parents in importance. As a result, many teenagers go through a rebellion against their parents and a passionate conformity to the norms of their peers; the "in" clothes, the right slang and the current fad in music. The eventual outgrowth of this is a healthy relationship to family, society and God.

However, in today's world, with shaky family structure and a society with no well-defined values, many people grow up without a core sense of self. Lacking a firm sense of self, they end up with insecurity, low self-esteem, frustration and despair. They cannot build a personality from the transferral process, because the first two building blocks, family and society, are missing or damaged. They, therefore, have to start the personality-building process at the final stage, seeking closeness to God.

We grow spiritually not by becoming superior, but by gradually transferring our feelings of intense fear and love from our parents to the One who is truly all-powerful and all-knowing. We actualize ourselves not by overcoming our inferiority in relation to society but by finding the absolute model and taking pride in trying to imitate Him. We overcome our inferiority by trying to be like God. If we make this our goal, we don't have to strive to turn the tables on our parents. We can appreciate all they did for us, forgive them for not being perfect and continue to love and honor them, even though they are human.

As we have seen many times, Torah shines a clarifying light on life's perplexities. All the psychologists quoted in this chapter sensed that there was more to life than superiority, status and success, but they couldn't quite see beyond the ceiling imposed by a secular viewpoint. Erikson, with his notion of developmental stages, each having its own developmental task (for example, in adolescence, identity vs. role confusion), realized that in order for people to reach their highest potential, their development had to include stages that transcend the self. But his theory maintained that at the final, mature stage the task was one of integrity vs. disgust. Beyond that, he could really conceive of no further development.

Adler believed that people could not be understood as individuals isolated from their social context. He maintained that the rules of communal life were an "absolute truth"[8] which made demands and placed limits on man. He further believed that all mental and emotional problems had a common cause—failure to abide by the "absolute truth" of social necessity. Does that mean that someone who failed to abide by the "absolute truth" of Nazi society had emotional problems?

In his day, Adler was psychologically right about the relationship between personality and society, but he was morally wrong about the "absolute truth" of societal rules because the values of society can be wrong. Today, with society in such a state of flux, the whole process to which Adler referred has been destroyed. Values change so rapidly and dramatically that people lose trust in the process of value formation. They simply make up their own values and "truths." In today's society, Adler is both morally and practically wrong.

Maslow, with his theory of hierarchical needs, acknowledged that it is necessary for man to go on to his higher needs in order to avoid illness and psychopathology, but he denied that there were elevated experiences that are supernatural and go beyond the jurisdiction of science.[9] All three men had, at best, a shadow of the glory that awaits those who advance above the social level.

Let's look at someone who is living at the social level of the life force ladder.

PERSONIFICATION OF A "LIFE FORCE SOCIAL"

A person living a Torah life is not likely to be completely stuck at the social level of the life force ladder, but "life force socials" may well become *baalei teshuvah* and then be in conflict about their status needs. It is also possible for people raised within the Torah framework to have unresolved needs for status and success that interfere with their spiritual growth.

Herschel is an example of a young man with unresolved status and success needs. He was always a very precocious little boy. He learned quickly and got a lot of attention from his parents for being able to recite the correct *berachos* (blessings) at an age when many children still have difficulty stringing three words together. Even as a young child he loved to learn and to receive praise for his accomplishments. He couldn't wait to get home from *cheder* (school) to tell his proud parents what he had learned and what grades he had gotten. He wanted to be the best, and if anyone else did nearly as well as he did, he was spurred on to higher achievement.

Herschel shied away from things that he was not particularly good at, because he couldn't stand not being the best. He would rather not participate at all than be in a game where he might not come out on top. Therefore, when the other children were out playing, he would stay inside and study. They could excel on the playground, but he would excel in class the next day. His motivation never flagged because he anticipated the thrill of being the one who knew the answers.

Unfortunately, Herschel's parents' own status needs were being fed by his cleverness, and they were blind to the stunting of his character development. They justified his asocial behavior as "normal for such a bright child" and reinforced his striving to be the best.

Herschel managed to be the top student in his *cheder*, but when he eventually went on to *yeshivah* he came into contact with the best students from many schools. He worked very hard, but he just couldn't be the best anymore. He was dispirited when some of the other boys were more advanced than he was. He was very lonely, because he was contemptuous of those boys who were not as smart as he, and antagonistic toward those who were as smart or smarter than he. He saw people as his adversaries, and he was unable to relate to others on the basis of common human needs and interests.

When Herschel finished *yeshivah*, he went on to college. He developed an interest in computers. He liked working with computers, because he found he could excel easily in this area. He became an expert, and he graduated with top honors. He soon got a good job in the software industry and became a topnotch programmer. His skills were very much in demand, and before long, he had an impressive title and earned lots of money. Herschel had to work very long and hard to keep ahead of the many bright ambitious people in the industry. He had an advantage in that he was single and didn't have to take anyone else's needs into account. He spent less and less time on Torah study and *davening*, and more and more time on work. He grew more and more unbalanced, but his status at work had become all important to him. His entire identity was based on being successful. Business was the one area where he had a clear edge. He believed that if he poured all his life energy into it, he could get to the top and stay there. And that is the only place he wanted to be.

If Herschel doesn't break out of this pattern and broaden his sources of identity, he is running a high risk of suffering irreversible emotional and spiritual crippling. Inevitably, the day will come when there will be another computer "star" on the horizon, and he will then face a major life crisis. He will be fortunate if that day comes when he is still young enough to reevaluate his life and make significant changes. There is hope for Herschel if he can realize that his self-worth is not dependent on being "the best," that he has intrinsic worth by virtue of being created in the image of God.

CORRECT USE OF STATUS AND SUCCESS

How can we avoid getting stuck at the social level of the life force ladder? Where do the needs for status and success fit in Torah life? All our needs and feelings are God-given and thus, by definition, all are essentially good. Our task is to learn to use them for elevation, to have them spur us on to higher spiritual levels. Let's take these needs and see how they fit into a Torah framework.

We are endowed with the needs for status and success so that we will be motivated to move toward perfection. These needs help us reach the ultimate goal for which we were created—which is to make active choices to draw closer to God. Without the esteem needs, we would be content to be mediocre, to take the easy way out. Living a Torah life, a life of evaluating ourselves against the standard of the Absolute, is not the easy way out. It is a life of constant challenge, constant striving. In Torah life there is no title we can achieve that confers upon us the right to stop striving, to feel that we have "arrived." In fact, we learn that the higher we elevate ourselves, the more we are tested ("According to the camel, so the load").

There is no place in Torah life for fulfilling identity, status and success needs through reliance on professional or vocational success. Instead of eliciting our identity through our vocation, we use our vocation to express our identity. As doctors, lawyers, accountants, teachers, etc., we have an opportunity to put our Torah values into practice. "It is not the position that honors the man, but man who gives honor to the position." (*Taanis*, 21b)

In fact, the concept of "career" is foreign to Torah. A man is expected to earn a *parnassah* (a livelihood) in order to be able to live a Torah life. The late Irving Bunim wrote in his commentary on *Pirke Avot:* [10]

> If you would live in the faith of a Jew, the Torah cannot
> be a secondary, extracurricular, spare-time hobby; it is to

be your first and foremost vocation, your primary concern and interest, your veritable life-work. If you would live with a Jewish sense of values, occupy yourself less with business and more with Torah. Let this rule determine your life-style; let this rule guide you in allocating your time, your energy and your money.

Although work is secondary to Torah learning, great value is placed on productive labor. Torah teaches us that we must use every possible means to support ourselves. We should not consider any honest work beneath us: "Skin a dead animal in the street to earn your bread, but do not say, 'I am a priest, a great man, it is not fitting for me.'" (*Pesachim* 113a)

Here are four ways in which work can be integrated into our spiritual lives:

KIDDUSH HASHEM

If we are honest, conscientious, responsible and diligent workers, we bring honor to God. If we conduct ourselves according to these Torah principles, we reflect well on God. We show that His Torah is very special and that God expects a high level of ethics from us. We show that by training seriously according to Torah principles, we refine and elevate ourselves.

CHESSED (LOVINGKINDNESS)

Rabbi Dessler[11] explains the story in the *Midrash* of Hanoch the cobbler, who "achieved mystical unions with his Creator with every single stitch that he made." (*Midrash*

Talpios) This *Midrash* does not mean that Hanoch's mind was on mystical subjects while he stitched shoes. The "mystical unions" were

> nothing more nor less than the concentration which he lavished on each and every stitch to ensure that it would be good and strong and that the pair of shoes he was making would be a good pair, *giving maximum pleasure and benefit to whoever would wear them.* In this way Hanoch achieved union with the attribute of his Creator, who lavishes his goodness and beneficience on others.

RESPONSIBILITY

In *Bereishis* 31:36-42, when Lavan catches up with Jacob after seven days of pursuit, Jacob says, "What is my crime, what is my sin that you have hotly pursued after me?" Jacob points out to Lavan that in the twenty years he served him he did not demand all that was coming to him. He took on extra responsibilities. He was "consumed by heat by day and by frost at night." He got very little sleep. And his wages were changed ten times. Rabbi Samson Raphael Hirsch[12] says that in the merit of his exemplary work, Jacob's life was spared. "Deeds, active work is worth more than the merit of one's forefathers . . ."

TZEDDAKAH (CHARITY)

The more money we earn, the more we must help others.

So we see that in Torah life, man does not live to work, to surround himself with possessions or to establish a position of status. He makes a living to support himself and his family and to do good deeds, and he uses work as an opportunity for spiritual growth. Therefore, the needs created at the social level of the life force present us with a great test. As we strive to fill our needs for status and success, we must not forget that

> everything comes to man from the hands of Heaven—strength, wealth, health, cleverness, beauty and all the other good things man enjoys. You have been diligent, you have worked hard, and you have succeeded in acquiring wealth and knowledge. Quite so; for without hard work and diligence and toil we get nothing. But will you be proud on this account? Who is it then who had to give you strength and opportunity and blessing in order that you might acquire wealth and knowledge? Is it not God?[13]

In order to progress to the religious level of the life force ladder, we have to use the needs for status and success as a springboard to God-identity, not as a stopping place for self-identity. We have to maximize our God-given skills and talents and use them *not* for self-glorification but to fulfill our needs for spiritual elevation.

SUMMARY

SUCCESS AND STATUS

At this level the social soul adds a spiritual quality to our lives. It is no longer enough just to be alive and secure. We are now concerned with success and status.

1. The needs for success and status are God-given and are

therefore essentially good. They can be used for elevation or they can become an obstacle to growth.

2. Our success and status needs can motivate us to move toward perfection or they can become so central to our identity that we get stuck at the social level.

The Senses and Emotions: True and False Love

Genuine love is an active striving for the growth and happiness of the loved person, rooted in one's own capacity to love.[1]

We have now arrived at the second rung of the ladder of the emotions and senses.

The yearning of the soul has prompted us to raise ourselves from the elemental level to the social level of the senses and emotions. Remember that the essence of the social soul is a desire to make progress, and that the two main themes of the social level are self-awareness and self-identity. At the social level, one of the major sources of our identity is how we express our sensory/emotional needs; where, how and

253

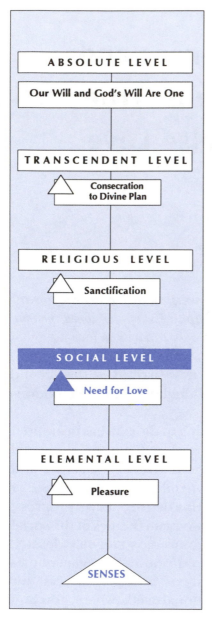

ABSOLUTE LEVEL

Our Will and God's Will Are One

TRANSCENDENT LEVEL

Consecration
to Divine Plan

RELIGIOUS LEVEL

Sanctification

SOCIAL LEVEL

Need for Love

ELEMENTAL LEVEL

Pleasure

SENSES

with whom we find sensory pleasure.

At this level, we feel a spiritual stirring, and our primitive demand for immediate gratification of our sensory needs is transformed into a desire to satisfy our selves in a framework that establishes and confirms our identity. Our search for pleasure becomes a search for love. Our relationships are central to our identity: we are strongly identified by whom we love and by who loves us. Therefore, the main theme of the social level of the sensory/emotional ladder is love.

OUR SOCIAL SENSES

What happens to our senses and emotions when they are activated by the social soul? Are we still sensual? Do we still want pleasure? The answer is emphatically yes! We still need and desire sensory stimulation and we still desire pleasure. In other words, we still have the sensory needs and desires activated by the elemental soul. And we still have our general need for connection. But both our sensory/emotional and general needs are transformed by being elevated to the social level. They can no longer be satisfied in primitive ways.

What are these transformed needs like? For one thing, they are much more discriminating. We cannot be satisfied just by turning up the volume or keeping ourselves constantly busy. Something inside of us demands meaning and refinement, not just sensory bombardment. We want pleasure, but gulping down "fast foods" does not please us. Now we want good food served in nice and pleasant surroundings. We still long for connection, but stimulation-based relationships aren't enough. They leave us feeling empty and unconnected. Life is not worth living if we are lacking love and a sense of belonging to something that transcends the boundaries of our personal selves. This is the first step in self-transcendence.

THE NEED FOR LOVE

What is this thing called love? Is it a "a wondrous state, deep, tender, and rewarding"?[2] Is it "a feeling of tenderness and affection with great enjoyment, happiness, and satisfaction"?[3] Is it the "passionate torment that leads to madness, melancholy and disease"?[4] Is it nothing more than a projection of competitiveness with a parent,[5] a sublimated passion?[6] Is it the outcome of a behavioral system which leads to "attachments" and "affectional bonds" because these states yield a survival advantage?[7]

The above elemental and social level definitions of love are all narrow, and they lead to distortions of our sublime, God-given ability to love, an ability crucial to self-transcendence. In the Torah system, love is a feeling, but it is also a way of acting and a means to spiritual elevation—from love of self to love of others and, ultimately, to love of God.

If love is trivialized and seen as nothing more than a feeling (elemental level), it can give great pleasure or agonizing torment; on the other hand if it is aggrandized and made an end in itself (social level), it is accepted as a substitute for spirituality. It then becomes an obstacle to spiritual growth by clouding the real longing for progress and closeness to God.

Erich Fromm is an example of someone whose thinking led to an inflated view of human love. In his influential book *The Art of Loving*, Erich Fromm said:[8]

> Man's awareness of his aloneness and separateness, of his helplessness . . . all this makes his separate, disunited existence an unbearable prison. He would become insane could he not liberate himself from this prison and reach out, unite himself in some form or other with men, with the world outside.

So far so good. But Fromm added, "Without love, humanity could not exist for a day . . . I shall call love the *mature answer to the problem of existence.*" (p.18, emphasis added) Fromm saw love through the eyes of a humanist. He defined humanism as a

> global philosophy which emphasizes the oneness of the human race, the capacity of man to develop *his own powers*

and to arrive at inner harmony and the establishment of a peaceful world." (emphasis added)

Fromm further stated that in the development of the Old Testament and post-biblical Jewish tradition, "Man, the obedient servant, becomes the free man, who makes his own history, free from God's interference" (p. 177) and thus becomes a "being who is alone in this world, but who can feel at home in it if he achieves union with his fellow man and with nature." (p. 178)

Fromm believed that we have no savior but ourselves. Being alone and omnipotent in this world, we have nothing to uplift us and comfort us but our love for each other. Fromm copied the Jewish concept of love as a potentially ennobling feeling, but he placed its roots in our human nature, rather than in our Divine souls. He made all of us gods, complete in and of ourselves, *if only we can love each other*. He took noble spiritual yearning and froze it at the social level.

What happens when our love is stuck at the social level, when our highest aspiration is human love? Our understanding of love is perverted and our growth is stunted. We turn human love (be it romantic love, companionate love, conjugal love, parental love or genuine love, to name just a few categories studied by psychologists) into an ultimate value. It becomes the primary source of our identity, which gives it its awesome power to catapult us from the heights of ecstasy to the depths of despair. We lose ourselves if we lose love.

If our powerful feelings of love are cut off from their divine roots and idealized in their own right, the consequences are disastrous. When we are in love with love, we not only keep making the same painful and humiliating mistakes, but we never learn how to really love and how to make love last.

In the secular view, we "fall" in love when we meet the "right" person. "Rightness" has nothing to do with the character traits or background of the beloved. It is a "chemical" response, not a rational one. The intense, irrational passion called love in the secular world is a consuming flame; the lover burns with desire and is obsessed with fantasies of the unique irresistibility of the beloved. When they are together, the emphasis is on excitement and romance, not on spiritual growth. And eventually, the flame of passion, which was fueled by fantasy, is snuffed out by reality—she is too demanding, he is always late—and the flame flickers and dies. They "fall" out of love, only to repeat the chemical sequence over and over.

From our discussion of the soul's yearning for God in Chapter 6, we can recognize this relentless searching for the perfect lover and the obsessive preoccupation with the beloved as a distortion of the yearning of the soul for connection with God. Here at the social level, however, the yearning of the soul is experienced primarily as a longing for confirmation of identity: I am someone if someone loves me and needs my love, I am no one if no one loves me.

Those who idealize love "question everything but the quest itself . . . when love decays, the quest for love continues . . . "[9] Actually, it is not the quest itself that is the problem, but the object of the quest: idealized love. The powerful bond of enduring love that can develop between people *is* worth seeking.

How do we foster the kind of love that results in devotion and harmony between people? By doing just the opposite of what is done in the secular world. The divorce rate is about fifty percent. What happens when a couple seeks counseling for their marital problems? The counselor observes their interaction and says, "You have a communication problem." The next couple is told, "You have an intimacy problem." The next couple is told, "You have a compatibility problem." It may be true that the first couple has a communication problem, the second couple has an intimacy problem, the third couple has a compatibility problem, etc. But why do fifty percent of marriages have problems serious enough to cause divorce?

To get some perspective on the situation, let's look at a different kind of problem. Let's suppose an airplane crashes (we'll call it a Jet 550). An investigation will be conducted to determine the cause of the crash. Suppose another Jet 550 crashes soon after. There will be another investigation to determine the cause of this crash. Now suppose that, over the next few weeks, four or five more Jet 550's crash. At this point, the aeronautics board will realize that there is probably something wrong with the design of the Jet 550. All flights scheduled for Jet 550's will be canceled, and production of new aircraft will be postponed until the design is thoroughly evaluated.

The investigation reveals a major design flaw which puts too much pressure on the aircraft in flight. Therefore, individual investigations would show a different problem for each crash because each Jet 550 would crack *at its weakest point*. If the inquiry had been limited to investigation of each individual crash, the underlying problem would never have been discovered.

In order to understand the problem with modern marriage, we have to take the approach of the aeronautics board. We have to assume that with a fifty percent crash rate there is something wrong with the design. Each marriage is failing at its weakest point, because too much pressure is put on the relationship. When we analyze each couple independent of their social context, we miss the underlying problem.

What is the design flaw in the secular approach to love? In order to understand the problem, we have to go back to our parable of the horse and the rider. Remember that we all have two parts, body and soul, horse and rider. And remember too, that the "horsy" part (physical pleasure) declines, while the rider part (spiritual pleasure) increases.

We get our identity from both parts and we want to be loved for both parts. In the context of love, we will talk about man/woman (horse) and person (rider). Imagine how a woman would feel if her husband said to her , "I love your mind. You're very smart, and you have great ideas, but if you don't mind, just don't touch me." Or how a man would feel if his wife said to him, "You're very strong and handsome, but please, would you just be quiet?" No one would want this kind of love. We want our love to combine both parts.

FLAWS IN THE SECULAR APPROACH TO LOVE

SEPARATING HORSE AND RIDER

The first problem we can identify in the secular approach to love is that it separates horse and rider. As we said earlier, in the secular world, love is often a chemical, not a rational response. People sometimes fall in love and get married on the basis of physical attraction alone. They then tend to fall out of love when the attraction fades or when they find out they don't really like each other's rider.

ACCEPTING THE PERSON (RIDER)

The secular approach is to accept the person part: "Love me for who I am, don't try to change me." Being accepted as a person is very nice if all we want to do is give each other good feelings. But since our whole destiny in life is to make progress, if we really love each other we will encourage each other to grow, not stay the same. If we accept the person part of each other, we are actually negatively reinforcing spiritual growth. This is a serious mistake, because spiritual pleasure is a very tender shoot that has to be cultivated. If accepted as it is, it will not thrive. By giving the rider unconditional love we rob ourselves of spiritual pleasure in marriage. Love, as designed by the secular world, actually damages our potential for spiritual growth.

PREFERRING THE MAN/WOMAN (HORSE)

The secular approach is to prefer the man/woman part: "I am attracted to you now and so I prefer you to all others. We will stay together as long as we are still attracted to each other." Preference based on attraction is very vulnerable because:

1. We are in competition with all other "horses." We are constantly stimulated by an endless supply of young ones proudly strutting their stuff. We see them all over in the street, we work with them, and they peer out at us from every billboard, newspaper and magazine. Therefore we

desperately try exercise, cosmetics, face lifts, nose jobs, hair transplants and liposuction to keep us in the competition.

2. We adapt to physical stimulation, so the same stimulus gives less pleasure over time. Physical excitement inevitably fades, and when we compare our present level of arousal with our memory of the past we conclude that we must have fallen out of love. All because the thrill is gone!

3. Our horses inevitably decline with age. Even our top physical specimens, the star athletes, are "over the hill" before the age of forty.

These three factors lead to frustration and dissatisfaction in relationships based primarily on physical attraction and pleasure.

THE TORAH APPROACH TO LOVE

COMBINING HORSE AND RIDER

The Torah approach combines horse and rider. Attraction and preference are important, but the decision to join with someone for the journey through life is a rational one. "Is this the kind of person I can grow to love and make progress with?" Body and soul are united; the physical part of the love is used as fuel for spiritual growth.

GIVING PREFERENCE TO THE PERSON (RIDER)

In the Torah approach we choose a person we prefer, but we expect the person to make spiritual progress. *Loving someone as a person does not mean to accept them as a person.* In Jewish marriage, we don't accept each other just as we are.

It's not that we point a finger at each other and say, "I expect you to change." Torah tells us that man and wife are one flesh. We are a unit. We have a mutual goal, and we unite to help each other achieve that goal. As we ascend spiritually, we encourage and support each other, each being strong when the other is weak, wise where the other is ignorant, inspiring when the other is discouraged. Ideally, the Jewish marriage is a greenhouse for spiritual elevation.

ACCEPTING THE MAN/WOMAN (HORSE)

The Torah approach is to accept the declining man/woman part: "I love you and will always be very faithful to you." Our love does not depend on physical youthfulness, strength and beauty. It depends on strength and beauty of character.

CONTRASTING THE TWO APPROACHES

In relation to love, we have two parts, horse (man/woman) and rider (person), and two needs, to be accepted and to make progress. The horse is always declining while the rider has unlimited potential for growth.

THE SECULAR APPROACH TO LOVE

The powers of the horse and rider are separated, and they often pull us in opposite directions.

Pressure is put on the wrong part. Progress is demanded from the declining power of the horse.

The rider is reinforced to stay at the status quo, thus

wasting its unlimited potential for spiritual growth.

The secular design for love works in opposition to our God-given powers. What chance do we have for love to last?

THE TORAH APPROACH TO LOVE

The powers of horse and rider are combined.

The declining power of the physical part is accepted.

The increasing power of the spiritual part is encouraged.

The Torah design for love is matched perfectly to our powers. By uniting horse and rider, *accepting* that which declines (the horse), *supporting progress* in that which can grow (the rider), Jewish love is enhanced. It deepens and ripens with age. (In the next chapter, we will discuss the third factor, sanctification, or how to combine the horse and the rider.)

We see the Torah ideal in the story of Isaac and Rebecca. Rebecca was selected as a suitable wife for Isaac on the basis of her family background and her *midos*(character traits). After they were married, "Isaac . . . took Rebecca and she became his wife, and he loved her." (*(Bereishis*24:67) Notice the sequence of events. He did not fall in love with her and then marry her. He married her and then loved her. Shraga Silverstein[10] quotes Malbim on this verse as saying:

> Their love was like the growth of a tree, which begins from a small seed that the water makes cling to the soil, which grows and expands, more and more, from day to day. So was their love. In the beginning, it was only the seed of love that was planted in the furrows of their hearts; and it was through beauty of deed that this seed grew more and

more, from day to day, so that love was at its fullest only *after* marriage . . .

It is very difficult to nurture the seed of love and make it sprout and flourish through the vicissitudes of life. Every day, we all face really difficult questions about how to behave in relation to those we love. For example, the fact that I love a child tells me little or nothing about what to do when he pinches his little sister. After all, I love her too. The fact that a woman loves her husband tells her little or nothing about what to do when he sits and reads the paper while she rushes around trying to get ready for *Shabbos*. And the fact that a man loves his friend tells him little or nothing about what to do when the friend gets so distracted that he forgets their important lunch appointment.

In order to deal correctly with these and the hundreds of others more and less serious problems that arise in life, we have to learn Torah so we can know what Torah principles to apply in these situations. Love alone does not supply the answers.

Within a Torah framework, however, the ability to love and be loved are kept in perspective. Both are considered to be crucially important milestones in human development, but they are not deemed to be the ultimate stage of human development. They are but the second rung of development on the sensory/emotional ladder. And as we know, in the Torah system, there are three ladders, each having five rungs or levels of growth.

Every step in development is important in order to create a balanced, integrated Torah personality. Knowing this helps us put our need for love and belonging in perspective. Love and belonging are crucial elements of a good life; they are steps on the journey to sanctification of life and love of God.

IS SELF-LOVE IMPORTANT?

It's impossible to talk about love without discussing self-love. We often hear that if we don't love ourselves, we can't love others, and that the root of all negative behavior is low self-esteem. Erich Fromm[11] says "my own self must be as much an object of my love as another person." Is this true from a Torah perspective?

The Torah answer is both yes and no. Yes, because there is, of course, an element of truth in the idea that high self-esteem is necessary to mental health and well-being. No, because the importance of self-love is often badly misinterpreted and exaggerated, and when it is, we get shipwrecked at the social level.

YES, SELF-LOVE IS IMPORTANT

Let's expand on the "yes" part of the answer first. Of course self-love is crucial, but only if "I" am both horse and rider, body and soul combined. If I identify just with my "horse," self-love will lead to self-centeredness. If I identify only with my rider and disregard my horse, self-love may lead to abuse and neglect of the body entrusted to me by God. If I think my horse is not important, I will lose the powers of the body which were designed to help me. I can't make progress without these powers.

The proper balance (as we saw in the discussion of love

above) is a combination of acceptance of my horse and encouragement of growth from my rider. In order to really love myself, I have to be grateful to my horse and give him the best care I can. I have to know and accept that he is declining, but I also have to know that all his energy is not going to waste. It is being transferred slowly but surely to my rider. From my rider I have to demand progress. If, for example, I hate myself for being short, chunky and unathletic, I will make myself quite miserable. I have to learn how to be a *happy*, short, chunky, unathletic person. But I should not try to learn to be a *happy*, mean, selfish, cruel person. I should be dissatisfied with those *midos* and work on improving my character. (Of course, this does not imply that I should hate myself for those qualities, just that I should try to change.)

Now we turn to some Torah views on self-love. We are told in *Avos*, 2:18, "And be not wicked in your own estimation." In his comments on this *Mishnah*, Rabbi Shneur Zalman of Lubavitch[12] says that if a man considers himself wicked he will be grieved at heart and depressed and be unable to serve God joyfully. And according to Rambam, the problem is that if you consider yourself defective, no sin will be too big for you. You will tend to behave in accordance with your low self-evaluation and thus create a vicious cycle of negative behavior and plummeting self-regard.

Torah also tells us that we must love another as we love ourselves. (*Vayikra* 19:18) The key to loving others, then, is to love ourselves. But, if we stop here, our understanding of self-love cannot go beyond the social level. We gain real understanding by reading the whole verse, which elevates us to the religious level. Verse 18 ends with, "I am your God." We are being taught that it is impossible to really love ourselves without acknowledging our relationship with God. Torah provides us with the only real basis for belief in the intrinsic worth of ourselves and others the concept that we are *betzelem elokim*, created in the image of God. If we are nothing more than bodies, if we are random mutations of physical matter, we have no intrinsic worth. We have inherent dignity and value only because God breathed the breath of life into us, because we are sparks of the Divine.

When we fail to live up to the greatness inherent in ourselves, we suffer from low self-esteem. Some of us fail because we were not treated with dignity and respect when we were children and hence did not grow up feeling good about ourselves and others. We then tend to treat ourselves and others the way we were treated. Some of us fail because our impulses and desires get the best of us. No matter what the reason, we can improve. We can work on developing the belief that all people, ourselves included, are endowed with value by their Creator.

Once we get started on strengthening the underpinnings of our ability to love ourselves and others, we have to work on the specifics. The next step is to ask ourselves, "What kind of a person do *I* have to be to like myself?" Here again we have to remember that we are horse and rider combined. When it comes to our horses, we have to check out our standards and make sure that they are realistic and achievable. If not, we have to work on bringing them in line with reality. If our horses have weak legs, we probably should give up plans to be professional soccer players. On the other hand, when it comes to our riders, we have to make sure that our standards are consistent with Torah. Torah is our only real guide to proper personality development.

Our primary goal in Torah is to become more like God.

How can we love ourselves when we see how far we are from this goal (or even the secondary goal of being very righteous people)? In order to love ourselves while we strive to elevate ourselves, we have to have a process orientation; we have to learn to set sub-goals and get joy out of effort and progress. We have to be patient with ourselves and appreciate every step along the way. This is one way to achieve our goal of being more like God because we are taught that God gives us credit for our efforts. Let's consider two people who seldom get angry. One was born with an easy-going temperament, and the other was born with a highly arousable temperament. They are now at the same level on the *midah* (characteristic) of anger, but only the highly excitable one got there by struggling to control outbursts of anger. The one who worked hard on self-discipline will get more credit than the one who came to it naturally.

The analysis above sheds light on a problem that psychologists deem one of the biggest obstacles to self-love: perfectionism. But this creates a dilemma for us. We are told that God is perfect and we are supposed to imitate God. So why is perfectionism, or trying to be perfect, a problem? First of all, God's essence is perfection. We humans can point ourselves in the direction of spiritual perfection and continually take steps to improve ourselves, but we have to realize that we will never be perfect the way God is. Secondly, perfection as an end is correct, but demanding perfection in the means to the end is wrong. For example, we are told to beautify the *mitzvos,* so we try to make *Shabbos* as beautiful as possible. We set the table with our finest linen and dishes; we make delicious food; we polish our candlesticks. Fine. But if we drive ourselves to the point of exhaustion trying to make a gourmet meal, or if we can't have guests unless we have complete silver, crystal and china service, we are confusing the means with the end. We are channeling the goal of perfection to the wrong thing. It is a spiritual goal, not a physical goal.

▲ SELF-LOVE IS NOT ALL IMPORTANT

Now, let's expand on the "no" part of the answer to the question, "Is it true from a Torah perspective that I must be as much an object of my love as another person?" When this idea is exaggerated, it gets distorted and leads to a misuse of the power to grow and make progress, resulting in self-absorption and selfishness. I have seen many cases where people try to feel good about themselves by making themselves "number one" and satisfying their own needs exclusively. I have even heard Torah observant people say, "First I have to like myself, then I can work on being more friendly (giving, disciplined, etc)." Yes, it is true that it is hard to be friendly when you don't like yourself, but it is also hard to like yourself when people avoid you because you are sarcastic and rude.

How can we break this vicious cycle and become people who are really capable of loving ourselves and others?

▲ FOUR STEPS TO SELF-LOVE

INTRINSIC WORTH

First and foremost it is crucial to know that we have intrinsic worth because we are sparks of the Divine. This is a religious level concept, and at the social level we have no way to internalize the concept of intrinsic human worth. We may believe it intellectually, but we have not really related it to God and taken it "into our hearts," where the well-springs of feeling and behavior lie. If we don't start from the base that all people have intrinsic worth, we are dependent on a social-level "Consumer's Guide" approach to human worth. We have to score ourselves competitively and others on a rating scale of human worth. "Ruth is better than me because she is much more popular and gets higher grades than I do, but I am better than Ellie because I am more popular and get better grades than she does." Obviously, this is a poor way to evaluate human worth.

We said earlier that the only real basis for the belief in the intrinsic worth of ourselves and others is the fact we are *betzelem elokim*, created in the image of God. God breathed His own breath into us. Why did He create us and give us a divine soul? So we could compete with the rest of humanity for physical pleasure and status? No! We were given this wondrous gift so that we could earn eternal life and the ultimate pleasure of *dveikus*, or union with God.

When we identify with our souls, we transform our self-concept. We can sense the "light of seven suns" shining within us, filling us with a longing for God. When we identify with our souls we know that each one of us has a unique purpose that no one else can fulfill. And we know that each of us is uniquely fitted to fulfill our purpose. There has never been and never will be another person just like you, my dear reader. You are a spark of the Divine. The whole world was created for you. You are the purpose of the whole creation. Everything you do affects you and it affects the world. Any small righteous thing you do counts. You can choose to change your life right now.

IDENTIFYING THE IDEAL

In order to love ourselves, we have to know where we are going. As we said earlier, if our goals don't match our powers, we are in a no-win situation. The ideal for our limited horses is realistic and achievable goals. The ideal for our riders is to become more like God.

ASSESS THE REALITY

It is crucial for us to have a realistic perception of ourselves which includes both our horse and rider. In order to set sub-goals and know what steps to take, we have to know our strengths and weaknesses. We have to know where we are in order to know how to get where we want to go.

GIVING MEANING TO OUR DIFFICULTIES

How can we give meaning to our difficulties? By knowing that our purpose in life is not to compete with others but to elevate ourselves by our own efforts. We have a Judge that looks into our hearts and evaluates us according to our effort, not according to our objective standing in the world. The measurement is subjective: how much am *I* struggling with *my* difficulties? *My* difficulties are *my* challenge. God is looking to see how I handle my problems, not how I compare with someone else. As we said earlier, we get more credit for struggling to improve the *midah* of anger than for being born with an even temperament.

There are two different kinds of difficulties, physical and

spiritual. Physical difficulties would include illnesses and disabilities, as well as the fact that even within the normal range, we are better at some things than others. A relative weakness becomes a difficulty only if it interferes with accomplishing a goal. For example, I cannot sing very well, but since singing was never very important to me, I never thought of my poor voice as a difficulty. On the other hand, since I used to dream of being a concert pianist my mediocre piano playing was very frustrating to me. Why don't my fingers move faster and more accurately? Why can't I make the sounds my ear wants to hear? Why can't I hear what the teacher hears?

Spiritual difficulties are conditions that interfere with our spiritual growth. Suppose we were spiritually disabled by being indulged as children. No demands were placed on us, we had no responsibilities, and we got everything our hearts desired. Now we find it very difficult to discipline ourselves. We want to do *teshuvah*, but it's so hard to take on *mitzvos*. We just don't feel like getting up early every morning to pray. We're used to giving in to our impulses, and every fiber of our being longs to take the easy way out.

From a secular point of view, the best advice we can get is to accept ourselves and do the best we can with what we've got. "All right, so you won't be a concert pianist. Go with your strength and become a psychologist." "All right, so you don't feel like praying every day. Pray when you feel like it." This kind of advice is fine for our horses, but it destroys our riders. It's all right to tailor our goals to the strengths and weaknesses of our horses, but we must stick to Torah goals for our riders. The Torah gives us a way to give meaning to our difficulties, the more difficult, the more valuable.

There is a great deal more to say about self-love, but the

rest of the discussion will have to wait until we have climbed to the next level, the religious stage (see Chapter 16), because it is there that we will develop the concepts needed for a deeper understanding of self-love, e.g., love of the higher self. So far, our discussion of intrinsic worth was at the social level; we felt pride because we were created in the image of God. At the religious level, our reaction to having intrinsic worth will change. Rather than feeling pride at being in the image of God, we will long to perfect ourselves and be more like God.

THE "SENSUAL SOCIAL"

Just as it is virtually impossible for a Jew living in complete accord with the Torah to be a sensual primitive, it is impossible for such a person to be a sensual social (someone stuck at the social level). But as Rabbi Berel Wein said, "No matter how *frum* we appear on the outside, our inside reflects the American way of life."[13] Therefore many religious Jews have aspects of sensual social development more appropriate to secular society.

For example, Joel is a thirty-three year old married man. He comes from a religious home, went to Jewish schools and attended a *yeshivah* in Israel before starting college. He has an MBA, works as a financial analyst and earns a good living.

Joel met his wife Chaya while they were both college students. They fell in love, got married when they finished college and now have two children, a four-year-old girl and a two-year-old boy. The family lives in a lovely home in an Orthodox neighborhood. Joel goes to *shul* regularly and learns *Chumash* and *Gemara*. Chaya used to be a teacher but she now stays home with the children. She dresses stylishly but modestly. They are *shomer Shabbos* (they observe the laws of the Sabbath) and keep a kosher home. They would not consider a non-religious life, but they both believe that it is important to be part of the general society in which they live. They keep up-to-date on books, movies, current events, etc.

They had a good marriage at first, but even the best marriage can be affected by contact with secular culture. For example, Joel can't help but compare Chaya with the gorgeous women whose pictures enter his consciousness through the media. (Whether we realize it or not, images stay in our minds and become uninvited intruders.) Joel finds himself wondering if perhaps he didn't marry too young, if he didn't miss some exciting opportunities, if he shouldn't have had more experience before making such an important decision. He compares his feelings now with the passion he felt when they first got married, and he thinks something has gone very wrong. He knows that Chaya is very devoted to him and the children, but he sometimes finds her boring and feels stuck with her. This leads to resentment and lack of appreciation for all that she does for him.

Unfortunately, Joel has never sought help from a rabbi or suitable counselor and so his dissatisfaction festers within him. He still loves Chaya, but somehow not quite as much as he did when they first met. He responds to his doubts and his waning feelings of love by imagining what it would be like to be married to someone more stimulating. He is less attentive and affectionate to Chaya then he used to be, but he sees that as an inevitable consequence of familiarity and boredom.

Chaya senses that something has gone wrong with their

marriage, but when she tries to talk to Joel about it he tightens up and either denies the validity of her experience or assures her that he loves her, that he is just preoccupied with work and expenses. Chaya reads magazine articles with titles such as "Still Madly in Love After Ten Years," and she feels depressed about what is missing in her marriage. Every time she and Joel check in with secular culture their problems are exacerbated. His comparisons to other women became more vivid, and her romantic expectations are raised even higher.

Chaya is not worried about Joel leaving her, but her heart aches for more closeness. Marriage has turned out to be a big disappointment. She can't wait to go back to work when the children are in school.

We could write different plausible endings to this story, depending on whether Joel and Chaya decline or grow in response to their problems. If they decline, they stay married but drift into living parallel rather than complementary lives. They both seek completion outside of marriage through work, friends, activities and entertainment.

Or Joel and Chaya start blaming their frustration on each other and having angry quarrels. So much antagonism develops that they begin to hate each other. They end up seeking a divorce.

If they grow, Joel and Chaya seek help to learn how to have the kind of love that "grows and expands, more and more, from day to day." In this case, they would realize that although they had not become complete "social sensuals," the secular influence in their lives had thrown them off course. They both make a commitment to bring their marriage within a Torah framework and work on elevation together.

THE NEXT STEP

By the time we have reached the social level, our needs for stimulation, pleasure and connection have been elevated and we need to love and belong to something beyond ourselves. We have transcended narrow self-interest and are now capable of giving and loving. We have earned the self-respect and stability that result from taming our "horses" into becoming social animals.

Now we can look back at the elemental level and see that the climb was well worth the effort. The rewards of the social level are a much deeper sense of satisfaction than mere sensual gratification could ever yield. We can use this knowledge to help us face the challenges of the next stage of development: Onward and upward to sanctification of life and love of God.

SUMMARY

At the social level our elemental sensory/emotional needs are transformed into a desire for satisfaction that confirms our identity. Our search for pleasure becomes a search for love.

1. Life is meaningless if we don't have love and a sense of belonging to something that transcends our personal selves.

2. If love is trivialized and seen as nothing more than a feeling, or if it is aggrandized and made to be an end in itself, it is distorted and becomes quite an obstacle to spiritual growth.

3. In the Torah approach, the physical and spiritual are

united , with physical pleasure serving as fuel for spiritual growth.

4. Self-love is the basis of mental health and well-being, but it is often misunderstood and exaggerated.

The "self" we should love is the horse and rider, body and soul, combined.

We have *inherent* self-worth only by virtue of being *bętzelem elokim*, in the image of God.

The Quest for Meaning

Man is always reaching out for meaning, always setting out on his search for meaning; in other words, what I call the "will to meaning" is even to be regarded as man's primary concern . . .[1]

We have now climbed to the second rung of the ladder of intellectual development. At this level, the intellect is activated by the social soul. As we saw in Chapter 10, the social soul adds an exciting, dynamic quality to our lives; it brings us the need for progress and identity and the power of awareness. Intellectually, it is no longer enough to satisfy our elemental level need for curiosity. As psychiatrist Viktor E. Frankl said above, we now have

CHAPTER 13

279

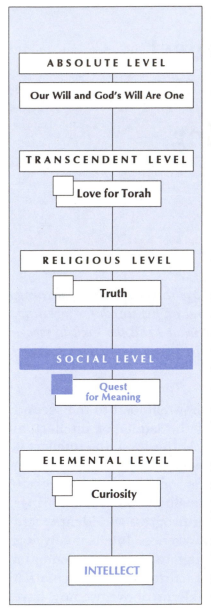

ABSOLUTE LEVEL

Our Will and God's Will Are One

TRANSCENDENT LEVEL

Love for Torah

RELIGIOUS LEVEL

Truth

SOCIAL LEVEL

Quest
for Meaning

ELEMENTAL LEVEL

Curiosity

INTELLECT

a "will to meaning," a driving need to find purpose in our lives. With our new-found ability to be aware of ourselves, to view ourselves from the outside, we search for the answer to the question, "What is the meaning of my life?"

QUEST FOR MEANING

The search for meaning is crucial to the development of our identity. Without meaning we are condemned to live out our lives in what Frankl called an "existential vacuum," pursuing in vain the ultimate elemental satisfaction, the satisfaction that will end our restless search and bring us peace. Frankl says that there is an "unheard cry for meaning" in contemporary society. "Ever more people today have the means to live, but no meaning to live for."[2] He sees people "haunted by the experience of their inner emptiness, a void within themselves."[3]

On the basis of both his personal experience as a prisoner in Nazi death camps and on clinical and research data, Dr. Frankl believes that the need for meaning is the primary motivating force in man. He sees our need for meaning as a distinctive characteristic of being human, a true manifestation of our humanity. While it is true that the need for meaning, like any other need, creates tension and disequilibrium in us, this kind of tension is inherent in being human. We are always poised somewhere between what we have and what we need, between what we are and what we ought to be. This tension motivates and mobilizes us to search for a way to fill our needs and become what we ought to be. It is thus indispensable to our growth and well-being. In fact, Frankl sees the presence of the "will to meaning" as a reliable criterion of mental health.

While interned at Auschwitz and Dachau, Frankl studied the effects of the death camps on the prisoners. He found that the risk of degeneration, demoralization, despair and death was greatly increased if the prisoners lost their sense of meaning and purpose.

> Besides these physical causes [for degeneration and death], there were mental ones . . . The majority of prisoners suffered from a kind of inferiority complex. We all had once been or had fancied ourselves to be 'somebody.' Now we were treated like complete nonentities.[4]

Dr. Frankl noted that those prisoners who could keep a hold on their moral and spiritual selves, who could maintain a positive self-identity in the face of extreme deprivation and humiliation, fared better psychologically than those who succumbed to the Nazi view that they were nothings. (Dr.

Frankl hastens to add that this did not necessarily mean that they could avoid being killed. A sense of meaning was a necessary, not sufficient, condition for survival.) Psychiatrist Joel Dimsdale studied survivors and found that they benefited from focusing on a purpose for survival (e.g., to be reunited with their families, to bear witness to the atrocities). Many fought off defeat by retaining a sense of mastery over some aspect of their lives. For example, they managed to observe *Yom Kippur* in the face of all odds.[5] Research done in other concentration and prisoner-of-war camps (Japanese, North Korean and North Vietnamese) reports the same conclusion.[6] The quality of the prisoners' existence depended on their ability to transcend themselves and to find positive meaning for their lives. Some people lived for a cause they wished to serve, others for a person they loved.

After the war, Frankl continued to study the "will to meaning" and developed logotherapy, or meaning-centered psychotherapy. In the course of his work, he found that patients who had supposedly been successfully treated by other methods were often left with an "existential vacuum":

> The patient was beautifully adjusted and functioning, but meaning was missing. The patient had not been taken as a human being, that is to say, a being in steady search of meaning; and this search for meaning ... had not been taken seriously . . . but was seen as a mere rationalization of underlying unconscious psychodynamics. (p.20)

Frankl emphasizes that the "will to meaning" is a primary psychological force, not a secondary rationalization of instinctual drives. If the therapist debunks the patient's need for meaning and sees it as neurotic striving, the patient will be left with a gaping void in his psyche. Along similar lines, the renowned cognitive and developmental psychologist Jerome Bruner says that "the major activity of human beings is to extract meaning from their encounters with the world."[7] He considers it to be an arrogant error to assume that "the meaning people assign to the world is a mere rationalization or an artifact."

(I cannot help wondering what happens to the unfortunate patients of psychiatrist Irvin Yalom, who wrote in *Love's Executioner and Other Tales of Psychotherapy* that there are four "givens" to be dealt with in psychotherapy: the inevitability of death; the freedom to make what we will of our lives; basic aloneness; and the lack of any real, sustaining meaning to life. He sees the role of therapist as helping patients to "accept" theses "facts of life.")

In his book *The Unheard Cry for Meaning*, Frankl quotes[8] a study of sixty students at an American university who had attempted suicide. The reason given for the suicide attempt by eighty-five percent of the students was that "life seemed meaningless." An even more striking finding was that ninety-three percent of the students who complained of meaninglessness "were actively engaged socially, were performing well academically and were on good terms with their family groups."

Frankl also refers to a dissertation study of 416 students[9] which reported a highly significant relationship between drug usage and low purpose in life. No differences were found between the extent of drug use and having a weak father image or a strong father image. In many studies reviewed by the author of the dissertation, heavy drug use was correlated with a search for meaningful experience.

It is clear that a sense of meaningfulness is a powerful force in human life. Meaningfulness has survival value, it enhances the quality of life, and it even helps us withstand the most cataclysmic events without demoralization and degeneration.

LEVELS OF MEANING

Meaning can exist at many levels. Surely, there is a difference between the person who says "I live to shop" and the person who says "I live to help create a just society." One categorization of meanings is the distinction between "terrestrial" and "cosmic" meaning.[10] Terrestrial meaning deals with one's personal goals and purposes. Cosmic meaning deals with whether life has some overarching, grand significance that applies equally to all people whether they think it does or not. This difference between terrestrial and cosmic meaning may explain why some researchers[11] found far lower reports of lack of meaning (5%) than those reported by Frankl (50%). If the definition of meaning is left vague, people may report meaning in life for the most superficial kinds of terrestrial meaning, thus greatly deflating the estimate of meaninglessness.

Our model gives us a more precise way to look at levels of meaning. We can look at meaning from the vantage point of our three levels of personal development—the elemental, social and religious levels. We might say that the person who "lives to shop" has elemental meaning. However, if the word "meaning" has any meaning, it is doubtful that the elemental level even deserves to be included in the definition. The difficulty here is caused by confusing identity and meaning.

Shopping may give a person a superficial sense of identity ("I am someone who loves to shop"), but it does not give meaning to that person's life. At the elemental level, there is no meaning, just identity. It is one thing to say, "This is important to me," but it is quite another thing to say, "This gives significance and purpose to my life." It is also doubtful that such trivial meaning would confer the above mentioned benefits of survival value, enhanced quality of life and ability to endure cataclysmic events without demoralization and degeneration. If I live to shop or to eat in fine restaurants or to wear trendy clothes, what is left to live for if those things are taken away from me? Without values that transcend our individual lives ("I have to go on living to help rid the world of tyranny"), we can quickly descend into moral degeneration in order to survive (the infamous Kapos, or Jews who served the Nazis) or sink into depression and despair. We will therefore limit our definition of meaning to the social and religious levels.

In this chapter, we are talking about the social-level person and are therefore focusing on the social level of meaning. People at this level find meaning in philosophies ("It is really important that we all love each other"), causes ("My goal in life is to help clean up the environment"), relationships ("I only feel really alive when I have a meaningful relationship"), society ("I dedicate myself to work for a society where all have equal opportunity"), life work ("I am making a contribution to society by pushing back the frontiers of ignorance") and personal growth ("I want to know myself and like myself and realize my potential"). Social level people often long for meaning in the form of immortality or self-perpetuation ("I was so happy when I had my first grandchild because I saw that my lifeline was going on for another generation"). This wish for eternity often takes the form of yearning for fame and/or memorials ("Seeing my painting on the museum wall thrilled me because I knew my work would live into the future," and "I endowed the university library so my name would be on the lips of all the students"). As Rabbi Yechiel Tucazinsky says:[12]

> Not only those who believe in the survival of the soul, but even (and perhaps more so) those who imagine that they deny man's immortality, strive all their lives to ensure that their memory will not be expunged from among their people.

The story is told about the king who had a wonderful life—riches, honor and power—but after his death his rivals destroyed everything he had and erased his memory from the face of the earth. Would we choose a great life if we knew that nothing would be left of us after we were gone?

THE PROBLEM WITH SOCIAL-LEVEL MEANING

The search for meaning at the social level has brought many benefits to the world. To name just a few, hospitals have been built, lives have been saved, children have been educated, scientific research has been endowed and great art has been preserved. Nevertheless, social level meaning is dangerous spiritually. What is the problem with social-level meaning? Why isn't it enough to find meaning in social causes, philosophies, relationships, etc.?

Social-level meaning is dangerous, because it can lull us into a false sense of completion and significance which may stunt further striving and growth. We may get such a wonderful feeling of noble self-satisfaction from attending a rally and waving a banner saying "Release the hostages!" that we don't realize that we still don't know how to act in business, how to treat our spouses, parents and children and how to relate to God.

The problem is that social-level meaning is based on the values of the society in which we live. But we all live in many sub-societies (family, neighborhood, religion, school), and every society has many values. What criteria do we use to pick the values on which we base our personal meaning? We tend to get meaning from those values that fit our personalities and experiences. For example, imagine two brothers growing up in a liberal, sociable, athletic family. One of the brothers is very intellectual and intense, the other is easy-going and casual. The intense child will probably be deeply affected by dinner table talk about endangered species and third-world suffering, while all that "serious stuff" goes right over the head of the easy-going child. The intense child is more likely to get his meaning from involvement in liberal causes, while the easy-going child is more likely to get his meaning from social status and sports.

What happens to these two boys if family values change (their parents become more conservative), or they go on to other societies with different values (e.g., summer programs abroad, college), or if their personalities change as they grow older so that their old meanings no longer fit ("I've got a Type A personality so I had to slow down and stop taking everything so seriously," "I've got to get serious about life so I can get married and have a family")? They are left with a feeling of meaninglessness. They can search for new sources of meaning, but if they find only social-level meaning, the whole cycle may repeat itself. After a few repetitions of this cycle, they may, as many people do, give up on meaning. They may conclude that since there is no meaning to life, they ought to devote themselves to making money and having pleasure. They live with an underlying sense of despair and futility that may manifest itself as depression, boredom and drug and alcohol abuse. This pattern is especially common in societies with relative, rapidly shifting values.

> Meaning is sustaining only if it is based on absolutes. Consider the doctor who was asked the question, "What gives your life meaning?" The doctor answered, "I get meaning from saving people's lives." The questioner then said, "Yes, but what is the meaning of the lives of the people you save?"

Ultimately, there has to be some absolute meaning to life that is independent of role, relationship, status, causes, etc. All these things can be taken away from us, and we can still find meaning in life. Just imagine a person who is standing in line for soup at Auschwitz. He has been stripped of his family, his career, his place in society, his possessions. We approach him and ask, "Who are you?" What answer is there? What is the "I" when you have lost everything? We find an answer to this question from Aryeh ben Leah Kornblit. In a *shul* in Brooklyn, there is a Torah that is dedicated to the everlasting memory of Aryeh ben Leah Kornblit and his wife.[13] In 1943 Rabbi Israel Shapiro was in the death camp of Yanowska from which only 11 of 3,000 prisoners survived. Late one evening, a *kapo* called for the rabbi because he had an important message for him. With trepidation, Rabbi Shapiro came forward and was handed a crumpled envelope. He opened it and found the following note:

> My dear Rabbi Israel Shapiro, may you have a long and happy life!
>
> They have just surrounded the bristle factory in the ghetto where some 800 of us ... are about to be put to death. The only question they are still debating is whether they should shoot us on the spot or take us to the ovens.
>
> Please, dear rabbi, if you should be found worthy of being saved, and if you should be able to settle in the Land of Israel, see to it that, somewhere upon our holy soil, a little marker is put up with my wife's name and my own so that our names should not be forgotten. Or maybe—no matter where you will make your new home—you might have a Torah scroll written in our memory. I am enclosing fifty American dollars, which I hope the messenger to whom I am giving this will pass on to you.
>
> I must hurry, because they have already ordered us to take off our clothes.
>
> When I get to the Other World, I will convey your greetings to your holy ancestors and will ask them to intercede in your behalf so that your days may be long and happy.
>
> Your servant,
> Aryeh ben Leah Kornblit
>
> P.S. My sister's children are now living with a Gentile family ... Please take them away from there and turn them over to a Jewish family. Whatever happens, they must remain Jews. My wife, Sheva bat Chaya, was shot yesterday.

Rabbi Shapiro carried the letter with him wherever he went. When the war ended and he came to the United States it was his only possession. He eventually raised money to carry out the last wish of Aryeh ben Leah Kornblit. The Rabbi said:

> Consider what strength God gives to His people. Here you have a man who saw his wife shot, who himself was about to die and yet found it in his heart to think of those who would live after him—not only his sister's children, but also the people whom he would never know and who would hold his *Sefer Torah* in their arms.
>
> How great is our portion, how magnificent our heritage.

This is religious-level meaning. At the religious level, our meaning comes from knowing that we are created in the image of God and from trying to become more and more like Him. Religious-level meaning gives us direction, purpose and detailed instructions on how to live our lives under all conditions. Nothing can strip us of this kind of meaning. It is eternal, and it gives us eternity.

After meeting Ken, our personification of the person at the social level of the intellectual ladder, we will discuss how to elevate meaning to the religious level.

THE INTELLECTUAL SOCIAL

Ken is a very successful thirty-five year old lawyer. He works with a prestigious law firm. He was raised in a Conservative Jewish family and got a strong sense of identity from being a member of his Temple Boy Scout group. He worked very hard for all of his badges and became an Eagle Scout. Although he was a good athlete and he liked sports, games just didn't give his life the meaning he got from being a scout. He chose scout meetings over soccer matches and scout camp over the Little League.

As an adolescent, Ken followed up some of the interests he developed as a scout. He got meaning from starting an environmental protection club in high school. He won an ecology prize for outstanding achievement based on the club's recycling project.

While in college, he got involved in student political activities. He was outraged by (among other things) poverty, discrimination against women and the dictatorial methods of the university administration and most of the faculty. He marched in protests, worked on raising his own and others' consciousness of their chauvinism and organized rallies to demand relevant courses and to eliminate grades.

When he graduated from college, he went on to law school. He was still politically active, but he now believed that he could wield more influence by working within the system to elect liberal candidates. He reasoned that if he became a successful lawyer, he would have much greater political power in the future. He dreamed of running for office someday.

Ken graduated from law school and got a job in a law firm. He worked long hours and was richly compensated for his efforts. What little time and energy he had left after work were spent in relaxing social activities. He just didn't seem to have time for politics anymore. And as much as he hated to admit it, he was even beginning to lose faith in his causes. The world didn't seem like a much better place now than it was when he was an idealistic boy scout. In fact, it might even have become a little worse. He still believed in his old values and causes, but he couldn't figure out why they didn't seem to have the desired results. His youthful optimism just didn't seem to fit him anymore.

Beneath the pleasures of success, Ken felt a gnawing emptiness that told him that something was wrong in his life. He was trying to get his identity from being a successful lawyer and his meaning from helping people with their legal problems. But in truth, he was becoming more and more cynical and frustrated. He was in danger of completely losing his cherished idealism and sensitivity. He was at the point where he could either go up or down. He could give up on meaning entirely, or he could search for new sources of meaning.

And then, something strange happened. Once a week, during lunch hour, at the request of some of his colleagues, a rabbi came to the firm to give a class on the Torah portion of the week. Ken was indifferent at first. He needed his lunch hour for work, and besides, he had learned all of those Bible stories in Sunday School. But he felt such an aching void that he decided to give it a try. He didn't expect to find much of interest, but to his amazement, he found the classes fascinating. He learned things that gave depth and substance to Judaism. Rather than the series of disconnected children's stories he had learned in Sunday School, he began to see an integrity and cohesiveness throughout the whole Torah. He enjoyed spirited, intellectually stimulating discussions with the other lawyers about what they were learning together.

A few of the other Torah students invited Ken to their homes for *Shabbos* meals. He loved the atmosphere of peace and sanctity that settled over their homes when the *Shabbos* candles were lit and all distractions were put aside. He began to think seriously about getting married and having a family, and he even felt a little nostalgic for the Friday night meals with his family when he was growing up.

Ken started to go to services with his friends occasionally. He felt uplifted by praying with a group, and he could feel his soul thrill to the ancient rhythms and melodies. He got a feeling of regeneration when he didn't work on Saturday, and he found that he missed *Shabbos* when business took precedence.

Ken finds himself being drawn into a way of life different from anything he has ever known. He is in great conflict, however, because he feels himself being pulled in two directions. He still believes in social activism, freedom of speech and equal rights and opportunities for all. He still believes in relative morality and free choice for the individual conscience. Yet, this Judaism that he finds so compelling, emphasizes obligations and responsibilities rather than rights and privileges. It is full of circumscribed roles—for men, women, children, parents, husbands, wives. The *kohanim* (priests) not only have a special status but they are born into it. There are absolute, inviolable, immutable laws. Why then, does he feel liberated by *Shabbos* and by his burgeoning awareness of the presence of God?

It is becoming clear to Ken that if he continues on the Torah path, some of his most revered ideals will be challenged. He doesn't know exactly where it will all end up, but like Uri Zohar (see Chapter 6), he finds the prospect of change at once exciting and frightening. He is sometimes embarrassed to tell people where he is going on Friday nights, and the thought of publicly wearing a *kippah* (skull cap) is mortifying. His parents, who were at first happy that he was rekindling his interest in Judaism, are now afraid that he will go too far. Some of his old friends are already teasing him about becoming a religious fanatic. If Ken is too threatened by the challenge to the life-style and social level of meaning that he shares with most of his friends, family and associates, he will step off the Torah path. He will conclude that Judaism is fine for people who need a crutch, but that he can manage without it. If he has the kind of intellectual honesty shown by Uri Zohar, he will accept the challenge and follow the Torah path wherever it leads.

THE PROPER USE OF THE NEED FOR MEANING

Once again, we turn to Rabbi Tucazinsky for deep insight into the human personality:[14]

> You can find people who claim they do not believe in any intangible spirituality yet would give their lives for spiritual ideals, such as justice and the like . . . We see people sacrificing their lives, going to their deaths for the sake of principles, their nation and society, or for the honor that will be given to them after their death . . . This feeling reveals that man, consciously or unconsciously, whether he believes or does not, possesses subconscious stirrings which confirm the spirituality in him, his soul and spirit, that aspire to ascend on high and to survive . . .
>
> This aspiration derives from a higher source, from the soul's sensing that it indeed survives even after its separation from the body . . . the self therefore longs that its remnant not be wiped out . . . that it be exalted.

Rabbi Tucazinsky is telling us that we long for meaning and perpetuity because we sense the immortal soul within us. The self is shouting, "I want eternity too." The self knows only this world, so it seeks a worldly monument. But the divine soul drives us relentlessly toward fulfillment of our real purpose here on earth, which is to draw closer to God and achieve immortality in the World-to-Come. Paradoxically, the only way we can achieve immortality in this world is to strengthen our immortal soul while we are alive. If we allow ourselves to be sidetracked by the lure of social level meaning and memorials, we are in danger of wasting the precious gift of life. As Rabbi Tucazinsky says:

> This [life in this world], then, is not a process of living but of dying. Life kills life. Every moment slips by and disappears. Every minute kills a minute; every day kills a day; every year kills a year. (p.153)

In order to use the gift of life well, we have to learn to find our meaning at the religious level. In general, this means finding the significance and purpose of our lives— yours and mine. At the personal level we have try to find our individual way of being *betzelem elokim* (in the image of God). Each of us has to try to realize *his own potential.* (No one else on earth is exactly like you, my dear reader, and no one else has your abilities to express your way of expressing them.) At the cosmic level, we each have to make our unique contribution to the building of the perfect society as described in Torah.

As Rabbi Samson Raphael Hirsch taught, Torah has to be the filter for testing our ideas, dreams, desires and plans. Some of our most cherished secular beliefs may show up as impurities when we try to pass them through the filter of Torah. But the Torah is a much more trustworthy filter than society. We need Torah to help us separate the good from the bad, the moral from the immoral and the blessing from the curse.

And so, if we want to raise ourselves to the religious level, we, like Ken, may have to struggle with our priorities and face challenges to familiar, cherished values and practices. We may have to acknowledge that some of the things we consider crucially important don't really bring us fulfillment. Promotions, beautiful homes, smart and beautiful children, recognition for achievement, our pictures in the newspaper, the Nobel and Pulitzer Prizes—none of these things, important as they may be, are enough *in and of themselves.*

Are we ready to admit that we are restricted by our human, finite perspectives? That we are hemmed in by the limitations of space and time? That we can't understand the present in its relationship with eternity? That we are not aware of all the forces—physical and spiritual—impinging on us at any given time? Are we ready to admit that we can rationalize any course of action we want to take and make it sound moral? When we see that we *must* have ultimate meaning, and that the fulfillment of all our fondest social aspirations will not give us that meaning, then we can look to the Torah. If we are ready for the Truth perspective (see Chapter 17), we can elevate ourselves to the religious level, where, with a shudder, we say, "What does Torah tell us about this?"

SUMMARY

At the social level of the intellect, mere curiosity is

transformed into the need to have meaning and purpose in our lives.

1. At the social level, meaning is relative. You have your meaning, and I have mine. We find meaning in philosophies, causes, relationships, society, life work, personal growth, and immortality via memorials and lasting contributions to society.

2. We long for meaning and perpetuity because we sense the immortal soul within us. The self knows only this world, so it seeks a wordly monument.

3. Social level meaning is dangerous because it can lull us into a false sense of completion and significance.

4. Ultimately, in order to be really sustaining, there has to be some absolute meaning to life, and this we get from Torah.

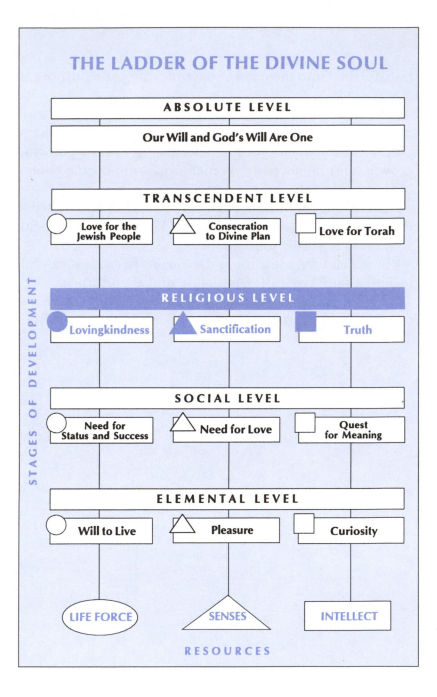

CHAPTER 14

The Theme of the Religious Soul: Unity

> *Hear, O Israel, God is our Lord, God is One.* (Deuteronomy 6:4)

> *Above all, the most vital lesson is that the One God is your God... You must comprehend your life with all its diversity as preceding from this One and you must direct it towards this One, in order that your life may be a unity, just as your God is One. With mind and body, thought and feeling, word, deed and enjoyment, in wealth and poverty, in joy and sorrow, in health and sickness, in freedom and slavery, in life and death, your life-task is everywhere and always the same . . . Strive to reach the One, and be one in heart as your God is One.*[1]

We have arrived at the religious level of the soul. The religious soul is purely spiritual, the very breath of God. In terms of our glass-blowing metaphor in

Chapter 4, the religious soul is the breath of the glass-blower while it is still in the craftsman's mouth. There is a direct connection, however, between the spiritual and the physical at this level. The mouth of the glassblower is in contact with the glass.

The theme of the religious soul is unity. We feel distress and unrest when our lives are fragmented and disjointed, when there is no overarching purpose that harmonizes all facets of our lives. Deep in our psyches, we feel a need to be like God. At the religious level we seek a coherent world view that unifies all aspects of our lives. We yearn to synthesize and integrate the profusion of phenomena which surround us, and we yearn for universal peace and harmony. At this level, we seek a source for our identity that is absolute, universal and eternal. We now strive to emulate God and to get our identity from Him ("How can I be more like God?").

At the religious level, the power of awareness transcends narrow ego boundaries and becomes the power to unify. Our ego-boundaries are expanded to include a sense of ourselves as part of others. We now have the ability to "love our friend as we love ourselves," because we realize that we really belong to each other, that we are part of the same divine root. We know that the best way to relate to God is to relate to others. We identify with our "rider"; we appreciate the divine spark in ourselves, and we can thus appreciate it in others. Just as we can see our own unlimited potential, we can see the unlimited potential of others. We now have the ability to work toward the harmony and well-being of others, and we are willing to put personal desires aside for the sake of peace.

At the religious level this theme of unity pervades every

phase of our lives. Our social level needs are transformed into religious level needs. The need for success becomes the need for *chessed* (lovingkindness); rather than competing and comparing ourselves with others, we seek unification with others through giving. The need for love becomes the need for *kedushah* (sanctity). At the elemental level we loved each other physically. At the social level we added the personality, and at the religious level we add the spirit. This enriches and deepens our love. Love becomes one of our main channels of elevation. The need for meaning becomes the need for truth. Pluralism and relative truth do not satisfy us; we seek the absolute.

The power of unity has a very interesting by-product: excitement (for a fuller discussion, see Chapter 8). When we succeed in uniting all our powers toward the goal of being more like God, we feel tremendously excited. Before we reach this stage, we can experience only partial unity and, therefore, only partial excitement. At the social level, for example, we may be able to combine sensual pleasure and love, which is very exciting. But our careers still seem like separate, unrelated compartments, untouched by the excitement of our love. Not until we reach the religious level do we have one overall goal that connects *all* parts of our lives into a harmonious whole. At this level we can see how all of our roles are related to our central purpose. We are no longer just businessmen fighting for status and wealth. We are businessmen who have the challenge of acting ethically while earning a living which will enable us to support our families and to give *tzeddakah* (charity). We are no longer just housewives doing the difficult and tedious job of raising children. We are Jewish women raising children who are the next link in the chain of transmission of Torah.

Mundane activities like changing diapers and doing laundry are infused with meaning and purpose because they are a crucial part of our sacred mission of building a Jewish home. Why is this mission so crucial? At the social level, where achievement is the most important thing, the home is a preparatory stage for real life, which is outside the home. But at the religious level, where spiritual progress is the most important thing, *home is real life*. And we are in charge of building the Jewish home, where we have a splendid opportunity to work on elevating ourselves and on helping our families elevate themselves. When we can relate our activities to the "big picture" we feel constant excitement.

Is Torah the only path to unity? There are two areas of life that are often discussed in terms of unity. One is Eastern thought and religion, the other is the arts. It is said that the power of cults based on Eastern thought is that they give a sense of unity. Cult members feel a oneness with each other and with the universe. Music and other arts can also create a feeling of sublime harmony. The danger in getting a sense of unity from these sources is that they don't unify all aspects of life. They detach you from the rest of life and create a false sense of wholeness.

Here at the religious level, we have an opportunity to unify our lives around the goal of becoming more like God. How wonderful it is to have the need for unity satisfied by "the real thing"!

In the next three chapters we will discuss the religious level needs of lovingkindness, sanctity, and truth, and how they relate to our goal.

CHAPTER 15

Lovingkindness and Seeking Peace

Come and consider how great is the power of those who are charitable and perform deeds of chessed, for they shelter neither in the shadow of the morning, nor in the shadow of the wings of the earth, nor in the shadow of the wings of the sun, nor in the shadow of the wings of the chayos or the cherubim, nor in the shadow of eagle's wings; but under whose wings do they shelter? Under the shadow of the One by whose word the world was created.

Ruth Rabba

Here at the religious level of the life force ladder a new power enters our lives; we are now being activated by the religious soul, which is purely spiritual. The religious soul, with its theme of unity,

303

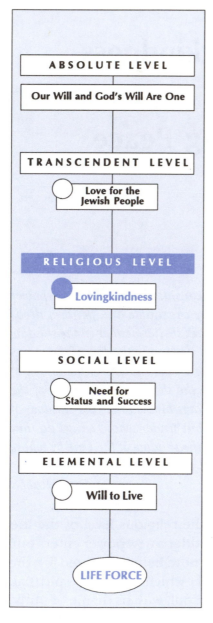

awakens the "holy virtue"[1] of *chessed* (lovingkindness) in us and radically changes our relationship with people. We now need people so that we can express our God-like identity by doing acts of kindness for them. Our center of gravity shifts from taking to giving.

GIVING AND TAKING

The switch from taking to giving is the central feature of the religious level of the life force ladder. Rabbi Dessler relates a story[2] that illustrates the essential difference between giving and taking. The story is about a meeting between the world-conqueror Alexander of Macedonia and the King of Cassia. The king offered to show Alexander the Cassian a system of justice. Two men came before the court. The plaintiff had bought a piece of property and found a treasure buried on it. He insisted that the treasure belonged to the vendor. The vendor argued that he had sold the land and all that it contained to the plaintiff and thus insisted that the plaintiff keep the treasure. The King of Cassia asked whether they had sons or daughters, and it turned out that one had a son and one a daughter, each of marriageable age. The king decided that the two children should marry and the treasure would "stay in the family."

Alexander was astonished by the decision. He said he would have had both parties put to death and would have confiscated the property for the royal treasury.

According to Rabbi Dessler, the plaintiff and the vendor were "givers," neither wanting to take from the other or get more than he deserved. The decision of the Cassian "king of givers" was that they unite for their mutual good. Alexander, the "king of takers," would have condemned the givers to death and taken their property. He would have added to himself by diminishing them.

Rabbi Dessler concludes:

> We can now derive a general law: Takers harm each other, for the taker makes the person from whom he takes a taker in his turn; his aim now is to try his best to get back what was taken from him. *But givers complete each other.* The giver arouses a spirit of giving in the recipient, whose aim is now to give back in gratitude that which he has received.

Notice that Rabbi Dessler talks about the recipient, because there must be a recipient of kindness. Givers need receivers, but there is a great difference between recipients and takers. The taker takes for himself and people take from him only if he is unable to prevent it or if he has to do so in order to be in a position to take from them again.

> There is another person: one who *gives* and *receives*. He is the giver, whose giving flows from the source of pure goodness in his heart, and whose receiving immediately fills his heart with gratitude—in payment for whatever he receives.

Rabbi Dessler is teaching us that giving and taking are fundamental character traits. They are the pivots on which the personality turns, determining how we act toward others, whether we will be takers who harm each other or givers who complete each other. We move on now to explore the motivation behind giving.

THE MOTIVATION BEHIND CHESSED OR GIVING

Chessed is the sublime ability to give to others without thought of reward. It is a wish to give as God gives. But can we ever give the way God gives? Aren't we always motivated, at least partially, by thoughts of praise or gratitude for our acts of kindness?

Let us see what the behavioral sciences have to say about this subject. What we are calling *chessed* or giving would be categorized as prosocial or altruistic behavior in psychology. Prosocial behavior is defined as

> those behaviors in which the emphasis is . . . upon actual *concern* for others. They include those acts of helpfulness, charitability, self-sacrifice and courage, in which the possibility of reward from the recipient is presumed to be minimal or non-existent and which, on the face of it, the prosocial behavior is engaged in for its own sake.[3]

According to psychologist C. Daniel Batson, most psychologists don't believe that people engage in prosocial behavior for its own sake. They believe that

> the only persons we are capable of caring about, ultimately, are ourselves. We value others instrumentally; we care for their welfare only to the degree that it affects ours. Our behavior may be highly social, our thoughts may be highly social, but in our hearts, we live alone. *Altruism,* the view that we are capable of valuing and pursuing another person's welfare as an ultimate goal, is pure fantasy. We are *social egoists*.[4]

Psychologists do not debate the fact that people *do* sometimes help each other, but there is a controversy over the motivation behind prosocial behavior. They generally attempt to explain it with concepts which imply covert reward: self-reward ("It makes me feel good to help others"), empathy ("Since I feel distress at your pain I am alleviating my own discomfort when I help you") and evolutionary advantage ("We sometimes act for the good of others; the human species is presumably more likely to survive if people generally help each other").[5]

Support for the covert-reward hypothesis can be found in a phenomenon called "helper's high,"[6] which is a sense of calmness, freedom from stress, increased energy, enhanced self-worth and a feeling of well-being associated with the act of helping others. The reaction to helping is the opposite of the body's response to stress. The benefits of helping seem to occur only when the helping is voluntary. Forced helping does not seem to yield a reduction in stress.

Many psychologists disagree with the view that all

prosocial behavior is self-serving. For one thing, research has shown that some people seem to be prosocially oriented.[7] They have three defining characteristics: a positive view of people in general; concern about others' welfare; and a sense of personal responsibility for others. Also, helping behavior starts very early in life. A group of researchers videotaped children three to five years old during thirty hours of free play and found about 1,200 acts of sharing, helping, comforting and cooperating. They concluded that altruistic behavior is just as "natural" as selfish behavior.

Batson argues that simply showing that "self-benefits follow from benefiting the other does not prove that the self-benefits are the helper's goal."[8] He reports a series of experiments in which subjects observed a "worker" (someone allegedly participating in an experiment involving electric shock) reacting badly to pain. The subjects were then given a choice between escaping from the situation or relieving the "worker's" pain by taking the shocks themselves. The results of the studies supported the idea that empathy evokes truly altruistic motivation.

Batson concluded that it is indeed possible that the goal of "empathically aroused helpers" is to help others. He points out, however, that the studies suggest that our capacity for altruism is limited to those for whom we feel empathy, and that concern for others is "a fragile flower, easily crushed by self-concern." (p. 344) He concludes that before we can nurture the fragile flower of altruism we need to know it is there. Says Batson after a decade of research, "I hope I have convinced you that it does exist or, at a minimum, that it is worth taking a careful look to see whether it exists."

Why is this topic so controversial? And why are conclusions based on the results of years of study presented so apologetically and tentatively? The answer is that the behavioral sciences are dominated by the principle of hedonism, which states that human behavior is motivated primarily by the pleasure principle. Their claim is that all behavior is motivated by an attempt to maximize pleasure and to minimize pain. In other words, our behavior is determined by the consequences of our acts; we keep doing things that are followed by rewards (either receiving pleasure or avoiding pain), and we stop doing things that are followed by pain. Belief in this principle is a matter of faith among many psychologists. Most behavioral scientists simply cannot conceive of acts done without reward or reinforcement of some kind. From their point of view, the child who helps his mother has the same motivation as the child who doesn't help. The helper gets self-reward ("What a good child I am"), and the non-helper gets to do what he wants. Morally, it's all the same selfish motivation.

In the absence of belief in God and the powers of the divine soul, this view makes sense. If we are little more than "the elaborate packaging and guardians"[9] of our genes, then we have no choice but to respond in terms of selfish interest. From such a position the following conclusion is warranted:

> It now seems modern evolutionary biology can . . . give some sort of objective and factually well-founded answer to the ultimate question: "Why are we here?" . . . Today we can answer this question with brutal frankness. We are here to reproduce ourselves; we are providing a temporary home for our genes . . . Many people, when confronted with such ungratifying answers to the deep questions of life, prefer to

console themselves with comforting ideas of some special creation by a reassuringly anthropomorphic God . . . *Furthermore, it [the idea of God] serves to place a fig-leaf over the most unmentionable element of all—the essential selfishness which underlies what passes for altruism.* [10] (Emphasis added).

While the behavioral scientists argue about the possibility of altruism, we can find the truth in the Torah.

TORAH AND SECULAR VIEWS OF CHESSED

What are the similarities and differences between the Torah concept of *chessed* and the secular psychological concept of prosocial behavior or empathy-altruism? The similarities are that Torah acknowledges that people do sometimes help each other, and that such seemingly altruistic behavior can spring from selfish motives. In fact, there is considerable similarity between Rabbi Dessler's[11] discussion of the motivation of the person who does *mitzvos* (commandments) *shelo lishmah* (out of concern for himself) and the secular view of motivation. Such a person

> will do things out of fear . . . of punishment for himself; and he will perform *mitzvos* . . . for reward for himself. And he will perform *mitzvos* with the idea of receiving "the portion allotted by the master to his servants". . . In *mitzvos* between man and man . . . he will act out of compassion and sympathy, which are not motives of pure, unselfish love, since basically they are self-centered, their aim being to avoid the pain caused by seeing the other person's distress . . . All these motivations are based on taking, since in the final test one is acting for one's own benefit.

Up to this point, Rabbi Dessler seems to agree with those secular thinkers who do not give any credence to altruism for its own sake. We do seem to act to maximize reward and minimize pain, even when doing *mitzvos*. But in the very next sentence, we see the profound difference between the secular and the Torah positions. Rabbi Dessler tells us that *we can use all our motivations for spiritual progress.* This is the meaning of the saying, "You shall love Hashem your God with all your heart—with both your inclinations, both the good and the bad." In other words, we can use the energy of our selfish urges to get us started on our spiritual journey. At first, we may do *chessed* for the promise of a reward, but if we sincerely strive to reach the point of *lishmah* (for its own sake), the selfish motive will be transformed.

We don't have to deny, suppress or glorify our selfish urges. We just have to use them with the right intentions.

Next, we can reach a middle ground between *shelo lishmah* and *lishmah*. As in Chapter 14, at the religious level, we can internalize that we are *betzelem elokim*, in the image of God. Because we can identify with our riders, we can recognize the riders of others. Because we know we are all sparks of the same divine root, we can identify completely with others. We can use these psychological powers of *self-identity* and *identification with others* to progress spiritually. At this point we can love others as we love ourselves, and we can give to them as we would give to ourselves, because giving to them is actually giving to ourselves.

We are all able to do this for our children. They are extensions of us. Their well-being is our well-being. Their pain is our pain. We joyously give them what they *need*, with no hesitation. In fact, if we can't provide what they *need*, we suffer terrible anguish.

At the religious level, our ego-boundaries expand to include others. We help a friend with the endless details of planning for her wedding, and we feel the same excitement and joy as if we were getting married. We share the benefit of our business or professional expertise with a friend because we want him to succeed as much as we want to succeed. When we are able to do this, we are well on our way to *lishmah*.

The idea of "spiritual progress" is the key to the profound difference between the Torah view and the secular view. Our bodies are indeed elaborate packages—but not for snippets of DNA. The body houses the divine soul. We are body and soul, and we have the capacity for spiritual as well as physical growth. The divine soul gives us the ability to recognize and want to emulate the attributes of God. Therefore, it is within the realm of possibility for us to do things the way God does them, *lishmah*, rather than for personal gain. When we do *chessed* we become a bit like God. This is why totally secular writers have had difficulty coming to grips with altruistic giving; they lack the acceptance of God as the ultimate "Giver" of everything we have.

In order to understand how we can reach the level of pure giving, we have to know that God has embedded two abilities in us, the ability to do things to fill a lack or satisfy a need, and the ability to do things out of fulfillment. For example, we can relate to our children from either root, need or fulfillment. We can look *to* our children for unconditional love and ego strengthening, or we can see them as needy recipients of our overflowing love, devotion and nurturance. The more we relate to them (and others) from need, the more problems we have. We will try to shape them to satisfy our ego needs, and we will be disappointed, angry and rejected when they don't reflect well on us. If we relate out of fulfillment, we can "train each child in his own way" and help each to fulfill his own potential. The closer we come to being able to give *lishmah*, the fewer problems we will have.

Lishmah is a lofty level of development, and it is difficult to reach. I was told by Rabbi A.H. Lapin in the name of Rabbi Eliyahu Lopian, that doing things *lishmah* is as difficult as breaking the cask and keeping the wine. Nevertheless, it is possible, and we do strive to reach that level.

CULTIVATING THE TRAIT OF CHESSED LISHMAH

How do we train ourselves to do *chessed lishmah*? There are a number of ways.

PRACTICING GIVING

According to Rabbi Dessler,[12] we first have to practice giving. If we are focused on taking, we will always want more and never be satisfied or grateful for what we do have:

> When a "taker" sees other people doing completely unselfish acts he simply does not believe what he sees. He insists on calculating and speculating what selfish ends these apparently unselfish acts must serve. It is obvious to him that everyone must be like himself. He has never experienced the doing of *chessed*, and therefore, he cannot admit the existence of such unselfishness. (p.142)

We have to turn away from taking and start giving.

RECOGNIZING HUMAN GIVING

Once we start giving, we become attuned to giving. We have probably all had the experience of not *really* noticing someone's *chessed* to us until we did the same *chessed* ourselves. For example, we might have taken it for granted that someone brought us a pot of chicken soup when we weren't feeling well. "No big deal, they were making soup for their family and made a little more." But until the day that we took time out of our own busy schedules to shop for the ingredients, make the soup, transfer it to a portable container, clean up the kitchen, get in the car and deliver it, we didn't really comprehend the effort involved. Similarly, as parents, we finally realize all that our parents did for us. Only a giver can recognize giving.

RECOGNIZING GOD'S GIVING

Once we begin to perceive giving, we can start noticing the manifold blessings that God bestows on us. Here are a few examples of God's *chessed* that we may take for granted:[13]

> The miracle of food is the greatest evidence of kindliness. This miracle includes also the tremendously complex miracle of eating. The ability to use the food is an overwhelming marvel. The eyes first scan the food to see whether the color indicates ripeness or deterioration. The nose tests the odor of the food to discover its eligibility for entry. The lips serve as a sucking disk and prevent liquids from spilling out. The front teeth are all sharp-edged, to cut off a piece which is conveniently-sized for chewing. The tongue and the elastic cheeks manipulate the morsel toward the rough-surfaced

back teeth which grind the food. Meanwhile, the saliva assists by softening the food, at the same time beginning the digestive process by chemical action upon the food. The teeth are coated with a marvelously hard and smooth enamel, and the jaws have a surprisingly powerful leverage which enables them to exert great pressure in biting and chewing. Meanwhile, the tongue darts to and fro, testing the food for admission to the inner body . . . It tests for decay, and when an improper taste is discovered, it warns the brain, which sets up an alarm: the sensation of disgust and nausea. Even if such food is swallowed because its taste was disguised, the nerves in the digestive organs give the alarm and the entire process is suddenly reversed to vomit out and expel the harmful matter.

[When holding a glassful of water, a Jew] considers the marvel whereby two gases, neither of which can quench his thirst, are united into a clear and sparkling liquid which pours down his throat in a life-giving stream. No liquid in the world can take the place of water for relief of thirst. This fluid is the most potent of all elixirs, although its availability and its inexpensiveness cause it to be overlooked. It is the universal solvent. It is the vehicle of digestion, of blood circulation, of the numerous body secretions and of the process of expulsion of waste materials. It is the cooling agent in the sweating process. It is the major part of the body's weight. If water could be obtained only from the pharmacist, it would be the most costly of liquors, both for its vital properties and for its enjoyment.

Even walking is a delight for the man who thinks. As his thigh swings forward in effortless motion, he considers the miracle of the smoothly-functioning joints, bathed in anti-friction liquid. He marvels as his knee bends and straightens again and again, without any sensation of chafing or scraping. The ankle joints and the complex arch bones flex and relax in easy motion. He delights in his ability to maintain his balance and in his ability to rotate his head to view the world around him. He considers the eye lenses, which can view distant objects and then can instantaneously be adjusted to focus on nearby objects. His two ears, equipped with whorls and hollows to catch and gather the sound waves, are perched strategically on both sides of his head like earphones. He collects from the world around him the sights, sounds and smells which he stores away in the infinite storehouse of the brain, to be recalled and chosen, when needed, from the millions of pictures and sounds and smells which are stored up therein.

Why don't we usually notice these (and other) examples of God's *chessed?* According to Rabbi Avigdor Miller: [14]

The universal benefits of men are ignored and bring no pleasure. The popular criterion of happiness is to possess more than others; but *that which all commonly possess* is despised. Air, light, water, food, clothing, shelter, health and the other gifts of man are not considered worthy of gratitude. If the happiness of life passes by unnoticed, *then it also passes by unenjoyed.* If one sees no happiness in his lot, *one will indeed not see reason to be grateful to the Creator.* It is only when one is about to leave the world that one looks back with regret, too late, at all one possessed but failed to enjoy.

ACKNOWLEDGING AND APPRECIATING GIVING

When we examine the details of life we discover infinite reasons to be grateful to God. We begin to notice the numberless kindnesses that God showers on us, and we can begin to develop the quality of *hakoras hatov,* or acknowledging and appreciating His *chessed.*

LOVE GOD AND GIVE AS HE GIVES

Think what our lives would be like if we felt truly grateful for everything we have, if we really perceived everything we have as a gift from God. Our hearts would swell with love and gratitude to God. Our cups would truly "run over," and we would give to others like "a river in flood whose life-giving waters overflow all its banks."[15]

SEEKING PEACE

At the religious level, we also develop a need for peace. Because we identify with others as children of the same Father, we want peace to prevail. Strife and contention upset us, and we try to smooth ruffled feathers and soothe hurt feelings. We try to be *rodfei shalom* (pursuers of peace), rather than pursuers of honor.

We will use our horse-and-rider metaphor to explain how this works. Suppose you were shopping in the supermarket. As you walk toward the checkout counter with the shortest line, someone shoves into you with her basket and says loudly, "I was here first. I saw you trying to get in front of me, but you're not going to get away with it." What do you do? If you think you are a horse, you kick back. You say, "Oh no, you're not going to beat me out. I was here first, and I can prove it." What do you do if you know that you are the rider? You realize that your horse has been kicked by an angry horse whose rider is asleep. You know that your own horse has a tendency to kick back. So the first thing you do is calm down your own horse. "Okay, I know you're hurt, but it will be all right." Then you try to calm down the other horse. You say, "I'm sorry. I must have been distracted and I didn't see you. I really appreciate your forgiving me. Please, go ahead." Then, you might even try to wake up the other rider. You might say, "How wonderful it is that we are all created in the image of God and we can solve our little problems and get along with each other." Obviously, the third step can't always be taken. If trying to awaken the other rider will only make the horse angrier, it is better to stop after the first two steps: calming down your own horse and calming down the other's horse.

Let us now meet two people who became *baalei chessed veshalom* (masters of giving and peace).

PERSONIFICATION OF THE LIFE FORCE

Mr. and Mrs. Gold are a married couple in their sixties. Mr. Gold is a retired architect, and Mrs. Gold is a retired elementary school teacher. They were both raised and lived most of their lives as Conservative Jews. They have three grown children and two grandchildren whom they don't see too often because they do not live nearby.

About seven years ago, while Mr. Gold was still working as an architect, a co-worker, Alan, invited the Golds to a *Shabbos* meal at his home. Alan was an observant Jew who lived in a very cohesive Torah community. The Golds were not particularly interested in the religious aspects of the visit, but they were both moved by the warmth, joy and dedication they saw in Alan's home and in the community.

Alan invited the Golds back again, this time for an entire *Shabbos*. After their complete *Shabbos* experience, the Golds felt they had found something they didn't even know they were seeking. They felt spiritually uplifted by the experience. They started going to the community *shul* occasionally, and eventually they joined a Torah class taught by the rabbi. Little by little, they took on *mitzvos* and attended more classes. They enjoyed the gracious hospitality of their community friends on many a *Shabbos* and holiday.

As they got to know the community better, the Golds were struck by the quality of giving and peace that they saw. People gave of themselves (*chessed*) and their resources (*tzeddakah*) willingly, joyfully and with love. And they didn't let little things come between them. For example, when the women in the community prepared the *seudah* (meal) for the *bris* (circumcision) of a friend's baby, it was as if they were all one family. And when the men got together to build a retaining wall in back of the *shul*, they did it as they would for their own homes. Everyone contributed what they could. There were no expressions of jealousy, and no contribution was more highly prized than another.

The Golds, who had always been generous people, realized that this giving was different from the kind of giving to which they were accustomed. Their friends were all self-sufficient and didn't need much help from each other. The few circumcisions they went to were catered, and all work was done by paid laborers. They sent cards to each other when sick and shared birthday and anniversary celebrations, but for the most part, they all led separate lives, coming together only for social events. Their main giving was *tzeddakah*, but there were so many "causes" competing for their donations that they seldom felt they had enough information to evaluate which were truly deserving.

The Golds' inherent generosity impelled them to give, but they seldom felt sure that they had done the right thing.

In fact, their giving often left them feeling guilty, dissatisfied and sometimes resentful. Maybe they should have given more to the Peace Fund than to the Anti-Pollution League. Should they have given to the boys who came to the door for money for uniforms for their baseball team, or should those boys be earning the money? And how about the request they got for a contribution to a fund for a specially-equipped classroom for handicapped children? Didn't their taxes cover that? Surely, these were all worthwhile causes, but "we just have to draw the line somewhere!" Sometimes they got so frustrated trying to decide where to draw the line that they felt like withdrawing their support from all causes.

The major difference they saw in the Torah community was that giving was an integral part of daily life. Everyone was involved in giving to the community and the larger Torah community in some way. After about a year, the Golds realized that the spirit of giving had touched them deeply. They woke up every morning feeling a debt of gratitude to God, their rabbi and their new friends for giving their lives a new sense of purpose and meaning.

A year after their first *Shabbos* experience, the Golds moved into the community so they could live a Torah life more fully. After a few months, everyone wondered how they had ever gotten along without them. Whenever anyone needed anything, the Golds were there. A young man from the community was immobilized with a leg injury, and at the Golds' insistence, he moved into their home to recuperate. The Golds were his nurses, cooks, secretaries and companions until he was back on his feet again.

Mrs. Gold was always available to babysit, cook for the sick, teach little girls to sew, make decorations for community celebrations, organize events and consult to the school.

She often helped her friends deal with their interpersonal problems, always helping them find a peaceful solution to their difficulties. There seemed to be no limit to the energy and time she had to do things for others.

Mr. Gold donated his architectural skills and life experience to the community in many ways. He designed and helped convert two small rooms into a large *beis midrash* (study hall), and he designed many of the community *sukkos* (temporary dwellings needed for observance of the holiday of *Sukkos*). He was a virtual fountain of technical wisdom to all who wished to drink from it. In addition, he was a father figure to many of the younger people whose own families were either far away or unsympathetic to their Torah lives.

The Golds now gave more generously of themselves and their resources than ever before. They had clear Torah guidelines as to which causes to support. They eagerly sought opportunities to give *tzeddakah* and do *chessed*, and somehow, they always seemed to have more to give. In some cases they could see and enjoy the fruits of their giving, but even when they couldn't see direct results, they enjoyed the satisfaction of knowing that their money and service were helping people who were living Torah lives.

CHESSED AND BEYOND

We have traced a process that starts with giving *shelo lishmah* and ends with loving God and being able to give as He gives, *lishmah*. It is crucial that we train ourselves in the "holy virtue" of *chessed* because, as Rabbi Dessler says:[16]

It is the power of giving which gives the final rectification and fulfillment to the whole of creation. Through it the barriers of selfishness are broken down and the divine *chessed* can come to its final fulfillment." (p.143)

We can—and must—contribute to the final rectification of the world and the fulfillment of God's plan to bestow the ultimate *chessed* upon us in the World-to-Come. Let us prepare ourselves for the splendor of the Divine Presence by clinging to His attributes and becoming lovers of *chessed*.

SUMMARY

At the religious level of the soul our center of gravity shifts from taking to giving. We need people so that we can express our God-like identity by doing acts of *chessed* for them and by seeking peace.

1. Takers harm each other, givers complete each other.

2. We can learn to give as God gives, *lishmah* (for its own sake), by starting out *shelo lishmah* (out of concern for ourselves). If our intention is to reach the point of *lishmah*, our selfish urges will be transformed.

3. To accomplish this we have to: practice giving; perceive human giving; perceive God's giving; acknowledge and appreciate giving; and love God and give as He gives.

When we truly identify with our soul and recognize our common divine root, we pursue peace rather than honor.

CHAPTER 16

THE RELIGIOUS LEVEL

Sanctification of Life

If the relationship to God is to be complete, it must engage man in his entirety. We can know nothing of the religion of a pure soul. Our task is to establish the religious reality of man. Since man is neither only soul nor only body, but both joined to each other, both these constituent elements within man must be related to God, each in a manner adequate to its own nature.[1]

Now we come to the religious level of the sensory/emotional ladder.

We are now being activated by the religious soul, with its theme of unity. We long for harmony, wholeness and sanctity in our existence. We still have our elemental needs for pleasure and our sensory

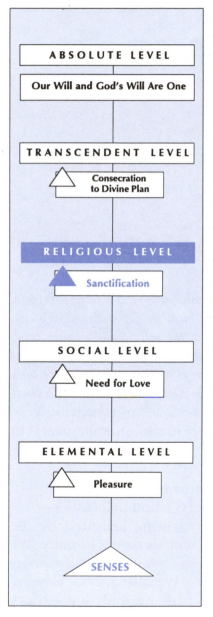

stimulation and our social need for love, but we now yearn to express these needs in sanctified ways.

SANCTIFICATION

What is sanctification? For many of us, the word may bring to mind the pursuit of religious ecstasy through denial of the body and abstention from the pleasures of life: contemplation, meditation, flagellation, the monk in the monastery, the guru high in the Himalayas. This is not the Jewish concept of sanctity! As Rabbi Samson Raphael Hirsch[2] tells us, in Torah, the body is just as holy as the soul:

> The Torah does not forbid the gratification of any legitimate and natural desire; it destroys no natural impulse. On the contrary, it purifies and sanctifies even our lower natural instincts

and desires by using them with wise limitation for the purposes designated by the Creator.

Rabbi Hirsch is telling us that in Torah life, we use our lower needs in the service of our higher needs. We sanctify ourselves by combining body and soul. Let's return to our horse-and-rider metaphor to explain this more fully.

A basic human need is to make progress. If we separate horse and rider, each will try to progress in its own way. The horse will try to get more physical pleasure and excitement with no concern for the sensibilities of the rider. And since we adapt to physical stimulation, the horse will always be looking for something new or trying a higher dose in order to get excited. In its quest for satisfaction, the detached horse will risk destroying itself and its rider, the soul.

The rider, in its turn, will try to progress spiritually by thinking of the horse as a necessary evil. Give it just enough to sustain life and treat it with contempt and disgust. The detached rider takes the joy out of life.

In Judaism we are taught how to connect the horse and the rider. And strangely enough, as we saw in our discussion of excitement in Chapter 8, together they are capable of excitement, pleasure, and elevation far beyond the reaches of either one alone. A combination of instinctive physical love with a spiritual dimension of inter-personal love is the Jewish concept of sanctity.

SANCTIFIED LOVE

What happens to the need for love and connection when it is brought within the influence of the religious soul? There are two kinds of human love to consider, the love of people in general and the love between man and wife. We will use our horse-and-rider metaphor to help us understand the difference between the two kinds of love. The love that we should feel for people in general involves only the riders. The love between a husband and wife, however, involves both horse and rider. The seed of love between husband and wife is an attraction between both horses and riders. If the attraction is for one part only, the love is self-destructive. Acceptance strengthens the love between the horses (we don't have to compete with other horses), and giving develops the love between the riders. Here at the religious level, we add one more dimension, and that is sanctity.

How do we sanctify the love between man and wife? Our answer starts with a reminder that there are two kinds of pleasure, physical and spiritual (see Chapter 8). Briefly, in the physical realm, pleasure is not cumulative and sensitivity decreases. In the spiritual realm, pleasure is cumulative and sensitivity increases. Physical pleasure is very intense and encompassing. Spiritual pleasure is more delicate and is directed upward. They each have a different essence, but if we combine them, we can have intensity that accumulates and is refined. This is the secret of sanctity, to combine the two pleasures so we get the benefit of both. We do this by taking the strong love between the horses and transferring it to the riders. Do we know how to do this? No! If not for the divine instruction of God we wouldn't have the vaguest idea of how to sanctify love. It is totally out of the realm of secular thinking. We need Torah to give us the laws of family purity and use of the *mikveh* (ritual bath). [3]

When physical love is transformed into spiritual love, it grows deeper and stronger in spite of the fact that we all age and become less physically attractive. Even though the engine is weaker, the love accumulates, and hence the bond grows stronger and stronger through the years. The two horses may be climbing more slowly, but they have already ascended to great heights.

When sanctity is very important to us, it doesn't really matter if we see more attractive horses. Our sanctified love has reached such great heights that no one can compete. It is always very touching to see old people who have spent a lifetime together and are very much in love with each other. All their combined love has accumulated. Judaism tells us how to do this.

Now we turn to the discussion of the love of people in general. Remember that at the social level, we felt very ennobled by human love, but we learned that it was really ennobling only when it was a step on the journey to love of God. All other kinds of love, as good and important as they are, can become substitutes for the love of God if they are seen as ends in themselves. When this happens, our spiritual progress is retarded, and we are prevented from elevating our capacity to love. Only when the powerful feelings associated with love are connected to their roots in the religious soul is the experience of love transformed. Then we are filled with the love of God. Human love is still very important, but it is not the final step.

As we said above, love (for people in general and between man and wife) is strengthened by giving. As Rabbi Dessler points out, love flows in the direction of giving, not in the direction of receiving: "the one who gives, loves."[4] We love our children more than they love us because we give to them more than they can give to us. In other words, the *feeling* of love is a consequence of the *action* of giving.

> That which a person gives to another is never lost. It is an extension of his own being. He can see a part of himself in the fellow-man to whom he has given. This is the attachment between one man and his fellow to which we give the name "love".[5]

At the religious level love arises from fulfillment, not from deficiency.[6] Love based on deficiency is basically taking. We attach ourselves to others to try to get our needs filled. The love of the horse is based on deficiency. Love based on fulfillment is giving. The love of the rider is based on fulfillment.

Deficiency-based love is strong at first, but does not accumulate. Fulfillment-based love is not strong at first, but it builds and builds. It is the spiritual overflowing from our souls when we feel happy and recognize and appreciate the blessings bestowed upon us. It is the way God, who lacks nothing, loves us.

When we feel fulfilled, we do not have to draw things to ourselves from outside. When we feel deprived and dissatisfied, however, we crave things beyond our reach. We may get so caught up in craving that we cannot give. If we cannot give, we cannot love. All we can do is try to fill the void we feel. We then focus on *being loved* and *getting*, rather than on *loving* and *giving*.

A case in point was a very attractive young woman who was quite unhappy because all of her friends were getting married and she was still single. She was introduced to many suitable young men, but all of the arrangements ended after one or two meetings. The problem was that she was so preoccupied with assessing whether she could get what she thought she needed from a husband that she never gave anything of herself. Her self-absorption and focus on getting made her so closed off that she couldn't give. And nothing anyone gave her was ever enough to fill the void she felt. Under these conditions, it was impossible for love to develop.

SANCTIFIED SELF-LOVE

Now that we know what happens to love when it is activated by the religious soul, we can return to the discussion of self-love which we started in Chapter 12. As we said, self-love or self-esteem is a necessary ingredient in the healthy personality. But here at the religious level, we need unity and we are beginning to think about concepts like peace, harmony and loving others the way we love ourselves. Just as the word "love" means very different things at the social level than it does at the religious level, "self-love" means something very different now than it did before.

To fully explain elevated self-love we will include some ideas from the transcendent level. We start by modifying our concept of the word "self." In Chapter 11 we discussed Rabbi Dessler's three levels of self-identity as represented by three kinds of thoughts: "I want" thoughts, which arise from our desires (elemental level); "you ought to" thoughts, which contain spiritual stirrings (social level); and "He wants me to" thoughts, which represent pure spirituality (religious level). Thoughts from this higher source don't seem to be our own; they seem to come from outside.

We learned in Chapter 10 that before we have elevated ourselves to the religious and transcendent levels we identify with the "I" of the lower soul. We perceive the voices of the higher levels as alien forces which make unpleasant demands on us. We don't realize that just the opposite is true. When we succeed in elevating ourselves to the higher levels, our reference for "I" changes. What used to be perceived as "He wants" becomes "I want." In other words, we begin to identify with the needs of the religious soul. They are no longer experienced as alien messages. They are acknowledged and accepted as our own deepest needs. We internalize the voice of our religious soul and love it. This is crucial, because if we are to continue to make progress, each of us must "treat the demands coming from his higher self with mercy and compassion."[7]

The promptings of the elemental "I" are still experienced, but they become much less central. We experience them in a more detached way. We feel them, but we don't allow them to determine our thoughts and actions.

Remember our horse and rider? Another way to say what Rabbi Dessler is saying is that we have to know that we are the riders, not the horses. We have to identify our sense of self with our higher level needs, not our lower level needs. Otherwise, we will act with "cruelty to our precious soul."[8] The horse will drag the rider through the dirt. Real self-love means loving our riders, our higher selves, and this in turn means that we will see our "selves" as divine sparks seeking connection with our root.

THE DIFFICULTIES OF SANCTITY

Activation by the religious soul causes profound spiritual and psychological changes in us. The religious soul wants exclusive domain over us. It wants us to dedicate all the forces of the body to our partnership with God. But, at the religious stage *both* the religious soul and the lower souls act on us. They "wage war against each other over the body and all its organs."[9] They both demand total obedience from the body. Unfortunately, the elemental soul wants just the opposite of what the religious soul wants. It wants us to see ourselves as the center of being, as ends in ourselves. It wants us to satisfy our sensory needs as quickly and easily as possible. The lower soul has no patience for the delays and restrictions required for sanctification.

We experience the war between the elemental soul and the religious soul as an internal struggle between what we think we *want* to do and what we think we *should* do, between what feels good at the moment and what we think is right. Let's translate this into a real-life term. The elemental soul says, "I'm hungry. There's the cookie jar. I'll eat some cookies." Along comes the religious soul and adds an entirely new dimension to eating—sanctification. The religious soul says, "I'm hungry. There's the cookie jar, but before I eat, I want to get closer to God by sitting down and saying a blessing to thank Him for the food He has given me."

How does reciting a blessing bring us closer to God? The purpose of the blessing, like any *mitzvah*, is to unite the body and the soul. In general, we know that we should be grateful to God for everything we are and everything we have. But the truth is that our gratitude is more strongly evoked by direct reinforcement of needs than by general principles. When we're hungry, we can use the physical pleasure of eating to reawaken our gratitude. We can be grateful for the hunger which reminds us that we depend on God to fill our needs, and we can be grateful for the food which tastes so good and gives us the strength to live and elevate ourselves. We express this gratitude by saying a blessing, both before and after we eat. By saying a blessing, we elevate our desire for food and use it as a tool to form a stronger connection with God.

The human dilemma is that both levels of the soul are directing us simultaneously. We are constantly being tempted to do things the easy way, to give in to impulses, to slip down to a lower level. One part of us is saying, "Go on, gobble up some cookies. They'll taste so good." Another part is saying, "You're not an animal. Don't eat like one." If we give in to temptation and grab a cookie and eat it without remembering the source of our sustenance, the elemental soul has won a victory.

This struggle is an essential part of the process of elevation and sanctification. Without conflict, there is no moral choice and no progress.

When we speak of sanctifying the senses, we are talking about sanctifying the most intimate and ordinary details of our lives. This includes the way we eat and drink and dress, the things we choose to see and hear, and the way we relate to each other at home, at work and in social situations. It even includes going to sleep.

Before we go to sleep at night we say a special *brachah* asking God to please let us awaken in the morning. It is an acknowledgment that life and death are in the hands of God and that we might die in our sleep. When we go to sleep we give ourselves to God. We ask God for another day of life that we can use to make progress. This makes life precious. It reminds us that sleep is a loss of awareness and a taste of death. It makes us aware that we have completed one more cycle of sleep and wakefulness. It gives us a chance to take account of the day we just lived, just as we have to take account of our lives when we die. For those who sanctify life, death is a constructive power and being reminded of it is uplifting. For those who don't sanctify life, death is a terrifying tragedy (see Chapter 7) and not something they would like to be reminded of just before going to sleep.

It is in these everyday events, the way we eat, the way we go to sleep, the way we relate to each other, that we are most apt to fail. Our habits are so deeply ingrained that it requires an iron will to stop ourselves and think about what we are about to do. In a way, it is easier to perform heroic acts than to be watchful of ourselves from moment to moment.

The religious soul helps us fight the battle by making us feel empty and desolate if we follow our senses and live as if we were animals. It prods us to search for something to fill the aching void which self-indulgence inevitably creates.

Let us look at two people who were able to raise themselves to the religious level.

THE SANCTIFIED SENSUAL

Nachum, his wife Naomi and their six children live in a Torah community. Nachum and Naomi are *baalei teshuvah* who have striven diligently for many years to take Torah "into their hearts." Nachum works as an engineer, and Naomi, who gave up a career as a graphic artist, devotes herself to family and home. She donates her talents to community projects as time permits. Their entire lives revolve around learning and living Torah. Nachum and Naomi both learn Torah with their rabbi and other teachers in their community. They also teach more recent *baalei teshuvah*; Nachum teaches a *shiur* on *davening,* and Naomi, who is fluent in Hebrew, teaches Hebrew to a class of women.

Nachum and Naomi have so completely integrated Torah into their lives that they don't have any conflict about being *shomer mitzvos* (keeping the laws of Torah). But they remember that when they first considered Torah life they said, "We can imagine keeping a kosher home and not working on *Shabbos*, but one thing we can't give up is eating in our favorite non-kosher restaurants." To their own amazement, when they became *shomer Shabbos* and started enjoying the sanctity and warmth of eating *Shabbos* meals with family and friends, they realized that "eating out" was no longer the center of their lives. They still enjoy good food, but taking their "horses" out to eat is just not as important as it used to be now that they know the harmony and joy they feel when both the horse and the rider are satisfied in a unified way.

And so it is with their relationship. They were initially very skeptical about being able to keep the laws of family purity. Naomi, whose first experience of spirituality was as a Sixties "love child," thought that the rules would stifle her spontaneity and deaden her responsiveness. But she was delighted to find that when she and Nachum sanctified their needs for connection and stimulation by expressing them within the Torah framework, their love and pleasure grew.

Nachum and Naomi found that their marriage had much more meaning to them when they were able to see it as a holy union. One of the results of their shared commitment to spiritual elevation was that their love for each other deepened. From the change in their love they began to sense the delight that they could experience from loving God and feeling His love for them: ("If human love is capable of bringing us such joy, how much more so is love of God"). In a paradoxical way, their human love was reduced by being seen as secondary to the love of God, but it was also elevated and enhanced by being expressed in a sanctified way. They loved more, but they also knew that there was something beyond their human love.

Nachum and Naomi are certainly not free of conflict. Since both the lower and higher levels of the soul are still acting on them, they still get caught up in struggles with more elemental impulses. But the battleground of their struggles is at a much higher *bechirah* (free will) level. Nachum struggles to concentrate more on his learning. Naomi struggles to fulfill the *mitzvah* of honoring her mother and father even though they are critical of her religious "fanaticism." There are struggles at every stage of development, but Nachum and Naomi have raised their struggles to the religious level.

THE NEXT STEP

At the religious level, both the lower and higher levels of the soul still demand complete dominion over the body. We are often tempted, if only for a moment, to take the easy way out and give in to the demands of the elemental soul. But by the time we have reached the religious level, we have had a taste of something so much deeper, so much more satisfying, so enriching, that we are less easily influenced by the deceptions of the lower soul. We can't be tempted to drive on *Shabbos* or eat *treif* food. Those things are now in conquered territory; they are below the *bechirah* point.

But, as we saw with Nachum and Naomi, we face new conflicts all the time as we struggle to elevate ourselves. We struggle to be able to dedicate *all* of our resources to our partnership with God. At this level we can at least sense what an enormous relief it would be to be freed from the ceaseless, futile demands of the elemental soul.

SUMMARY

At the religious level of the sensory/emotional ladder, our elemental needs for pleasure and stimulation, and our social level needs for love and belonging, are transformed into the need for sanctification.

SANCTIFICATION

1. We sanctify ourselves by combining body and soul.

2. We use the intense immediacy of physical feeling as fuel for spiritual elevation. Our hunger reminds us that we depend on God to fill our needs, and eating reawakens our gratitude to God for His bountiful sustenance.

3. We express our awareness of God's *chessed* by saying blessings.

DIFFICULTIES IN ACHIEVING SANCTITY

1. Both the religious soul and lower levels of the soul act on us simultaneously, each wanting dominion over the body. We experience this as an internal struggle between what we want to do and what we should do.

2. Struggle is an essential part of the process of elevation

and sanctification. Without conflict, there is no moral choice and no progress.

SANCTIFIED LOVE

1.Love between man and wife: The Torah's laws of family purity teach us how to take physical attraction and use it as fuel for spiritual love.

2. Love between people in general: Love is strengthened by giving. When we feel happy and fulfilled, and when we recognize and appreciate the blessings bestowed on us, our love for others is a spiritual overflowing from our souls.

SANCTIFIED SELF-LOVE

1. We identify with the voice of the religious soul and recognize it as an expression of our own deepest needs.

2. We know that we are riders, not horses, and we love ourselves for being divine sparks.

CHAPTER 17

The Need for Truth

For He is a God of truth, His Torah is true, His Prophets are true, and He performs an abundance of deeds of goodness and truth.[1]

We have elevated ourselves to the religious level of the intellect. Here at the religious level, the soul gives us a *need* for unity and the *power* of unification. We have a need for a coherent world view and a drive to harmonize all the needs and powers of the previous levels into one overarching identity.

What happens when the religious soul activates the intellect? We develop a burning need for *truth*. We are still curious, but it is not the idle curiosity of the elemental person. We want to know the truth about the world so that we can marvel at God's creation and direction of the universe. As the Chazon Ish said: [2]

> If a person possesses a noble soul . . . the world looms imposingly as an impenetrable riddle, wondrous and mystical. His heart and mind are enwrapped in this riddle. He feels anguished, lifeless; his only interest is in this riddle. His soul pines away to know its secret.
>
> We still want meaning in our lives, but we are no longer satisfied with meaning based on our own biased preferences and beliefs. We look for purpose based on truths that transcend the human limits of perception.

At the social level, we tried very hard to give our lives meaning. We tried philosophies, causes, personal growth and relationships in an attempt to go beyond the narrow self-absorption that characterized us at the elemental level. Here at the religious level, however, where we develop a need for truth and integrity in our lives, we come to see that we cannot trust our own meanings. If we are scrupulously honest with ourselves, we have to admit that it is almost impossible for us to be objective and logical when dealing with matters that affect us personally. We tend to take positions that support our world view and dismiss those that contradict it. We see and hear only what we want to see and hear. As the seventeenth century philosopher Gabriel Pascal said, "The heart has a thousand reasons which reason does not know."[3]

To cite a personal example, I once owned a home alongside a beautiful, historic canal in verdant farmland. I could walk out my front door and stroll along the wooded tow path, canoe in the quiet waters and see abundant wildlife in their natural habitat. At that time, I was opposed to proposals to develop the area with parks and recreational facilities. I was convinced that making the area more accessible would destroy it by bringing in people who would not respect its special qualities. In my own eyes, my position was a noble one; development was ecologically and historically unsound. However, when I no longer owned property near the canal, my position switched. From my new perspective, I saw very clearly (I thought) that the uniqueness of the area could be preserved while *at the same time* providing pleasure to a wider range of people. I now felt even more noble supporting the development of public parks in the canal area. My new position was not only ecologically and historically sound, it was also egalitarian. The truth was, of course, that in each instance I tried to justify my own selfish motives and interests with noble sentiments.

Rabbi Dessler explains[4] this phenomenon beautifully. He points out that every individual is prone to becoming

> ensnared in the pitfalls of self-deception, as a result of the almost imperceptible, subconscious influence of his own subjective desires. Thus, the individual may find that his entire thought-process will become beclouded, and that he will become blinded to the truth, whenever a situation arises

which may come into conflict with his own personal *negius*—his subtle, often subconscious, subjective motivations.

We see that it is very difficult to rise above our own personal desires to find the truth. How, then, is the need for truth manifested?

THE NEED FOR THE TRUTH

A woman has a treasured diamond ring, which she wears proudly. She loves to see it sparkle in the light. It is her most prized possession. One day, however, an uncle of hers, who happens to be a gemologist, comes to visit. She shows him her ring, hoping of course, to hear how valuable and beautiful it is. He tells her that the diamond is not the perfect blue-white jewel she thought it was. It has a flaw that reduces its value somewhat. The woman is dismayed. She looks at the ring, but she simply cannot see what her uncle's trained eye sees. Objectively, the stone looks exactly the same to her as before. But she trusts her uncle. She knows he wouldn't lie to her. The dance of sparkling light no longer thrills her. In fact, she wants to get rid of the ring. Her uncle says, "Don't be silly. No one but an expert could see the flaw. It is still a beautiful and valuable stone." But now that she knows *the truth*, she feels frustrated and angry every time she looks at the ring.

We see a similar demand for authenticity in the world of art ("Is this really a Rembrandt?") and the world of literature ("Who really wrote Shakespeare's plays?"). At a more trivial level, we have the brand-name phenomenon. Many of us insist on clothes emblazoned with the designer's crest to show one and all that we have the "real thing."

These demands for perfect diamonds, authentic art and brand-name merchandise are all superficial manifestations of the need for truth.

Another example of the need for truth can be found in the story of an actor who met the daughter of a millionaire. A whirlwind courtship ensued. He wined and dined her and professed undying love for her. She was deliriously happy with his attention, and after a few months, they became engaged. One day, he was at her home and was talking on the phone to a friend. His friend was telling him that he was making a big mistake because his fiancee was obviously not the right woman for him. The actor said, "I don't love her, but I want her money. As far as I'm concerned, being married to her is a job, and the pay is great." The fiancee's brother overheard the conversation and was enraged. He threatened to kill the actor unless he broke the engagement. The actor said, "What's wrong with what I'm doing? I'll be faithful and make her happy. I'm a great actor and she'll never know the difference." But the brother was not pacified. He said, "It doesn't make any difference if she's happy. It will all be based on a lie."

Somehow, living a lie seems ugly to us. This is because God has implanted in us the need for the truth so that we will search for the ultimate truth.

ULTIMATE TRUTH

Psychiatrist Viktor Frankl (see Chapter 14) believed that yearning for meaning was essential for mental health: *We say that the need for truth is essential for mental health*. Frankl wrote a book entitled *The Unheard Cry for Meaning*. If we were to write the book, we would call it *The Unheard Cry for Truth*. Frankl believed that people settle for lust, power and status only when they repress their need for meaning. We say that people settle for meaning only when they repress the need for truth. The social level need for meaning is fine if it is raised to the level of a search for meaning *through truth*. The religious soul yearns for unified meaning, meaning which is consistent and all-encompassing. It will not settle for meaning based on anything less than the ultimate truth.

Truth is the cornerstone of the Torah personality. In *Alei Shur*[5] we are told that

> truth is one of the essentials of the soul ... The Almighty is truth, and the essence of the soul that emanates from Him is truth. Nevertheless, man is called "completely false" from the point of view of his physical body and its attributes. The Almighty desired that this completely false being turn into a man of truth. Truth exists potentially in a man because of his soul. His task in life is to make it his reality, so that his physical body and its attributes reflect truth.

Without truth we are miserable and lost. We need truth to elevate and unify our personalities. Without truth, how can we ever choose among the staggering array of competing values and life-style options available to us in contemporary society? Without truth, how can we strike a balance in *midos* (character traits)? Without truth, how can we ever achieve our real purpose in life of growing closer to God?

Truth is crucial both for our individual development and also for the development of a harmonious society. If we all have our own meaning or truth, if there is no cosmic meaning or absolute, universal truth which we can all recognize, then the search for truth divides and separates us: You have your truth, and I have mine. You go your way, and I go mine. Only absolute truth unifies and connects us.

Truth is a reflection of reality, and it is also a central and basic *midah* (character trait), one around which all other ethical traits revolve.[6] Truth is

> the foundation-stone . . . of all other traits, for only through truth will the individual learn to recognize his own shortcomings and weaknesses, as he strives to improve his midos, to refine his character traits and to fulfill himself as . . . a true Torah Jew.[7]

We need truth, and so God has given us two gifts which help us find truth. The first is the "truth machine." The second is the "truth perspective."[8] But before we discuss these two divine gifts, let us see what happens when the need for truth is cut off from the source of truth.

MISUSE OF THE NEED FOR TRUTH

We misuse the need for truth when we settle for relative truth. When cut off from the source of truth, the need for truth spawns a plethora of flawed and imitation truths: man-made religions, cults, psychological movements and spiritual highs through drugs, to name just a few. All these experiences may feel intensely real for the relatively short time we are experiencing them, but when they are done, they leave us with a vaguely dissatisfied feeling, as though we had just missed making contact with some fundamental reality. Just as junk food may taste great but leave us with malnutrition, spiritual junk food can feel great but leave us in despair.

Without being securely tied in to the source of truth, we can only stumble around in the dark. We, with our puny human intellects, cannot begin to comprehend our Creator or His Creation. As Rabbi Hirsch said, we must not try to understand God from the world but the world from God.[9] For us to imagine that we can be the arbiters of ultimate reality is audacious indeed.

Speculations about truth and reality are dangerous, because they may mislead us into thinking we have the real thing. Man-made "truths" may lull us into a false sense of security and well-being. Falsehood parading as truth is especially hazardous in the hands of influential and charismatic leaders. Listen to what Rabbi Eliyahu Kitov[10] has to say about the dangers of faith in the ultimate reliability of human reason.

> All idolatry is an abomination, but when Man himself becomes an idol, and all his faculties minister to the idol, he has then created an infinitely worse abomination. When wood and stone are worshiped, they inflict no greater harm or ruin than their worshippers do, because they have no spirit of their own. Whereas if man is deified, and ultimate faith is placed in the superiority of his good taste and the truth of his reason, he is then capable of evil and destructiveness without limit.

In the case of flawed or imitation diamonds, accepting falsehood as a substitute for truth may not really matter. But if we accept falsehood as a substitute for the truth about God and our purpose in life, we waste our precious lives. As Uri Zohar[11] said:

> This is a question of life and death—of a life of conscious purposeful actualization of the truth or the slow death of a misdirected and ultimately meaningless search . . .

If we turn our backs on the truth, we damage ourselves and the world. Nevertheless, those who stay open to the drive for truth can always return to the search, but those who harden their hearts against truth commit spiritual abortion.

God has given us two wondrous gifts to help us stay committed to the truth: the "truth machine" and the "truth perspective."

THE TRUTH MACHINE

People at all levels of development have a computer we call the truth machine. Built into this machine is the basic premise that "truth is good, falsehood is bad." The truth machine is programmed to do one thing and one thing only: to discriminate between truth and falsehood. When data is entered into the computer, one command is given: check the data according to the definition of the truth. Is the data true or false?

Our built-in need for the truth is so strong that we usually abide by the answer given by the truth machine. Why then, is there such a multiplicity of opinions on every subject? And why is the world torn apart by the actions of people who are passionately committed to the truth as they see it? There are three main reasons: the truth machine is not programmed to find absolute truth; some people change their definitions of truth at will or bypass the truth machine; and some people have primitive truth machines.

SHORTCOMINGS OF THE TRUTH MACHINE

First, the truth machine is not programmed to find absolute truth. The "truth" of the truth machine is relative truth, not absolute truth. We all write our own programs for the truth. An example of relative truth can be seen in two friends, Gail and Jean. Gail believes that the only real differences between men and women are physical and that even these differences are greatly exaggerated. Her definition of the truth leads her to conclude that women should be allowed to do just about everything men can do. Therefore, she has applied to an all-male club to fight discrimination against women. Jean believes that there are fundamental emotional and intellectual differences between men and woman. Her definition of the truth leads her to conclude that all-male (and all-female) social groups fill a need and should be allowed. She thinks that her friend's protest is ridiculous. Once Gail and Jean define the truth, they both follow the dictates of their truth machines. Obviously, however, each fervently believes the other is wrong, which causes a serious rift in their relationship.

Our definitions of the truth are seldom based on hard facts. They are most often based on our impressions of the world as we saw it through the eyes of childhood. These early "truths" are hard to change, but they can be changed by all-powerful authority figures (for example, a teacher, therapist or spiritual leader), or by the destruction of a person's identity and reprogramming (cults, brainwashing), or by tapping into our deepest needs and ways to fulfill them (advertisements which pair our needs for love and security with expensive gifts, e.g., a beautiful woman wearing a diamond necklace looks adoringly at a handsome man, while a resonant voice says "Diamonds are forever"). This suggestion of being able to satisfy psychospiritual needs with material acquisitions has been called "the consumable life, the buyable fantasy." (For a fuller discussion of the destructive effects of the media see Chapters 9 and 10.)

As we said above, most people are led by their own truth. Even in cases where truth doesn't seem to matter, the truth machine may be operating. It's just that the program for the truth is very distorted. A criminal might truly believe, "I need to succeed. I'll never get anywhere by working. Society is my enemy. I'm a wimp and a loser if I don't fight for my truth." Does robbery and violence fit that definition of the truth? Yes. We have to know what people's truths are in order to understand their behavior.

Second, the definition of truth can be changed. Although most people do follow the truth, there are some who create new truths at will and others who ignore even their own truth. People who do this are governed by their lower needs and values. This can happen to people at the elemental, social and religious levels. At the elemental level, the need for pleasure might take precedence over the need for the truth: "I hear all this stuff about the dangers of drugs, but they make that up just to scare you. I can take drugs without hurting myself." At the social level, if the need for status is stronger than the need for truth, a person might pass off an imitation diamond as real by redefining the truth: "It looks real, and most people can't tell the difference, so for them it is real." At the religious level, if a person has a value ("I should fit into the society around me"), he might change the commandment to wear a head-covering and say, "It's not good for the Jews to stand out, so we only need to cover our heads in *shul*."

Third, the truth machine may be too primitive. Some people have such strong lower needs, and have lied and deceived so often, that they no longer know the difference between truth and falsehood. They have accumulated so much *tumah* (for an explanation of *tumah*, see Chapter 6) that they have completely destroyed their sensitivity to the truth. Their truth machines are still active, but the command has been changed from "Find the truth" to "Take care of yourself; the world is a jungle." Such people cannot be trusted and are truly dangerous.

The most important point for us is to know that *we are the programmers*; we have to decide how to program our truth machines. Shall we look for truth or settle for something easier? This is one of the most crucial decisions we shall ever make.

A crucial decision: Let's go to court. We see a lawyer and a judge. They are both very smart. They both have enough brainpower to find the truth. The lawyer wants to demonstrate beyond the shadow of a doubt that his client is innocent. The judge, on the other hand, wants justice to be done. Which one has a better chance of finding the truth? The judge, of course, because he is looking for the truth. The lawyer is less likely to find the truth, because he is not looking for it.

We have to choose! Shall we be our own lawyers or our own judges?

In the chapter on free will (Chapter 3) choice was

defined as choosing between truth and our needs, preferences and values. People often think that we choose between good and bad, but actually that's no choice at all. Who would really choose the bad? No, we choose between truth and something that feels good to us. "I know I should visit my mother tonight, but I really want to go to my friend's party." What happens when we say, as many do in today's society, that "whatever is good for us is the truth"? Once we define truth that way, we have so blurred our choices that we have nothing from which to choose. We have lost our free will; we have lost sight of the image of God. That definition of truth is very destructive to our fundamental humanity.

THE TRUTH PERSPECTIVE

When we reach the religious level we have a programmer who yearns for the truth. So we change the program for the truth machine. We tell the truth machine to check the definition of the truth—is it absolute truth?—before it analyzes the data. This is the truth perspective: a programmer who yearns for the truth and a program to check for absolute truth.

When we have achieved the truth perspective we can resist the inclination to make the truth fit our needs and values, *even when the truth goes against our own lower level interests*. We can achieve this state of mind only if we love truth so much that we are willing to do battle with our character flaws and destroy bias at its source.

According to our Sages, the only way we can destroy bias is by learning Torah, which is the quintessence of absolute truth. In the words of Rabbi Dessler:

> Our holy Torah is "a Torah of truth." It is "from Heaven," that is, immeasurably far above human pettiness and prejudice. The ideas and outlook of the Torah are completely free of the fog of materialism which obscures our own vision. How great is the lovingkindness of Hashem, who has handed this precious treasure down to us in the midst of our darkness! He has enabled us, even in our lowly state, to use its bright vision to light up our own path . . . To the extent that we strive . . . to make its views our own, we may hope to free ourselves from our bias, gain clarity of vision and see the truth about our world and ourselves.[12]

In order to make the Torah's views our own we have to immerse ourselves in Torah learning and observe its commandments meticulously. The Chafetz Chaim said that if we devote ourselves to learning and living Torah, we will eventually reach the point where we feel as if we have already heard the *halachos* we are learning. At this point, we are penetrating into our innnermost heart where truth is natural and undistorted.

If we do not make the effort to elevate ourselves spiritually, all we will find at the bottom of our hearts is what was put there by our conditioning. There will be a "dullness of heart" which keeps us from discerning the truth. A case in point is the story of a social worker in a detention home for girls who was trying to inspire the young inmates to get an education and set higher goals for themselves. One of the girls said to her, "You're trying to change us, but I don't want to change. Who wants to be like you? I'm only sixteen, and I've already had prettier clothes, more money and more pleasure than you'll ever have." The girl saw the world through the distorted lens of her own bitter life experience. From her point of view, the truth was that she should grab all the primitive pleasures she could from a world full of abuse and hardship. Without the hard work of purification of the soul, we tend to believe that our own limited experiences represent the truth about the world, and we lose our ability to recognize the truth.

Even when we have achieved the truth perspective we can ignore the truth to follow our own whims. This is referred to in Torah as being "stiff-necked." According to Rabbi Ovadia Sforno:[13]

> It is impossible for fairness and honesty of heart to go together with stiff-neckedness. The stiff-necked person is one who follows the arbitrary will of his own heart and intention. Even if a righteous teacher shows him by the clearest proof that his intention is not good and will inevitably lead to destruction, he will not turn to the teacher; it is as if his neck is as hard as an iron sinew making it impossible for him to turn in any other direction but the one his will originally dictated.

Rabbi Dessler explains that "not turning to the teacher" means that we will not apply the truths we know to our own hearts.

Why, if we know the ultimate truth, do we become stiff-necked? Why do we harden our hearts against the truth?

God has implanted in us a very strong inclination to accept falsehood as truth. If we didn't have this inclination, we wouldn't have the power of free choice. If the truth could present itself unopposed, in all its glory, we would have no choice but to follow the path of the truth. So we are inclined to satisfy our lower level needs cut off from our religious need for unity. For example, at a business luncheon we might find ourselves thinking of our needs for pleasure (Level 1) and belonging (Level 2): "The catered lunches (non-kosher) everyone else is eating look so delicious. Why should I be different? And why should I settle for some uncut fruit for lunch? It will ruin my business relationships to set myself apart, and I won't be able to concentrate on business if I don't eat well. So for the sake of my family, I'll just eat what everyone else is eating when I'm doing business. I'll still keep kosher at home."

When we sever lower needs from higher needs we risk impairing the sensitivity of the religious soul. As Rambam[14] said, just as we can be sick in body, we can be sick in soul. When we are sick in body, the bitter can taste sweet and the sweet bitter. When we are sick in soul, falsehood can seem like truth, and truth can seem like falsehood. We can reach the point where we are so committed to falsehood that we no longer have the choice to choose truth.

So how can we be sure we are not fooling the truth machine and capitulating to self-deception? For this, we have to develop the "truth perspective."

The words of Torah, if studied with sincerity, intense effort and humility, have the power to sanctify and elevate us, to lift us beyond the mundane and give us a grasp of the ineffable and eternal. Rabbi Luzzatto[15] tells us that:

> The only reason the Torah has any power at all is because God bound His most precious Influence to it ... If God had not made it so, then the Torah would be no different from any other educational book involving the various aspects of natural inquiry.

The influence of the Torah is a Godly thing.

God, whose "signature is truth,"[16], has given us a way to become more like Him and to grow closer to Him. By learning His Torah, we can strengthen the truth perspective in ourselves and give truth primacy in our lives.

THE RELIGIOUS INTELLECT

Let us meet Donna, a woman whose yearning for truth has elevated her to the religious level of the intellect. Donna was raised in a secular Jewish home. Her loving parents taught her that there were no absolute truths. Whatever she believed was okay as long as it made her happy. She was not given any religious education because her parents believed that they shouldn't bias her world view. They wanted her to have an open, clear mind so that she would be free to find her own values and her own authentic way in the world.

Donna, however, always had a very strong drive for the truth. She felt very empty without a sense of meaning and reality. Her life just didn't seem worth living if she couldn't believe in something. And so, as she grew up, she tried to believe in many things. During her teens, Donna was deeply disturbed by pictures of terrified children with wartime injuries. She decided that there was no reason ever to go to war; nothing justified maiming innocent children. Donna believed that the truth was that the world would be saved if people became pacifists. She wrote letters to the President and Senators opposing the funding of arms stockpiling and weapon development. Her parents were very proud of her.

Donna went to college and became a psychology major. When she studied Freud's psychodynamic theory, she thought she had found the truth about the human personality. But when she got to Jung's analytical theory, it too sounded like the truth. And yet Freud and Jung disagreed so vehemently about the fundamentals of human nature that their friendship ended on a bitter note. She was very confused, but after studying all the theorists, she concluded that each had a piece of the truth. Her parents were very proud of her.

Jung's emphasis on the spiritual sparked an interest in learning more about spirituality, so Donna took a comparative religion course. She was fascinated by Eastern religion, joined a Buddhist organization and spent weekends at the country Zendo, meditating and working in the gardens. She thought for sure that she had now found the truth about the nature of reality. Her parents were very proud of her.

Donna graduated from college, and she went on to get a master's degree in social work. She decided that the Buddhist practices were all right if you wanted to live in a monastery, but they didn't solve the problems of the world. The truth was that she had to get out in the world and help people. Upon completing her graduate work, she got a job in a clinic that served homeless and impoverished people. Donna's parents were very proud of her.

The problem was that Donna wasn't happy. And she didn't feel she had found the truth or even her own authentic self. She went into psychotherapy in the hope of finding herself, but after a year she still felt lost. The truth still eluded her.

Let's step out of the story and analyze this situation. According to her parent's philosophy, Donna should be happy. She has personally meaningful values, values which she chose herself. And she lives according to her values.

Why, then, isn't she happy? Actually, however, for people who are sensitive to the truth, meaning is not enough. They can never really be satisfied until they find the truth. Donna could spend the rest of her life frustrated, searching in cults, philosophies and political movements for the truth. Or she could be influenced by philosopher Albert Camus[17] to believe that she has to give up her quest for the truth. But fortunately, her story has a happy ending.

Jake, one of the young men Donna dated, was involved with an organization that gave a variety of classes on Judaism. He invited her to attend a program with him. She wasn't particularly interested in the subject matter, but she liked Jake and agreed to go. Since Donna had no religious background at all, most of what she heard sounded very strange. Almost everyone she had ever known was a secular humanist or a Buddhist. It amazed her to hear that there were people who actually believed in an Almighty God, divine origins of Torah and absolute truth. In spite of the strangeness of the ideas, she found the experience fascinating and pleasant and decided to start taking classes in Judaism. Donna's parents were a little worried about her.

Donna began to learn the history of the Jewish people, how the Torah was faithfully transmitted from generation to generation and how God was revealed in nature. After a few months of classes, Donna felt that a laser beam had been focused on the world and her life. Putting God into the picture had caused a radical shift in her world view. Seeing herself as a divine spark gave her a new, uplifted sense of herself. She was exhilarated by the feeling that although she was just a beginner and couldn't put it all together yet, she had finally found the truth. She realized that she had had this feeling before, but somehow this time it seemed different.

Now Donna's parents were very worried about her. They felt she was being brainwashed into betraying her liberal upbringing.

Donna continued to learn Torah. And she continued to date Jake. She found that her relationship with him was deepening as no relationship ever had before. They shared a spiritual quest that drew them together. Within a year, Donna and Jake decided to get married and make a commitment to Torah life together. They became *shomrei mitzvos* (keepers of the commandments of the Torah) and continued to learn Torah. Within another year, Donna had a baby and stopped working. She took great pleasure and pride in developing her identity as a Jewish woman and in learning how to create a Jewish home and raise Jewish children. Donna's parents were still concerned about her "rigid" lifestyle, but they had to admit that she seemed happy. They were sure she could be just as happy without all the ritual, but they were committed to letting her do her thing and so they didn't interfere.

Donna now finds her life very satisfying. She feels authentic as a Torah Jew and has a profound sense of purpose. Not that everything is perfect, not that the truth is always easy to hear. For example, Donna found the laws of modesty very difficult to accept. They just didn't seem "natural." In her former belief system, "natural" and "good" were synonymous, so she found herself caught in quite an internal struggle. How could "unnatural" be good?

Donna's love for the truth of Torah is so great, however, that even when she can't see the logic in *Halachah* (Torah law), she takes it on. She realizes that she does many things she doesn't really understand. Even though she knows nothing about the physics of flying, she travels on jet planes, because she trusts the engineers and crew. She has started to trust the Torah to guide her even if she doesn't always understand the basis of Torah law, because when she does, her life invariably improves. Dressing modestly, for example, gives her a sense of dignity and femininity that she never dreamed of. From experiences like this, she has come to realize that while "good" used to be a prerequisite for truth, truth must be a prerequisite for good.

Donna has reached the point where she no longer doubts the truth of *Halachah*. She has found that, as her understanding of Torah deepens, things which were incomprehensible at first begin to make sense. She knows that if something about Torah doesn't seem right to her, she has to work on her *hashkafah* (outlook). She still struggles with herself, but not with Torah. Donna is well on her way to developing the truth perspective.

THE NEXT STEP

At the religious level of the intellect, we have a burning need for the truth. We delight in living and learning Torah. Being Jewish is central to our identity. If we continue on this path, we have an opportunity to elevate ourselves to an even more spiritual level where our need for faith and strength of devotion to God increase. As we grow spiritually, we free ourselves from the demands and deceptions of the ego and become able to achieve the truth perspective.

Day by day, as we learn Torah and put our learning into practice, we experience the sublime joy of being a partner with God in the act of creating ourselves in the His image.

SUMMARY

At the religious level of the intellect we develop a burning need for absolute truth.

ABSOLUTE TRUTH

We realize that we cannot trust our own meaning because we are so easily "ensnared in the pitfalls of self-deception."

Truth is the cornerstone of the Torah personality. Without it we are confused and lost.

THE TRUTH MACHINE

We all have a truth machine, or a computer programmed to discriminate between our definition of the truth and falsehood.

THE TRUTH PERSPECTIVE

1. The truth perspective is an elevated truth machine. At the religious level, we program the truth machine to discriminate between absolute truth and falsehood.

2. In order to develop the truth perspective, we have to immerse ourselves in Torah learning and observe the Torah commandments meticulously.

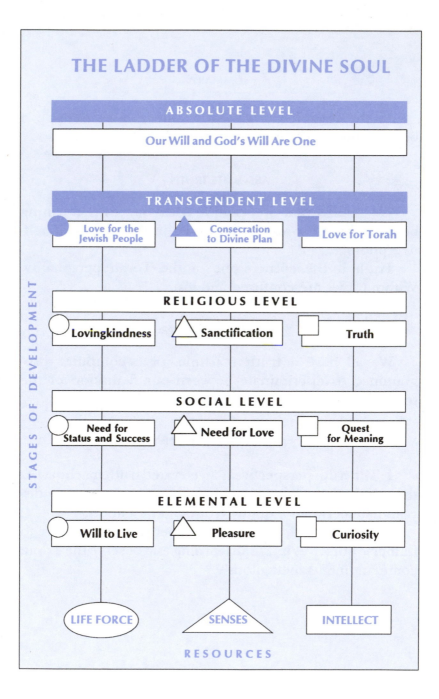

The Transcendent and Absolute Levels: Beyond the Ego

CHAPTER 18

We can now see why such importance has been placed through the ages on studying the Torah. Since it is a manifestation of the divine mind on the human level, its study assumes a dimension totally different from disciplines produced by the human mind. The person who devotes himself to penetrating the depths of the Torah internalizes the supreme knowledge. Through it one is able to be purified by attaching oneself to the Eternal.[1]

Here we are at the two levels of the soul that go beyond the ego and the body: the transcendent and absolute levels.

How does one describe a color to a blind man? All one can do is describe the impact of the color. I cannot really explain the transcendent and absolute levels, because I feel that these are beyond my limited and imperfect experience. I will just put forth some principles that I have learned which can be traced back to those whose spiritual path has reached such exalted heights.

The soul is purely spiritual at the higher levels. The vocabulary of our physical world is inadequate for this ephemeral level of existence, but the horse and rider metaphor may help us catch a glimpse of the ineffable.

At the first three levels (elemental, social and religious), there is a direct connection between the rider and the horse, the soul and the body. The rider is directly influenced by the horse, and the horse is directly influenced by the rider. For example, if the horse is old and tired, the rider has to be satisfied to go slowly, and if the rider pulls at the reigns, the horse turns in the direction of the tug.

At the fourth and fifth levels, however, there is no direct communication link between the horse and the rider. Picture the horse and rider traveling homeward. To the horse, home is where he gets to rest and eat hay. To the rider, home is the place where his beloved wife is waiting for him. His longing for his wife is the transcendent level. The home to which he is returning is the absolute level.

This metaphor gives us some idea of what it means to say that, through the chain-like structure of the soul, we may be affected by the highest influences from above, but only indirectly. The horse cannot understand that the rider is in love with his wife and is eager to see her. The horse cannot know what the man's home means to him. The horse cannot realize that the rider is motivated by higher powers. Yet, the faithful horse follows the commands of the rider and takes him where he wants to go.

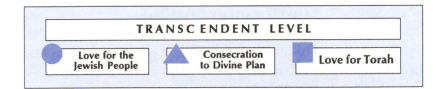

Do His will as you would your own, that He may do your will
as though it were His. Negate your will before His, that He may
negate the will of others before your will. (Ethics of the Fathers, 2:4)

This passage from *Pirkei Avos* defines the difference between the religious and transcendent levels. "Negate your will before His" fits the religious level. "Do His will as you would your own" fits the transcendent level.

At the religious level, we still have a very strong will. If our will clashes with His will, we try to dissolve it and submit to His will. For example, we sometimes pray at the appointed time even though we don't feel like praying, or we may give *tzeddakah* grudgingly. At the religious level, we are working hard to elevate and perfect ourselves, and we often have to nullify our own will and yield to His will.

At the transcendent level, we still have a will, but we are now able to do His will "as if" it were our own. We do His will joyfully and energetically, but still with the knowledge that it is His will, not our own.

The themes of the transcendent level are the need for faith and the power of devotion. At this level, faith is the air we breathe; we cannot live without it. The intensity of faith and devotion elevates our religious level powers. *Chessed* becomes love for the Jewish people, sanctity becomes *kiddush Hashem* (revealing the glory of God) and the need for the truth becomes *Torah lishmah* (learning Torah for its own sake).

LOVE FOR THE JEWISH PEOPLE

At the religious level, we could love others as ourselves, because we identified with our riders and could identify with the riders of others (see Chapter 15). At the transcendent level, we can also identify with the concept of Am Yisrael (the Jewish people). Am Yisrael has a role in the world, the role of *kiddush Hashem*. All Jews, all over the world, are partners in this goal. Everything that happens to every Jew is related to this goal. We are one army on one mission, and we feel responsible for each other's physical and spiritual welfare. At the religious level, we are very nice to our family, friends and "*shul*" members. We are concerned about the fact that the Russian Jews are assimilated, but we don't consider it our problem. At the transcendent level, we identify totally with the plight of our fellow Jews.

TORAH LISHMAH

Rabbi Shneur Zalman[2] defines *Torah lishmah* as "study with the intent of binding one's soul to God by comprehending the Torah." How can we ever achieve that level of comprehension?

Our Sages assure us that we don't have to worry, we are not expected to jump suddenly to such a high level. We have the elemental, social and religious levels, which are crucial steps along the way. And when we talk about the higher levels, we're not talking about isolating them. We're talking about combining them with all the levels that went before. So when we talk about *Torah lishmah*, we're talking about first combining it with *Torah shelo lishmah*. We're grateful that the Torah appreciates our need for *shelo lishmah*. As the *Mishnah* teaches:

> A person should always occupy himself with Torah and *mitzvos* even if not for their own sake (*shelo lishmah*), because out of doing them from ulterior motives one can come to do them for their own sake (*lishmah*).

Rabbi Dessler[3] explains that it is essential to learn Torah *shelo lishmah* before we can learn it *lishmah*. By way of illustration, he relates that his father and uncle used to get up at midnight on long winter Friday nights and learn Torah together until the morning service. His mother used to get up early to study the weekly Torah portion, and he (at the age of nine) used to get up and learn with his *rebbe* for a few hours. When it was time for morning services, his mother served them all cups of steaming hot coffee and delicious *latkes*.

> It goes without saying that the real reason I got up was in order to learn, but there is no doubt that the thought of those *latkes* made quite a difference in the way I got out of bed.[4]

Getting up to learn was *lishmah*, but getting a boost from the thought of *latkes* was *shelo lishmah*. Rabbi Dessler reassures us that it's perfectly all right to get a little help from *shelo lishmah*, as long as the goal is for the ulterior motives to be converted to pure motives.

Why is the stage of *shelo lishmah* essential for the development of *lishmah*? Because God arranged the path back to Him like a ladder planted firmly on the ground with its top reaching up to Heaven. We have to work our way to the top, progressing laboriously from step to step. Rabbi Dessler adds:

> The greatest service of God lies in the purification of motive. At the beginning of each advance toward *lishmah,* the tender plant of purity is too weak to stand on its own; it needs assistance from *shelo lishmah.* But with redoubled effort that point of *lishmah* can be won; and then on to the next advance, until one comes as close as possible to complete *lishmah.* (p.99)

At first, *lishmah* is only a fragile shoot. Therefore, we have to retain the *shelo lishmah* incentives in order to keep our motivation high while we nurture and develop the purity and strength of the *lishmah.*

At the transcendent level we reach the point of almost complete *lishmah.* Torah becomes a driving force in our lives. Learning of Torah is central to life. At the religious level, where the main goal was elevation and perfection, we needed the Torah for worldly reasons. We needed the truth of Torah to measure ourselves against, and we needed it for our identity. We loved the Torah, because we needed it. At the transcendent level, however, we love the Torah, not because we need it, but just because it is the truth. For us, God is the source of the truth, and we love God and identify with His Torah.

As we advance in our Torah learning we come to understand that:

> The very essence of Torah study is the revelation of mystery, to delve ever more deeply into the depth of Torah. The same knowledge of Torah assumes a new dimension when one immerses oneself into it more deeply. Whatever

such a person has already attained through his intense effort becomes the simple meaning; and he plunges ahead, he plumbs more deeply, he reveals the unknown, the incomprehensible. He is always occupied with the revelation of mysteries.[5]

Every insight reveals more, and every revelation yields more mystery. We see a new world unfolding infinitely before us. Torah learning is different from any other intellectual pursuit, because Torah is not bound by this world. As Rabbi Mordechai Gifter says:

> The wisdom of the holy Torah is infinite and unbounded, so its study cannot tolerate limitation. Therefore, the human being who studies it must . . . be engaged with all his strength and be preoccupied with it. Only so can Torah be studied.[6]

If we study Torah the right way we will be bound and united with its mystery. What is the right way to study Torah? We have to immerse ourselves in it. We must learn the intellectual content with awe and reverence, "return it to our hearts" and apply it to our actions. Rabbi Dessler[7] tells us that

> there is a vast empty space in the human psyche, situated between intellectual knowledge and its realization in the heart. Only when he achieves a close association of "knowledge" and "heart," with no gulf in between, will a person's actions accord with his knowledge.

When we are able to persist in our learning with a sense of reverence and awe until the learning becomes our own, the sanctity of Torah will penetrate our hearts and pervade our very being. We will truly bind our souls to God.

KIDDUSH HASHEM

> The most basic *mitzvah* of all is *kiddush Hashem*, the
> sanctification of God. This concept is all-embracing. All
> *mitzvos* and all forms of worship and service of God are
> basically forms of *kiddush Hashem*. Whenever we conquer
> our baser self to fulfill God's will we sanctify God. This is the
> stated purpose of creation.[8]

How can we sanctify God? The simplest way is to act as
good examples. Whatever we do, wherever we go, we serve
as examples of how Jews behave. If we behave in a way that
makes people say, "If that's what the Torah does for them,
it's great,"that is a *kiddush Hashem*. If, on the other hand, our
behavior makes people say, "If that's what Torah does for
them, I don't want any part of it,"that is a *chillul Hashem*.
Our behavior either makes people love God or not. In this
sense, we have a profound effect on the spiritual fate of the
world.

In the quote above, after defining *kiddush Hashem* as the
sanctification of God, Rabbi Dessler points out that God
does not need us to sanctify Him. "The whole concept of the
glorification of God is man-oriented. It is only for our
good." (p.89)

How is it beneficial to us to sanctify and glorify God?
Remember our parable about the king of extraordinary
wisdom and kindness who wanted to bestow the greatest
possible kindness on his subjects? He selected the simplest
person in his kingdom, brought him to the palace and

showed him the royal treasures and the Book of Wisdom. The man was filled with such delight that he never wanted to leave, but the king explained that, in order to earn the honor of sitting beside him, the man would have to leave the palace and go back and tell others about the glorious wonders he had seen. And then he would have to find his way back to the king and show others the way. In essence, this is *kiddush Hashem*, revealing God in the world by personal example.

There are basically four levels of motivation for us to want to return to the palace. The first is the fear of what will happen if we don't fulfill our mission (elemental level). The second is the desire for the honor of sitting next to the king (social level). The third is the desire for elevation to enable us to deserve the honor (religious level). And the fourth is longing for the king (transcendent level).

At the transcendent level we have accepted our mission of *kiddush Hashem*. We have risen above narrow ego considerations ("What are we getting out of this?"). Now we ask, "Do our actions reveal the glory of God?"

All right, let's say that I accept my role of *kiddush Hashem*. Does that mean I have be to just like every other Jew? Is there no room for individuality? Of course there is. The *mitzvos* are the tools by which we express our personalities, but each of us has an entirely different personality to express. We'll use a musical metaphor to show how this happens. Let's say that, at birth, each of us gets a group of instruments. As we grow, we are taught how to play each one. We are also taught the rules of composition and harmony. Each of us has the same task, which is to compose beautiful music with our instruments. Every composition is unique, but there is an underlying unity because they are all based on the same rules. We see this unified diversity in the lives of religious people. There is the woman who is devoted to her home and family. She raises her children to be Torah Jews, sanctifies her marriage, makes guests feel welcome, does acts of kindnes and grows closer to God. Her music is a great personality, home and family. Another woman becomes manager of a school. In addition to raising her own children, she is like a mother to hundreds of other children. Her music is an overflowing heart. There are businessmen who put *kiddush Hashem* before profit, and great scholars whose Torah learning enriches thousands of lives. Each meticulously observes the *Shabbos*, each does *chessed*, each invests mundane events with sanctity, *but each writes different beautiful music.*

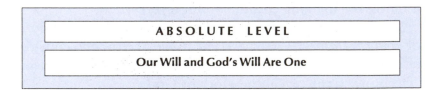

ABSOLUTE LEVEL

Our Will and God's Will Are One

Israel, the Holy Blessed One and Torah are one.[9]

At the absolute level, His will and our will are one. At this level, our will cannot clash with His; it unites with His. We know longer have to act "as if" His will were our will; it is. Now we work on strengthening our God-like will. At this point, *betzelem elokim*, or being in the image of God, has literal meaning. When our will and His will are one, we really become like Him.

We cannot really comprehend the absolute level. In the great moments of our lives, we might touch it. In rare moments, we might have a sense of being one with God. This level inspires us, but it is not where we live. The only one who lived at this level was Moses.

Now we see that the transcendent and absolute levels are tantalizingly close, and yet very difficult for most of us to attain. Step by step, as we work on elevating and unifying our personalities, we hope to come closer and closer to these sublime levels, and someday, with the help of God, to attain these great heights of spiritual development.

CHAPTER 19

How to Apply Torah Wisdom to your Life

Man is regarded as one who is constantly moving. For he must perpetually move from one [spiritual] level to another. If he will not go steadily upwards, he will decline steadily, God forbid, for it is impossible to remain on one level.[1]

This book is about spiritual progress and unification of all the parts of our bodies and souls. We each have our own unique way of making progress, we each go at a different pace, and we each start at a different place. Some of us are struggling to raise ourselves from the elemental to the social level. Others have put that struggle behind them and are now reaching for higher levels.

It is crucial to know that it doesn't matter where we start our climb. All that matters is that we start, and that we keep climbing. Before we review some of the fundamental Torah ideas presented in this book, let's return to the ten commonly held secular assumptions, presented in the Introduction, which are responsible for the kinds of problems which exist in the world today: drug abuse, broken homes and shattered children, teenage pregnancies, crime, immorality. These assumptions, if you accept them as true and use them as guidelines for your decisions, may be ruining your life. Now let us examine the contrasting Torah principle for each assumption:

SECULAR: The world is a chance phenomenon. It exists with no plan or design.

TORAH: The world is designed as a training field for our spiritual elevation.

SECULAR: There are no absolute rights and wrongs.

TORAH: There are absolute rights and wrongs. We learn them from the Torah.

SECULAR: Truth is in the eye of the observer. It is, therefore, relative and does not exist in "absolute reality."

TORAH: Relative truth is no truth at all. It is meaningless. It is nothing more than a psychological need. Torah Truth is reality.

SECULAR: Human beings are merely a link in the evolutionary chain. They are *not* of divine origin. They do *not* have any particular purpose.

TORAH: Human beings were created by God. Human development is the goal of the whole divine creation. God breathed a unique soul into man, one that sets them apart from every other species.

SECULAR: People have inherent rights, and the world is obligated to fulfill them.

TORAH: People have inherent sanctity, which obligates them to behave in the image of God.

SECULAR: Human behavior is determined by genetics and conditioning. Therefore, people are not responsible for their actions.

TORAH: People, unlike animals, have freedom of choice. Their ability to choose makes them responsible for their behavior.

SECULAR: All phenomena can ultimately be explained and controlled by science.

TORAH: Science describes physical phenomena. It cannot explain or control spiritual phenomena. It deals with what is, not what should be. Therefore, it can shed no light on values or morals, or on the purpose and meaning of human life.

SECULAR: Being happy is the most important thing in life.

TORAH: Seeking the truth is the most important thing in life. Happiness is a by-product of pursuing the truth.

SECULAR: Freedom means having as many options as possible.

TORAH: Freedom means being led by the rider, not by the horse, that is, by the soul, not the body.

SECULAR: If there is a God, His existence has nothing to do with the way the affairs of men are conducted.

TORAH: There is a God, and He is actively involved in the affairs of men. He influences us through three main channels: personal providence, whereby God gives each of us the opportunities for growth that we deserve and from which we can benefit;

He delights the soul with the level of sanctity to which we open ourselves; He moves history towards its destiny.

The contrasting Torah principles will have just the opposite effect on your life. The ten Torah principles above, plus the additional ones below, will enrich and ennoble life *if you take them into your heart and let them guide you.*

TORAH PRINCIPLES TO APPLY TO YOUR LIFE:

1. The Torah is the word of God. There is compelling logical evidence for this fact (see Appendix).

2. You are a divine spark, created by God, in His image.

3. You have a God-given purpose: to "find your way back to the palace" so that you can experience the ultimate pleasure of reunion with the King.

4. While you are searching for the palace, your goal is to train and elevate yourself and reveal God to the world by your self-example as a Jew. Remember that, as a Jew, God chose you to be a pillar of light to all. Don't try to get rid of the yoke. Be proud of the great challenge that was given to you.

5. The driving force in your life is your soul's yearning to fulfill its purpose. Your soul has awesome, uplifting powers. It beams its subliminal message to you, urging you ever onward and upward. Don't ignore the yearning of your soul; don't try to get rid of it or satisfy it with acquisitions and honor. Following your soul will bring you a sense of well-being and fulfillment.

6. The Torah was given to you by God to use as a

guidebook for your journey back to Him. The *mitzvos* are the tools you need. Use them.

7. You have free will. Through your choices, you can elevate or degrade yourself. You have the power of self-creation.

8. Spiritual progress includes two principles: elevation and unification. After climbing one rung on one ladder (elevation), it is better to catch up on the other ladders (unification) before moving up again. That way, no matter what level you are at, you will have a unified personality. Remember that the ideal Torah personality is the completely unified personality.

9. You are body and soul, horse and rider. You can use every sense, muscle, bone, organ, every impulse and desire for elevation and fulfillment.

10. Learn to identify with your rider rather than your horse. When you say "I," refer to your rider.

11. You experience two kinds of pleasure, physical and spiritual. Don't make the mistake of giving them equal status. Learn to differentiate between them. You will get the greatest pleasure from combining them.

12. Spirituality is not just prayer and fasting. It can be found in every cookie you eat (did it evoke gratitude toward God?), every tree you see (did it reveal God's wisdom and kindliness?) and every relationship you have (did you relate as a rider or a horse?). The *mitzvos* teach you how to sanctify every experience by transferring the energy of your horse to your rider.

13. The more parts of your personality you sanctify through unification, the more excitement and pleasure you will have.

14. Marriage is one of the best opportunities for sanctity.

There are three basic principles that create enduring, deepening love: accept each other's horse and create a secure atmosphere through modest thoughts and behavior; encourage each other's rider so you can progress spiritually together; combine the horse and the rider through observance of the Torah's laws of family purity.

15. Know where you stand in relation to the Truth. Remember that it's not important where you are at the moment. What matters is that you are doing your best to progress. If you do the best you can, you are on the path to righteousness. That's what God wants from you.

16. Don't avoid spiritual conflicts. Rather see them as a challenge and do your best to overcome them.

17. Judaism is not tradition. It is not a social club. It is a God-given, personal challenge. Accept it.

18. Motivation is the key to your spiritual growth. Here are some Torah principles to help you elevate and increase your motivation.

Know who you are. You have inherent dignity and infinite worth, because you are created *betzelem elokim*, in the image of God.

Your spiritual elevation depends on you and your actions, not on how you measure up to society's norms.

Internalize the "Jewish process orientation." You can live with a huge discrepancy between the real (where you are now) and the ideal (where you'd like to be) and still maintain your self-esteem. Just break your final goals down into *meaningful*, achievable sub-goals, and then take one step at a time. Know that God will give you credit for every step. He judges you by your effort, not by the final outcome. The difficulties you encounter are not just meaningless obstacles, they are purposeful challenges, tailored to your needs and abilities, designed to train you. God is your own personal coach.

19. You have a great chance to educate your children by making your home an island of sanity in a crazy world. You can create an atmosphere of sanctity, free of destructive influences. Just as you are careful to protect your children from physical contamination, protect them from spiritual contamination. Insure their high self-esteem by teaching them that they are *betzelem elokim*, in the image of God; that it is the truth that counts, not society's norms; and that they will be given credit for every small step they take to elevate themselves. Help them to set *meaningful*, achievable sub-goals and rejoice with them over their efforts. Remember that the example you set will influence them more than anything else.

20. The wisdom of the Torah is infinite. It has existed for thousands of years and has spread all over the world. If you haven't found just the right book, or just the right teacher, don't give up. Don't waste your life just because you have to struggle to find the right path. Search to find a place where you can learn Torah seriously and elevate yourself.

This brings us to the end of a shared journey. We have had a long and sometimes arduous climb from the elemental to the absolute level of spiritual development. I thank you, dear reader, for your attention, and hope that this book has been of value to you. At this point, I urge you to take action. Please, assess where you are on your spiritual path, and decide what step to take next to elevate and unify your personality.

A RATIONAL
APPROACH TO JUDAISM

BIBLIOGRAPHY

BIOGRAPHICAL
NOTES

GLOSSARY

INDEX

A RATIONAL APPROACH TO JUDAISM

This appendix has been provided for those readers whose interest may have been piqued by the ideas presented in this book but who need some reinforcement in their acceptance of the concepts of God and Torah.

Suppose you are willing to consider the possibility that God does actually exist. But being a person of rational mind and independent spirit, you cannot simply accept His existence without some kind of intellectually persuasive verification. Childhood notions of an old man with a long white beard peering at your hand in the cookie jar may have soured you on the idea of an Omniscient Being; and you have heard so many people justify their beliefs in all kinds of crackpot things by saying "I just know" that you are skeptical of anything which you are asked to accept on faith alone. I do not blame you. I am actually the same way. In fact, I often wonder if I ever would have "found" the Torah if I hadn't been introduced to it by my husband Don.

I met Don on a blind date and liked him very much. I really wanted to get to know him better—except for one thing. He was a religious Jew. He himself had recently returned to Torah learning and had not yet made a complete commitment to Torah life. If he had been exploring Hinduism, I probably would have thought it wonderful and begged to accompany him to interesting Oriental rituals. But Judaism? I was very turned off to it. First of all, I thought I already knew what Judaism was all about and second, living a Jewish life had many negative associations.

As I pointed out in the Introduction, I had, in effect, gone through an "immunization" process which left me very resistant to hearing the message of Torah. I had developed "emotional antibodies" which triggered intense rejection when the word "Jewish" was mentioned.

I was in a real bind. If I decided in advance that I just couldn't accept his way of life, it would be the end of a budding relationship with an attractive man. If I gave it a chance, there was the possibility of getting close and either ending up with a broken heart when the inevitable breakup came or, what seemed even worse at the time, actually living a Jewish life. My desire to get to know Don won out, and I opened my mind to possibilities I probably wouldn't even have considered under any other conditions.

I started going to Torah classes and hearing things that gave me a good case of what we psychologists call "cognitive dissonance." Cognitive dissonance occurs when we are confronted with new information which is inconsistent with currently held beliefs and attitudes. The usual psychological response to cognitive dissonance is discomfort and unease. The greater the investment in the beliefs and attitudes, the greater the dissonance and the greater the discomfort.

For example, suppose you recently bought a new car. You selected this particular car after doing a lot of research and concluding that it had the best safety record of all the cars in your price range. You are driving it proudly to work when you hear a news broadcaster reporting the results of a recent study of automobile safety. One of the main results is that another car in your price range has a much higher safety rating. You immediately feel very uncomfortable. You are experiencing the emotional consequences of cognitive dissonance.

At this point, you have to make a choice. You can deal with your dissonance and discomfort in three ways: by coming to terms with the new information, changing your perception of your new car and driving more carefully; trading in your new car for the other make; or completely rejecting the new information and continuing to believe that your car is the safest.

There is a very strong human tendency to take the third option and completely reject the unsettling information, because this option is most effective in getting rid of the dissonance and discomfort. No action need be taken, behaviorally or cognitively, since it is as if no new information has been received. The more attached we are to the old belief, the more likely we are to disregard the new information completely. In other words, anything that increases our sense of emotional investment in the old belief will increase our dissonance, discomfort and tendency to shut out the new. In our example, if you not only make safety your highest priority, but you also consider yourself to be an authority on the subject, you would have a very strong tendency to deny the results of the report. You would find ways to invalidate the research, e.g., "That's not really a scientific study." Or, "The research wasn't done in this part of the country, and the car handles differently in this climate." If, on the other hand, you felt that all cars were reasonably safe and therefore selected your car on the basis of style and comfort, you probably would not experience too much dissonance. There might still be a slight tendency to deny the new information, since we always want to believe that we have the best, but it would be much less upsetting. You could reduce your dissonance by saying, "It's not the safest car, but it is the classiest and most comfortable."

Now that you know about cognitive dissonance you know more about the position I was in. Later, I came to learn of a parable told by Rabbi Dessler[1] of a savage who saves the king's life and as a reward is taken into the royal treasury. He is given many empty sacks and told to fill them with whatever he wants. Not understanding the value of gold, silver and precious stones, he thinks he is being punished by forced labor for some unknown crime. Since no one is watching him he works very slowly and even takes a nap. At the end of the day, his sacks are almost empty, and when he is finally sent home with them, he is very proud of his cleverness in having outwitted the king and having such a light load to carry. But when he tells his story to some of his more sophisticated friends, they laugh at him and tell him what a fool he has been. He realizes—too late—that he should have worked with a will during that one precious day when the treasure was his for the taking.

I was that savage, and if not for the powerful attraction to Don, I might have stalked home with empty sacks, none the wiser for my first encounter with authentic Torah teachings.

What made it possible for me to open to the new information in spite of the threat to my ego? What I really believe is that I had a greater investment in developing a relationship with Don than in protecting my old beliefs and attitudes. I was therefore able to set aside my barriers to listening and really hear ideas I would otherwise have rejected automatically. Once I was able to listen, I heard intellectually compelling arguments, arguments which survived even the most rigorous philosophical scrutiny. I have come to believe in the existence of God and in the divine origin of the Torah because of the intellectual force of the arguments *and* because of the harmony and beauty of the Torah system. In this appendix I will present some of the arguments which I found so compelling.

As you read, you may find that you feel cognitive dissonance just as I did. You may feel some discomfort and a tendency to want to disregard or discredit certain conclusions even though you can't deny that they were arrived at rationally. To overcome the dissonance you will have to develop a tolerance factor. This will enable you to tolerate the emotional discomfort long enough to evaluate the arguments dispassionately. I wish I could give each of you an incentive as immediate and powerful as the one I had, but of course, that is impossible. I can only urge you, to open your heart and mind to ideas which have added new meaning and joy to my life (and the lives of thousands of others)—and just might do the same for yours.

I know that what I am asking you to do is very difficult. Many of us in today's society find it very unsettling to think of a Creator whose very existence may impose responsibilities on mankind. When confronted with this possibility we fight it all the way. This suggests a very high investment in the belief that there is no Creator, or at least no Creator who is directly involved in our lives. Why are we so attached to this belief that we are unwilling to seriously consider alternative ideas?

We may be blinded to the possibility that there is a God because we worship other "gods," gods which are palatable to modern secular minds because they parade in the intellectual disguise of "isms." The modern mind cherishes rational thought and is embarrassed and upset by the thought of the existence of something as seemingly irrational as an Absolute and Eternal God, a First Cause. The hidden gods of rationalism, relativism, liberalism, scientism, humanism or materialism, to name just a few, are much easier to live with. They exalt us to the highest position in the universe. They lull us into an illusory sense of security and control by telling us that we know best, that ultimately all the answers lie within us. They allow us to do whatever we can justify, and as I explained in the Introduction, we can use our so-called rational minds to justify just about anything. We do not want to believe that there might be a Will higher than ours, because then we just might have a responsibility to that Will.

Through the years, I have heard these attitudes expressed by clients. They have said things like: "I know what's best for me." "I make my own rules." "I don't have to do anything I don't want to do." "If God were to come down right now and tell me that was the right thing to do I still wouldn't do it if it didn't feel right to me." It is so difficult to admit that we don't always know what is best, that what we believed last year we no longer believe, that what we thought would work didn't work, that what we thought would make us happy didn't, that what "feels" so right at this moment may "feel" very different tomorrow. It is so hard to yield to the possibility that we might have to turn to a Higher Intelligence for eternal truths.

ESTABLISHING THE TRUTH OF TORAH

1. The revelation of divine design in nature. The obvious plan and purpose in nature reveals its divine origin and evokes the drive to know what God wants from us. Nature, however, cannot tell us how to relate to God. For this we need Torah.

2. The reliable process of transferring the knowledge of Torah, *unchanged*, from generation to generation.

3. The covenant God made with the Jewish people that, no matter what happens to them, they would survive. (The history of the Jewish people is, therefore, especially meaningful, revealing the deep patterns of Jewish prophecy and the fulfillment of His promise.)

4. God's covenant that the Torah will never be forgotten. No matter how oppressed, reviled and dispersed the Jews are, they will always be devoted to Torah.

5. The natural harmony between the soul of the Jew and the Torah. The truth of Torah matches the inner experience of the Jew. As Rabbi Mordechai Gifter says, "The Jewish heart is but an instrument upon which a Godly melody is played, which calls and summons Man to an awareness of God. Only this is a Jewish heart."[2]

6. Torah omnipotence. The Torah is relevant, wise and consistent. It is a living entity that survives as a unity. It is relevant for all generations in every culture.

Although design in nature and the transmission process have been discussed more fully elsewhere, we have included a section on these two subjects in this chapter. The main theme of this book is the resonance between Torah and the soul of the Jew. The other roots have been dealt with at length in the following books: Breuer, Y. *Moriah: Ysodos Hachinuch Haleumi Hatorasi*; Fendel, Z. *Challenge of Sinai*; Halevi, I. *Doros Rishonim*; Heller, Y. *Maoz Hadas*; Hirsch, S. R. *Collected Writings*; Malbim. *Ayeles Hashachar*; Nieto, D. *Hakuzari Hasheni*.

At this point, let's consider some of the intellectual arguments for a Higher Intelligence. We'll start with the "design" argument, which is one of the major approaches used to demonstrate rationally that there is a Creator.

DESIGN ARGUMENT

Basically, the "design" argument is that if something shows evidence of design in its structure, then there must be a designer.[3]

Consider the following example. Suppose you were a member of a space crew making the first manned flight to a newly discovered planet. While exploring the surface of the planet you were astonished to find a watch. What would you think? Would you think that the elements on the surface of this planet have the power to arrange themselves spontaneously into the materials that make up the watch, then form themselves into the parts of the watch, and finally arrange themselves into an intricate, perfectly calibrated mechanical system to measure time accurately? Stop reading for a moment and consider this. Can you seriously entertain the hypothesis that the watch was the product of millions of chance occurrences? Or do you really think that

the watch must be the product of design and that somewhere there must be a watchmaker (and a glassmaker and a
metalmaker, too)?

Now let us consider the complexity of design in just one
organ of the human being, as described by a contemporary
scientist:

> The eyes, for example, are formed on the sides of the
> head and are ready for connection to the optic nerves
> growing out independently from the brain. The forces that
> ensure this integration have thus far not been discovered,
> but they must be formidable indeed, since more than one
> million optic nerve fibers must mesh with each eye. Think
> for a moment about what is considered to be a feat of human
> engineering: the drilling of tunnels from both sides of the
> Alps that must somehow meet precisely and merge into one
> continuous highway. Yet any one of the thousands of things
> the fetus must do as part of the routine of development is
> far more wondrous . [4]

A Torah Sage, the Chazon Ish,[5] marveled that no matter
how much we see the eye does not get "full." He said that
while generation after generation will learn more about the
eye, and the treasure of wisdom which is hidden in it, they
will not get to the bottom of it. "How much wisdom there
is in the eye." [5]

Clearly, the eye is a system which was made to see. Is it
really rational to believe in the random development of the
coordinated activity of the billions of interdependent components in each eye (more than fifty million receptors alone)
and the incredibly complex electrical circuitry for processing and transmitting the data received to the brain? Does not
the complexity of the structure and the intentionality of

function of the human eye tell us there is a designer? And consider the design complexity of the brain:

> The development of the brain and nervous system and its rule of the integration of all systems remain one of the most profound mysteries of embryology . . . The nervous system eventually comprises the most efficient cable system in the world for the transmission of messages. Ultimately, each nerve fiber will be covered by a sheath of protective cells (sometimes 5,000 per fiber), and each will be able to carry messages at a speed of 150 yards per second, or 300 miles per hour . . . Where do these billions of cells in the nervous system come from? From the original fertilized ovum, which is still dividing after one month to form the tissues and organs that the child requires.[6]

The discoveries of science reveal the awesome beauty and complexity of the universe; therefore many of the greatest scientists have had a religious attitude toward the creation of life. Sir Isaac Newton said:

> Whence is it that Nature doth nothing in vain; and whence arises all that Order and Beauty which we see in the World? . . . Was the Eye contrived without Skill in Opticks, and the Ear without Knowledge of Sounds? . . . does it not appear from Phaenomena that there is a Being incorporeal, living, intelligent, omnipresent.[7]

According to Albert Einstein:

> The most beautiful experience that we are capable of feeling is that of the mystery of the cosmos . . . It is imperative to know that that which lies beyond our grasp is nevertheless

truly real. The mystery of reality is revealed in a supernal wisdom and sublime beauty that shines so exceedingly bright that our impoverished faculties can only comprehend it in the most primitive fashion. This knowledge, this feeling, lies at the source of all true religiosity.[8]

Einstein's perception of the "mystery of reality" stands in stark contrast to Darwin's theory of evolution. In the nineteenth century Charles Darwin theorized that living systems came into existence as a result of chance and "natural selection" *without the intervention of Divine Intelligence.* Evolutionists ignore copious research data which indicates that, although genetic mutations may create changes *within* a species, there has never yet been a case when one species actually *became* another species (which is what the theory of evolution proposes). This is true even in studies of insects which span millions of generations.

Although the data which purports to "prove" the theory of evolution has always been spotty and insufficient, the idea of evolution has captured the popular imagination. Many people believe that evolution somehow accounts for the complexity of design in the universe and thereby makes the idea of God as Creator obsolete. In fact, evolutionists have not come up with a viable alternative to God. The theory of evolution does not answer questions about the origin of the materials from which life supposedly evolved or the source of the pattern for increasing complexity of design in the development. Evolution says nothing at all about the awesome beauty of nature or the incredible balance of forces in nature. Darwin himself said, "The eye to this day gives me a cold shudder."[9]

A thorough discussion of the scientific evidence bearing on the theory of evolution is beyond the range of this book. The interested reader is referred to *Evolution: A Theory in Crisis* by molecular biologist Michael Denton. According to Dr. Denton:

> It is the sheer universality of perfection, the fact that everywhere we look, to whatever depth we look, we find an elegance and ingenuity of an absolutely transcending quality . . . which excels in every sense anything produced by the intelligence of man . . . Alongside the level of ingenuity and complexity exhibited by the molecular machinery of life, even our most advanced artifacts appear clumsy.[10]

Yes, yes, you say. Of course you can find scientists who rebut the theory of evolution. But there are also prominent scientists who do believe in evolution. Surely, they are not stupid. No, of course they are not stupid, but let's hear what one of the most honest of them has to say about evolution. We will quote a leading evolutionist, Professor George Wald (Nobel Laureate in Physiology, 1967):

> Organic molecules, therefore, form a large and formidable array, endless in variety and of the most bewildering complexity. One cannot think of having organisms without them. This is precisely the trouble, for to understand how organisms originated we must first of all explain how such complicated molecules could come into being. And that is only the beginning. To make an organism requires not only a tremendous variety of these substances, in adequate amounts and proper proportions, but also the right arrangement of them. The most complex machine man has devised—say an electronic brain—is child's play compared with the simplest of living organisms. The

especially trying thing is that complexity here involves such small dimensions. It is on the molecular level; it consists of a detailed fitting of molecule to molecule such as no chemist can attempt.[11]

The reasonable view was to believe in spontaneous generation; the only alternative was to believe in a single, primary act of supernatural creation. There is no third position. For this reason many scientists a century ago chose to regard the belief in spontaneous generation as a "philosophical necessity." It is a symptom of the philosophical poverty of our time that this necessity is no longer appreciated.[12]

One has only to contemplate the magnitude of this task to concede that the spontaneous generation of a living organism is impossible. Yet here we are—as a result, I believe, of spontaneous generation.[13]

Dr. Wald's statements could be a case study of cognitive dissonance. First, he talks about the incredible complexity of organic molecules; both the structure and composition are beyond the limits of a human inventor. Then he declares that the belief in spontaneous generation of these wondrous particles was a "philosophical necessity" to avoid the only alternative, the belief in a single, primary act of supernatural creation. He then says that the spontaneous generation of a living organism is impossible, and *yet, he believes in spontaneous generation.*

If no dissonance were created in you by the possible implications of the information presented above, if you could just calmly consider it on its own merits—would not the conclusion that there is a Creator be more logical?

"Despite all skeptical evasions, the ultimate agency of intelligence stares one in the face."[14]

Again—stop a moment, clear your mind, try to tolerate any dissonance evoked, and think about this rationally: How could the universe—the earth, one person, even one amoeba—have come into existence without a designer?

At this point, we will leave the "design argument" behind and go on to a different approach—the parable.

HOLOCAUST PARABLE

Difficult though it is to relate to the pain and anguish of the memory of the holocaust, the use of this contemporary cataclysmic experience as a parable to demonstrate the clarity of the tradition of a Torah given by God at Sinai is certainly pertinent and respectful to the memories of those who perished.

Let me tell you about a modern day dilemma. Many people consider the holocaust to be an event of such moral and historical significance *to all of humanity* that it is essential that its lessons be passed from generation to generation lest the lessons have to be learned again the hard way. These people see the holocaust as testimony to the fact that a seemingly civilized society can be bestialized if not built on a firm moral foundation. They see in the holocaust testimony that man can use his mind to justify and ennoble the most atrocious crimes. Hitler believed that he was doing a noble thing by implementing an evolutionary process found in nature—the process of strengthening a species by eliminating the weak.[15]

In another time and another place, another group might be exterminated for the "good" of mankind. Therefore, the events of the holocaust are significant for all humanity and must be passed down through history.

Here is the dilemma. In spite of the fact that survivors still exist and that there is copious documentation of the events of the holocaust, there are those who claim that it never happened. And there are many who believe them.

What do you do if you believe not only that the holocaust *did* occur, but that it is crucially important for mankind to *know* about it? How can you prove it occurred? What is necessary and sufficient evidence? Documents can be falsified, film can be made to show anything. There are two essential components of "proof." The first is the testimony of credible eye-witnesses, people who actually saw and participated in the events and who swear that they saw them, and the second is a reliable transmission process.

1. Participatory Eyewitnesses. It is given that the more people who participated in an event and give testimony to its occurrence, the more convincing the proof. This is how we "know" that George Washington was the first president of the United States, and that the Allies landed in Normandy in June, 1944. This is our basic connection with reality. If you deny the testimony of credible eyewitnesses, you may as well deny that you are reading this book now. But how do you prove something after the last eye-witness dies? How can you insure that there will be credible "witnesses" to transfer the message through the ages? For this you need the second essential component of "proof"—a reliable transmission process.

2. Reliable Transmission Process. One way to establish a transmission reliable process would be to form a "club" of survivors who accept the charge of bearing witness to the holocaust and transferring the message to their children, generation after generation. A crucial part of the transmission process would be to write a book to commemorate two things: the events of the holocaust and the foundation of the club. It is essential that both aspects, the historical facts of the holocaust and the foundation of the club of witnesses, be included in the book. Both aspects must pass through history *unchanged* in order to serve as conclusive evidence that the events in the book occurred. The club is living testimony to the events in the book, and the book establishes the legitimacy of the club.

Let's take a step-by-step look at this transmission process:

First, we must form the Holocaust Commemoration Club (HCC) by gathering all the survivors, men, women and children, in Israel. We must organize them into chapters according their place of internment. Then we must write the HCC Charter in a book that contains: a complete record of the events of the holocaust; a description of the foundation of the HCC; the rules of the HCC.

The complete record of the events of the holocaust would include the names of people who played key roles (e.g., German and Jewish leaders, leaders from other involved countries, key personnel), dates of events, extermination process (e.g., herding Jews into ghettos, wearing of yellow star, transporting Jews in cattle cars to prison camps, location of prison camps, conditions in the camps, number of people interned in each camp, number of people killed, extermination methods), the final liberation and immigration to Israel.

It would be written in the Charter that all the survivors

are gathered together to witness, to testify and to swear to the events herein. They will take the pledge: "We swear that this happened. We swear we saw it with our own eyes. We take upon ourselves the eternal duty to commemorate it and transfer it to our children so that our children can transfer it to their own children, forever and ever."

I think we can all see that except for those who are determined not to believe it, this process would serve as valid testimony to the events of the holocaust. But what does this holocaust transmission process have to do with our concerns—the existence of God and the divine origin of Torah? The point is, of course, that just as there are people who deny the holocaust, there are people who deny that the Torah is divine and was given to the Jews. And just as there are those who think it is crucially important for mankind to know about the holocaust, there are those who think it is *even more* crucial for mankind to know that the Torah is of divine origin.

The problem is that the Torah was given so long ago that it is difficult for many of us to grasp its significance. The holocaust, on the other hand, is an event that has directly touched the lives of most of us, and we are still shaken by its atrocities. The compelling relevance of the holocaust makes it easier for us to see that if the transmission method described above is legitimate, i.e., establishing a "club" of survivors who agree to transfer *credible* evidence of what happened via an unbroken chain of living "witnesses" through the centuries, then the same method would be legitimate for perpetuating the historical record of other events. This includes the unparalleled events that took place on Mount Sinai more than three thousand years ago.

In fact, this is the method that the Torah uses.

The events which led to the birth of the Jewish nation and the giving of the Torah are so significant to all mankind that God instructed Moses to gather all the Jewish people together and recount the events. Moses said to the entire Jewish nation:

> Only take heed and watch yourself very carefully, so that you do not forget the things that your eyes saw. Do not let [this memory] leave your hearts all the days of your lives. Teach your children and children's children about the day you stood before God your Lord at Horeb (Mount Sinai). It was then that God said to me, "Congregate the people for Me, and I will let them hear My words." (*Deuteronomy* 4:9-10)
>
> "Today you all stand before God your Lord ... You are thus being brought into the covenant of God your Lord, and into His oath that He is making with you today. He is establishing you as His nation, so that He will be a God to you . . . But it is not with you alone that I am making this covenant . . . I am making it both with those who are standing here with us today before God our Lord and with those who are not here with us today. (*Deuteronomy* 29:9-14)

According to Torah Sages, the words "those who are not here with us this day" refer to future generations of Jews. The same theme is born out in *Psalm* 78:5-7:

> He [God] established a testimony in Jacob and placed a Torah in Israel, which He commanded our fathers, to make them known to their sons, so that the last generation may know—sons yet to be born—they will arise and tell their own sons, so that they may place their hope in God, and not forget the works of God, but safeguard His commandments.

The Jewish people of every generation are the living "witnesses" that God gave them the Torah—and the Torah is the "club charter," the credible evidence that the events actually occurred. In *Deuteronomy,* God instructs Moses to write down the Torah as a witness for the day when the Jewish people question His existence:

> And it came to pass, when Moses had finished writing the words of the Torah in a book that Moses commanded the Levites, who bore the ark of the covenant of the Lord, saying, "Take this book of the Torah and put it by the side of the ark of the covenant of God, your Lord, that it may be there for a witness to you." (*Deuteronomy* 31:24-26)

When I heard the holocaust parable and reflected on the implications of the continuing existence of the Jewish people and the Torah, I realized that according to all the logical tests I usually use to determine whether other historical events actually occurred, the events in the Torah must have occurred too. (I had never doubted that Hannibal crossed the Alps, or that Socrates drank hemlock—yet the records of these and other historical events were less zealously guarded than the record of the events at Sinai.)

But even after I was intellectually convinced, I had difficulty accepting the idea that I had to live by the "rules." After all, times had changed dramatically, and some of the rules laid down centuries ago seemed obsolete and out-dated. Couldn't I be a witness just because I "feel" Jewish? Why did I have to follow rules? Once again, I turned to the holocaust parable for a new perspective. I was able to see that the rules and procedures of Torah Judaism make sense—even on the much smaller scale of something like our hypothetical "HCC."

The first rule of any system of rules is that you can't change the rules. If the club charter is to serve as an authentic record of the events and the foundation of the HCC, once completed and certified correct by experts, it can never be changed *by a member of the club.* Torah tells us that we can neither add nor subtract anything. (Since non-members are not bound by the rules of the club and are therefore free to make changes, it is inevitable that counterfeit versions of the Charter will eventually be produced. This makes it even more important to have authentic versions available to serve as standards.) To insure that there will always be authentic versions available for HCC members, copies of the Charter which are *exactly the same* as the original are made and distributed to the heads of the Chapters, and they in turn are required to make exact copies. Moses did just this. He made copies of the Torah and distributed them to the priests and elders of the Jewish people.

Safeguards, such as codes, are built into the text of the Charter to insure that it cannot be falsified. There are very specific rules of reproduction, because the constancy of the Charter through time is necessary to establish its validity. Chapter heads are therefore given rigorous training in the technology of the copying procedure. The parallel is, of course, that the Torah can never be changed: it is an eternal law to which nothing can be added and from which nothing can be subtracted. It is meticulously copied so that each Scroll is identical to every other—and to the original, which Moses distributed among the priests and elders in the presence of all the people.

Our hypothetical HCC has four major categories of rules in the Charter: membership, purpose, symbols, and holidays. I will give an example from each of these categories.

1. *Membership.* Since the club has to move in history *without change,* intermarriage is forbidden. However, membership in the club is open to all who are willing to make a commitment to live according to the rules and fulfill the purpose of the club. Members have a serious obligation to follow the rules and not to change them.

2. *Purpose.* The purpose of the HCC is to commemorate the importance of morality, to deny the validity of brute power and to bear witness to the horrific effects of the breakdown of morality. Therefore, the members must agree to live according to the rules of morality established in the Charter and serve as examples of moral living. To this end, members will set aside one day each week to rededicate themselves to their task. On this day, HCC members deny the importance of worldly power by not working. They will study and discuss the Charter and engage in activities which emphasize morality and values. They honor the day by dressing in their finest clothes and eating festive meals in the company of family and friends.

3. *Symbols.* All members will put a condensed version of the Charter on their doorposts. When they go in and out of their homes, members will see the Charter and be reminded of their roles as witnesses. Every member of the club will wear a yellow badge and every newborn son will be tattooed with a blue number.

4. *Holidays.* Liberation weeks will be established as a commemoration of being freed from the concentration camps. Members recreate some of the conditions of the

concentration camps in their homes. They cover furniture and curtains with ragged cloths and sit and sleep on the floor. When at home, they wear ragged, striped pajamas like those worn by the prisoners in the camps. The first night of the holiday they have special services at home, which include the telling of the events that led to the liberation and the eating of stale bread and watery soup. As part of the service, the children are taught to ask, "Why is this night different from any other night?" The father answers by showing them the Charter and saying, "This is the Charter, and I am going to read the story of the liberation to you. You will read it to your children, and they will read it to theirs." Active participation in the telling of the story is encouraged to insure that all feel as if they personally had been liberated.

Wandering Week is also established. Every year, all the members have to relive the wanderings of their ancestors. They have to leave home for a week and live on a ship.

Finally, Foundation Night is established. One night a year the members gather in their communities and stay up all night to learn the scroll. Fathers tell their sons, "Carry on, son. Learn this so you can teach your son. This is your heritage."

The parallels are obvious. The Charter is the Torah itself; the day set aside each week is *Shabbos*; the condensed version of the Charter on the doorpost is the *mezuzah*; Liberation Week is Passover; the Wandering Week is *Succos*, Foundation Night is *Shavuos*.

Having these modern parallels helped me to put Torah life in perspective. The parable helped me clarify my relationship to Torah and its rules, and understand the moral imperative of being a living witness. It made me realize that I am a link in the eternal chain of Torah transmission.

The two types of evidence I have presented, the mind-boggling, awe-inducing complexity of design in the universe, and the parable of the nature of reliable historical transmission, are, for me, intellectually persuasive. It was eye-opening to realize that everything I already believed about the origin of complex things was based on the design argument; and everything I already believed about the validity of historical events was based on a reliable and valid transmission process such as the one in the holocaust parable. When it became clear to me that the existence of God and the divine origin of Torah met these tests, my doubts were dispelled; I didn't have to believe just because someone told me to.

BIBLIOGRAPHY

INTRODUCTION (21-37)

1. Gardner, H. (1985). *The Mind's New Science* (p. 385). New York: Basic Books Inc.

CHAPTER 1: BEYOND PSYCHOTHERAPY (38-49)

1. Wallerstein, J., and Blakeslee, S. (1989). *Second Chances: Men: Women and Children a Decade After Divorce*. New York: Ticknor and Fields.
2. Maslow, A. H. (1969). Toward a Humanistic Biology. *American Psychologist, 24(8),* 724-735.
3. Ibid. (1968). *Toward a Psychology of Being.* Princeton, N.J.: D. Van Nostrand.
4. Ibid. (1969). The Farther Reaches of Human Nature. *Journal of Transpersonal Psychology, 1(1),* 1-9.
5. Ibid. (1970). New Introduction: Religions, Values and Peak Experiences. *Journal of Transpersonal Psychology, 2(2),* 83-90.
6. Marais, E. N. (1970). *The Soul of the White Ant* (p. 106). Plymouth, Great Britain: Clarke, Doble and Brendon Ltd.
7. Ibid. (p. 105).
8. Wood, G. (1983). *The Myth of Neurosis: Overcoming the Illness Excuse.* New York: Harper and Row Publishers.

9. Skinner, B. F. Invited address presented to APA Convention 1986. Reported in *APA Monitor*, Vol. 17, No. 10, Oct. 1986.
10. Ellis, A. (1986). The impossibility of achieving consistently good mental health. *American Psychologist*, Vol. 42, No. 4, pp.370-371.

CHAPTER 2: FREE WILL   (50-62)

1. Tucazinsky, Rabbi Y. M. (1983). *Gesher Hachaim* (p. 80). Brooklyn, New York: Moznaim Publishing Corp.
2. Berlin, I. (1970). *Four Essays on Liberty*. New York: Oxford University Press.
3. Wolbe, Rabbi S. *Alei Shur*. 2nd ed. (p. 45). Jerusalem: Bet Hamussar 5746 (1986).
4. Ibid. (p. 39).
5. Dessler, Rabbi E. E. (1985). *Strive for Truth*, Vol. 1. (A. Carmel, Trans.). (p. 53). Jerusalem and New York: Feldheim Publishers.
6. Ibid. (p. 55).
7. Tucazinsky, Rabbi Y. M. Ibid. (pp. 70–75).

CHAPTER 3: THE DIVINE SOUL   (63-82)

1. Dossey, L. (1989). *Recovering the Soul: A Scientific and Spiritual Search* (p. 1). New York: Bantam Books.
2. In Fine, R. (1973). *The Development of Freud's Thought* (pp. 4-5). New York.
3. Ryle, G. (1949). *The Concept of Mind* (p. 13). London: Hutchinson.
4. Rorty, R. (1979). *Philosophy and the Mirror of Nature* (p. 31). Princeton, N.J.: Princeton University Press.
5. Eccles, Sir J. C. ed. (1982). *Mind and Brain: the many faceted problems: selected readings from the proceedings of the International Conferences on the Unity of the Sciences* (p. 87). Washington: Paragon House.
6. Ibid. (p. 89).
7. Ibid. (p. 97).
8. Popper, K. R. and Eccles, J. C. (1985). *The Self and Its Brain*. Berlin and New York: Springer International.
9. Penfield, W. (1975). *The Mystery of the Mind: a Critical Study of Consciousness and the Human Brain*. Princeton N.J.: Princeton University Press.

10. In Popper, K. R. and Eccles, J. C. (1985). *The Self and Its Brain* (p. 558). Berlin and New York: Springer International.
11. Pribram. K. H. (1986). The cognitive revolution and mind/brain issues. *American Psychologist 41(5)*, 507-520.
12. Campbell, K. (1983). *Body and Mind.* Jerusalem: Hebrew University Magnes Press.
13. Eccles, ibid.
14. Ibid.
15. Planck, M. (1933). *Where is Science Going?* (p. 168). Cited in *Pathways to the Torah.* The Arachim Source Book, 5th ed. 1987. I:1.
16. Heisenberg, W. (1971) *Physics and Beyond.* In Eccles, Sir J. C. (1980). *The Human Psyche* (p. 244). New York: Springer International.
17. Maimonides. *Laws of the Foundations of the Torah* (1:1,6).
18. Penfield, W. (1975). *The Mystery of the Mind: A Critical Study of Consciousness and the Human Brain* (p. 60). Princeton, N.J.: Princeton University Press.
19. Gardner, H. (1985). *The Mind's New Science: A History of the Cognitive Revolution* (p. 153 and p. 388). New York: Basic Books Inc.
20. Goleman, D. (1985). *Vital Lies, Simple truths: The Psychology of Self-Deception* (p. 73). New York: Simon and Schuster Inc.
21. Gies, M. (1987). *Anne Frank Remembered.* New York: Simon and Schuster Inc.
22. Fromm, E. (1947). *Man for Himself* (pp. 45-46). New York, Chicago and San Francisco: Holt, Rinehart and Winston.
23. Russell, B. (1968). *The Autobiography of Bertrand Russell* Vol. 2 (pp. 95-96). Boston: Little, Brown.

CHAPTER 4: A MODEL OF THE SOUL (83-105)

1. Brawer, Y. (1990). Neurology and the Soul. *Chai Today* (p. 23). (Reprinted with permission from B'Or HaTorah Vol. 1).
2. Luzzatto, Rabbi M. C. (1981). *The Way of God,* (A. Kaplan, Trans.) 3rd ed. I:3:7.
3. Ibid. (3:1:4).
4. Ibid. (p. 181).

5. Rabbi Chaim of Volozhin. (1981). *Nefesh Hachaim* In *An Anthology of Jewish Mysticism* (B. Z. Trans.) New York: Judaica Press.
6. Lynch, J. J. (1977). *The Broken Heart: The Medical Consequences of Loneliness in America.* New York: Basic Books.
7. Justice, B. (1987). *Who Gets sick: Thinking and Health.* Texas: Peak Press.
8. Silverman, L. H., Lachmann, F. M. and Milich, R. H. (1982). *The Search for Oneness.* New York: International Universities Press.
9. Mahler, M., Pine, F. and Bergman, A. *The Psychological Birth of the Human Infant* (p. 27). New York: Basic Books.
10. Kaplan, L. J. (1978). *Oneness and Separateness* (pp. 94-95). New York: Simon and Schuster.
11. Rank, O. In Lifton R. J. (1979). *The Broken Connection: On Death and the Continuity of Life* (p. 57). New York: Simon and Schuster.
12. Lifton, R. J. and Olson, E. (1975). *Living and Dying* (p. 49). New York: Praeger Publishers.
13. Viorst, J. (1986) *Necessary Losses* (p. 10). New York: Fawcett.
14. Fromm, E. (1966) *You Shall Be As Gods.* Connecticut: Fawcett Publications, Inc.

CHAPTER 5: HOW THE SOUL GROWS (101-124)

1. Kegan, R. (1980). Where the Dance Is: Religious Dimensions of a Developmental Framework. In J. Fowler and A. Vergote (Eds.). *Toward Moral and Religious Maturity.* (pp. 403-440, p.407). Morristown, N.J.: Silver Burdett.
2. Dabrowski, K. (1964). *Positive Disintegration.* J. Aronson (Ed.). Boston: Little, Brown.
3. Snarey, J. et al. (1983). Ego Development in Perspective: Structural Stage, Functional Phase, and Cultural Age-Period Models (p. 305). *Developmental Review 3.*
4. Lopian, Rabbi E. (1975). *Lev Eliyahu.* (p. 3). Jerusalem: Goldberg Press.
5. Feldman, Rabbi A. (1990). *The Juggler and the King: The Jew and the Conquest of Evil* (p. 3). Jerusalem and New York: Feldheim.
6. Salanter, Rabbi Y. *Iggeret HaMussar.*
7. Feldman, Rabbi A. Ibid. (p. 4).

8. Steele, T. In Moldauer, E. (1983). Kashrus: The Ultimate Soul-Food. *Jewish Woman's Outlook.* Jan./Feb. 1983.

CHAPTER 6: WILL POWER AND THE NEED FOR SATISFACTION   (127-153)

1. Einstein, A. Attribution.
2. Frank, J. D. (1982). Therapeutic components shared by all psychotherapies. In J. H. Harvey and M. M. Parks (Eds.). The Master Lecture Series: Vol. 1. *Psychotherapy Research and Behavior Change* (pp. 5–38). Washington, DC: American Psychological Association.
3. Bandura, A. (1989). Human Agency in Social Cognitive Theory. *American Psychologist, 44(9),* 1175-1184.
4. Bednar, R. L., Wells, M. G., and Peterson, S. R. (1989). *Self-esteem: Paradoxes and Innovations in Clinical Theory and Practice* (p. 4). Washington, D.C.: American Psychological Association.
5. Harter, S. (1983). Developmental Perspectives on the Self-system. In E. M. Hetherington (Ed.). *Handbook of Child Psychology, Vol. 4. Socialization, Personality and Social Development* (4th ed.). New York: Wiley.
6. Baumrind, D. (1975). Some thoughts about childrearing. In Bronfenbrenner and Mahoney (Eds.). *Influences on Human Development* (p. 278). Hinsdale, Ill: Dryden Press.
7. Coopersmith, S. (Feb. 1969). Implications of studies of self-esteem for education research practice. Paper presented at the American Educational Research Association Convention. Los Angeles, Ca.
8. Bandura, A. Op cit., p.1180.
9. Dessler, Rabbi E. E. (1985). *Strive for Truth,* Vol. 2 (p. 13). Jerusalem and New York: Feldheim Publishers.
10. Southey. (1967). Remembrance 1,3. In Stevenson,B. *The Home Book of Quotations* (p. 453). Dodd Mead and Co.
11. Heschel, A. J. (1951). *Man Is Not Alone: A Philosophy of Religion* (p. 253). New York: Farrar, Strauss, and Giroux, Inc.
12. Ecclesiastes 6:7.
13. Luzzatto, Rabbi M. C. (1981). *The Way of God* 3:1:2. Jerusalem and New York: Feldheim Publishers.

14. Lopian, Rabbi E. (1975). *Lev Eliyahu* (p. 3). Jerusalem: Goldberg Press.
15. Gifter, Rabbi M. (1990). *Torah Perspectives* (p. 44). Brooklyn: Mesorah Publications Ltd.
16. Zohar, U. (1985). *Waking Up Jewish* (pp. 50-53, 202, 131, 214). Jerusalem: Hamesorah Publications.

CHAPTER 7: LOVE OF LIFE AND FEAR OF DEATH (154-179)

1. Hofmannstal, H. V. (1981). *Der Tod und Der Tod*. In Goodman, L. M. *Death and the Creative Life* (p. 17). New York: Springer Publishing Co.
2. Tucazinsky, Rabbi Y. M. (1983). *Gesher Hachaim: The Bridge of Life*. (N. A.Tucazinsky, Trans.) p. 52. Jerusalem: Moznaim Publishing.
3. Justice, B. (1987). *Who Gets Sick: Thinking and Health* (p. 269). Houston: Peak Press.
4. Ibid. (p. 203).
5. Weissman, A. D. and Hackett, T.P. (1979). In Lifton R. J. *The Broken Connection: On Death and the Continuity of Life* (p. 107). New York: Simon and Schuster.
6. Justice, B. Ibid.
7. Ibid.
8. Goodman, L. M. (1981). *Death and the Creative Life*. New York: Springer Publishing Co.
9. Butler, R. N. (1963). The Life review: an interpretation of reminiscence in the aged. *Psychiatry*, 119, 721-728.
10. Tobacyk, J. (1983). Death threat, death concerns, and paranormal belief. *Death Education*. Vol. 7 (2-3), 115-124.
11. Smith, D. K., Nehemkis, A. M., Charter, R. A. (1983-1984). Fear of Death, Death Attitudes, and Religious Convictions in the Terminally Ill. *International Journal of Psychiatry in Medicine*. Vol. 13, 221-232.
12. Danielsen, R. (1981). The Psychological Effects of Religion to the Dying Person. *Tidsskrift for Norsk Psykilogforening*. Suppl. 1. 34-39.
13. Brown, N. O. (1959). *Life Against Death: The Psychoanalytical Meaning of History*. New York: Vintage Books
14. Freud, S. In Brown, N. O. (1959). *Life Against Death* (p.99, 93). New

York: Vintage Books.

15. Brown, N. O. Ibid.

16. Jung, C. G. (1933). *Modern Man in Search of a Soul* (W. S., Well, and C. F. Baynes, Trans.) (p. 111). New York and London: Harcourt, Brace and Jovanovich.

17. Lifton, R. J. (1979). *The Broken Connection: On Death and the Continuity of Life.* New York: Simon and Schuster.

18. Osis, K. and Haraldsson, E. (1977). *At the Hour of Death.* New York: Avon.

19. Moody, R. A. Jr. (1975). *Life After Life.* Ga: Mockingbird Books.

20. Kastenbaum, R. (1984). *Is There Life After Death?* (p. 223). London: Rider and Company.

21. Noyes, R. Jr. (1977). Is there new evidence for survival after death? *The Humanist,* 31:51-53.

22. Moody, R. A. Ibid.

23. Moody, R. A. (1988). *Light Beyond.* New York and Toronto: Bantam Books.

24. Garfield, C. (1979). the Dying Patient's Concern with "Life After Death." In Kastenbaum R. (Ed.) *Between Life and Death* (p. 51). New York: Springer Publishing Company.

25. Kastenbaum, R. (1984). Ibid. p.51, p.209.

26. Kastenbaum, R. (Ed.) (1979). *Between Life and Death* (p. 23, 158). New York; Springer Publishing Co.

27. Tucazinsky, Rabbi Y. M., Ibid. p.45.

28. Ibid. p. 28-29.

29. Ibid. p. 44.

CHAPTER 8: THE NEED FOR PHYSICAL SENSATION AND PLEASURE (180-202)

1. Heschel, A. J. (1955). *God in Search of Man: A Philosophy of Judaism.* New York: Farrar, Strauss and Giroux.

2. Suedfeld, P. (1980). *Restricted environmental stimulation.* New York, Chichester, Brisbane, Toronto: John Wiley and Sons.

3. Freud, S. In Brown N. O. (1959). *Life Against Death: The Psychoanalytical Meaning of History* (p. 8). New York: Vintage Books.

4. Fromm, E. (1947). *Man for Himself* (p. 46). New York, Chicago, San Francisco: Holt, Rhinehart and Winston.

5. Frank, J. (1978). *Psychotherapy and the Human Predicament*. New York: Schocken.
6. Adler, A. (1938). *Social Interest: A challenge to mankind*. London: Faber and Faber.
7. Cushman, P. (1990). Why the Self is Empty. *American Psychologist, Vol. 45 No. 5*, 599-611, *Vol. 45 No. 5*, 599-611.

CHAPTER 9: CURIOSITY AND THE DRIVE TO EXPLORE (203-223)

1. Beiser, H. R. (1984). On Curiosity: A Developmental Approach. *Journal of American Child Psychiatry: Sept. Vol. 23* (5), 517-526.
2. Berlyne, D. E. (1960). *Conflict, Arousal and Curiosity*. New York: McGraw-Hill.
3. Harlow, H. (1950). Learning and Satiation of Response in Intrinsically Motivated Complex Puzzle Performance by Monkeys. *Journal of Comparative and Physiological Psychology, 43*:289-294.
4. Maslow, A. H. (1963). The Need to Know and the Fear of Knowing. *The Journal of General Psychology, 68*:111-125, 199-202.
5. McReynolds, P., Acker, M. and Pietila, C. (1961). Relation of Object Curiosity to Psychological Adjustment in Children. *Child Development 32*:393-400.
6. Maslow, A. H. Ibid. p.208-209.
7. Brazelton, T. B. (1980). Neonatal Assessment. *The Course of Life, Vol. 1*. S. Greenspan and Pollock. Washington DC: U.S. Government Printing Office.
8. Beiser, H. R. Ibid. p. 517.
9. Maslow, A. H. Op. cit.
10. Suedfeld, P. (1981). Environmental Restriction and "Stimulus Hunger" in Day, Hy I. *Advances in Intrinsic Motivation and Aesthetics*. New York and London: Plenum Press.
11. Schultz, D. P. (1965). *Sensory Restriction: effects on behavior*. New York: Academic Press.
12. Einstein, A. (1950). *Out of My Later Years* (p. 26). New York.
13. Chernievsky. *Between Science and Religion*. In *Pathways to the Torah*. The Arachim Source Book. 5th Ed. I:37:1.
14. Katzir, A. *Pathways to the Torah*. The Arachim Source Book. 5th Ed. 2:1:2.

15. Dessler, Rabbi E. E. (1985). *Strive for Truth* Vol. II (A. Carmel, Trans.) (p. 240). Jerusalem and New York: Feldheim Publishers.
16. Gifter, Rabbi M. (1986). *Torah Perspectives* (p. 55). New York: Mesorah Publication.
17. Ibid.
18. Luzzatto, Rabbi M. C. *The Way of God* (A. Kaplan, Trans.). Jerusalem and New York: Feldheim Publishers.
19. Ibn Paquda, R. Bachya ben Yosef. (1970). *Duties of the Heart,* Vol. 1 (M. Hyamson, Trans.) Jerusalem and New York: Feldheim Publishers.

CHAPTER 10: STABLE IDENTITY IN AN EVER-CHANGING WORLD (225-236)

1. Viorst, J. (1986). *Necessary Losses* (p. 61). New York: Fawcett Gold Medal.
2. Harter, S. (1983). Developmental Perspectives on the self-system. In E. M. Hetherington (ed.) *Handbook of Child Psychology*, Vol. 4 Socialization, personality and social development (4th ed.) New York: Wiley.
3. Markus, H. and Nurius, P. (1986). Possible Selves. *American Psychologist*, Vol. 41, No. 9, 954-969.
4. Browning, D. (1978). Erikson and the Search for a Normative Image of Man (pp. 264-292). In Homans, P. (ed.) *Childhood and Selfhood: Essays on tradition, Religion and Modernity in the Psychology of Erik H. Erikson.* London: Associated University Presses.
5. Erikson, E. H. (1964). *Insight and Responsibility* (p. 90). New York: W.W.Norton and Company Inc.
6. Dessler, Rabbi E. E. (1985). *Strive for Truth*, Vol. II (A. Carmel, Trans.). Jerusalem and New York: Feldheim Publishers.

CHAPTER 11: HOW TO BE A REAL SUCCESS (237-252)

1. Bunim, I. M. (1964). *Ethics from Sinai,* Vol. II (p. 79). New York: Feldheim Publishers.
2. Browning, D. (1978). Erikson and the Search for a Normative Image of Man. In *Childhood and Selfhood: Essays on Tradition, Religion and Modernity in the Psychology of Erik H. Erikson.* (Homan,

P. *ed.*) (pp. 264-292). London: Associated University Presses.

3. Steele, A. (1978). *Upward Nobility: How to Win the Rat Race without Becoming a Rat* (pp. 144-145). New York: Times Book Co.

4. McClelland, D. C. (1961). *The Achieving Society* (p. 303). Princeton: D. Van Nostrand Company Inc.

5. Maslow, A. H. (1970). *Motivation and Personality* (2nd ed.). New York, Evanston and London: Harper and Row, Publishers.

6. Ansbacher, H. L. and Ansbacher, P. R. (1956). *The Individual Psychology of Alfred Adler.* New York: Basic Books.

7. Ibid. p. 104.

8. Ibid. p. 128.

9. Maslow, A. H. Ibid.

10. Bunim, I. M. Ibid.

11. Dessler, Rabbi E. E. (1978). *Strive for Truth,* Vol. II (A. Carmel, Trans.) (p. 124). Jerusalem and New York: Feldheim Publishers.

12. Hirsch, Rabbi S. R. (1976). *The Pentateuch* (I. Levy, Trans.). Gateshead: Judaica Press Ltd.

13. Hirsch, Rabbi S. R. (1962). *Horeb* (Dayan Dr. I. Grunfeld, Trans.) (p. 41). New York, London, Jerusalem: Soncino Press.

CHAPTER 12: TRUE AND FALSE LOVE (253-278)

1. Fromm, E. (1956). *The Art of Loving* (p. 59). New York and Evanston: Harper and Row.

2. Harlow, H. F. (1975). The Nature of Love. In Montagu, Ashley. (Ed.) *The Practice of Love.* New Jersey: Prentice-Hall, Inc.

3. Maslow, A. H. (1975). *Love in Healthy People* (p. 91). In Montagu, Ashley. (Ed.) *The Practice of Love.* New Jersey: Prentice-Hall, Inc.

4. Burton R. (1963). *The Anatomy of Melancholy.* In A. M. Withespoon and F. Warnke, (Eds.) *Seventeenth-century Prose and Poetry.* New York: Harcourt Brace Jovanovich. (Original work published 1651).

5. Koenigsberg, R. A. (1967). Culture and Unconscious Fantasy: Observation on Courtly Love. *Psychoanalytic Review,* 54, 36-50.

6. Freud, S. (1955). Group Psychology and the Analysis of the Ego. In Strachey (Ed.), *The Standard Edition of the Complete Psychological Works of Sigmund Freud.*

7. Ainsworth, M. D. S. (1989). Attachments Beyond Infancy. In

American Psychologist, Vol. 44, 709-716.

8. Fromm, E. Ibid., p. 8 and p. 15-16.

9. Kazak, A. E. and Repucce, N. D. (1980). Romantic Love as a Social Institution. In Pope, K.S. and Associates. *On Love and Loving* (p. 225). California: Jossey-Bas Inc.

10. Silverstein, S. (1979). *The Antidote* (p. 31). Jerusalem and New York: Feldheim Publishers.

11. Fromm, E. Ibid., p. 60.

12. Zalman, Rabbi S. (1984). *Likuttey Amarim: Tanya.* Bi-lingual Edition. Brooklyn: Kehot Publication Society.

13. Wein, B. (1988). Being Truly Jewish in a Society of Plenty. *Jewish Observer. Vol. XXI, No. 3,* p. 11.

CHAPTER 13: THE QUEST FOR MEANING (279-297)

1. Frankl, V. E. (1978). *THe Unheard Cry for Meaning: Psychotherapy and Humanism* (p. 29). New York: Simon and Schuster.

2. Ibid. p. 21.

3. Ibid. (1959). *Man's Search for Meaning* (p. 107). Boston: Beacon Press.

4. Ibid. p. 62.

5. Dimsdale J. E. (1974). The Coping Behavior of Nazi Concentration Camp Survivors. *American Journal of Psychiatry, 12*(7) p. 792.

6. In Frankl, V. E. Ibid. (1978).

7. Bruner, J. (1989). Quoted in *APA Monitor,* July.

8. Frankl, Ibid. (1978).

9. Ibid. pp. 26-27.

10. Edwards, P. (1981). The Meaning and Value of Life. In E. D. Klemke (Ed.) *The Meaning of Life,* pp. 118-140. New York: Oxford University Press.

11. Ebersole, P. and DeVogler-Ebersole, K. (1985). Meaning in Life of the Eminent and the Average, *Journal of Social Behavior and Personality,* January, Vol. 1, No. 1, 83-94.

12. Tucazinsky, Rabbi Y. M. (1983). *THe Bridge of Life.* (Rabbi N. A. Trans.) (P. 133). Jerusalem: Moznaim Publishing Co.

13. *The Unconquerable Spirit.* (1980). *(S. Zuker, Compiler, G. Hirschler, Trans. and Ed.)* p. 135.

14. Tucazinsky, Rabbi Y. M. Ibid. p. 134-135.

CHAPTER 14: THE RELIGIOUS SOUL: UNITY   (299-302)

1. Hirsch, S. R. (1962). *Horeb.* (I. Grunfeld, Trans.)(p. 6). New York, London and Jerusalem: The Soncino Press.

CHAPTER 15: LOVINGKINDNESS AND SEEKING PEACE   (303-322)

1. Chafetz Chaim. (1976). *Ahavath Chesed: The Love of Kindness as Required by God* (L. Oschry, Trans.). 2nd (ed. P. 17). Jerusalem and New York: Feldheim Publishers.
2. Dessler, Rabbi E. E. (1978). *Strive for Truth,* Vol. I (A. Carmel, Trans.) (p. 153). Jerusalem and New York: Feldheim Publishers.
3. Rosenhan, D. L. (1978). Toward Resolving the Altruism Paradox: Affect, Self-reinforcement, and Cognition. Ch. 5 (pp. 101-113). In Wispe, L. (Ed.) *Altruism, Sympathy and Helping: Psychological and Sociological Principles* (p. 103). New York: Academic Press.
4. Batson, C. D. (1990). How Social an Animal? The Human Capacity for Caring. *American Psychologist, Vol. 45, No. 3,* 336-346.
5. Skinner, B. F. (1978). The Ethics of Helping People. Ch. 12 (pp. 249-262). In Wise, L. Ibid. p. 249.
6. Luks, A. (1988). Helper's High. *Psychology Today. October '88.*
7. Kohn, A. (1988). Beyond Selfishness. *Psychology Today. October '88.*
8.. Batson, C. D. Ibid. p. 340.
9. Badcock, C. R. (1986). *The Problem of Altruism: Freudian-Darwinian Solutions.* Oxford: Basil Blackwell Ltd.
10. Ibid. pp. 25-26.
11. Dessler, Rabbi E. E. Ibid. p. 144.
12. Dessler, Rabbi E. E. (1985). *Strive for Truth.* (Carmell, A. *trans.*) *Vol. 2 Jerusalem / New York Feldheim Publishers*
13. Miller, Rabbi Avigdor. (1962). *Rejoice O Youth!* (pp. 312-319). New York: Balshon Printing and Offset Co.
14. Miller, Rabbi Avigdor. (1973). *Sing, You Righteous!* (p. 18). New York: Balshon Printing and Offset Co.
15. Dessler, Rabbi E. E. Ibid. (1978). p. 142.

16. Ibid. Vol. 2.

CHAPTER 16: SANCTIFICATION OF LIFE   (323-337)

1. Berkovitz, E. (1959). *God, Man and history.* In Hirsch, Rabbi S. R. *Horeb* (I. Grunfeld, Trans.) (p. xciii). New York, London and Jerusalem: Soncino Press.
2. Hirsch, Rabbi S. R. (1981). *Horeb* (I. Grunfeld, Trans.) (p. xciii). New York, London and Jerusalem: Soncino Press.
3. Significant insights into the observance of the laws of family purity and *mikveh* are to be found in Rabbi Aryeh Kaplan's book, *Waters of Eden*, New York: NCSY/Orthodox Union 1976.
4. Dessler, Rabbi E. E. (1978). *Strive for Truth* Vol I, (A. Carmel, Trans.)(p. 131). Jerusalem and New York: Feldheim Publishers.
5. Ibid. p. 129.
6. Ibid. (1985). Vol II. .Jerusalem and New York: Feldheim Publishers.
7. Ibid. p. 139.
8. Rabeinu Yonah. (1967). *The Gates of Repentance* (S. Silverstein, Trans.). Jerusalem and New York: Feldheim Publishers.
9. Wienberg, Y. (1987). *Lessons in Tanya* (p. 139). New York: Kehot Publication Society.

CHAPTER 17: THE NEED FOR TRUTH   (338-359)

1. *Zohar, Vayakhel,* p. 206.
2. Chazon Ish (Rabbi Avraham Yeshaye Karelitz). *Emunah Ubitachon* p.1.
3. Dessler, Rabbi E. E. (1978). *Strive for Truth* Vol. I (A. Carmel, Trans.) (p. 114). Jerusalem and New York: Feldheim Publishers.
4. Wolbe, Rabbi S. *Alei Shur* 5745 2nd ed. (p. 528). Jerusalem: Bet Hamussar.
5. Fendel, R. Z. (1986). *The Ethical Personality.* New York: Hashkafah Publications.
6. Ibid. p. 129.
7. Dessler, Rabbi E. E. Ibid.
8. Hirsch, Rabbi S.R. (1981). *Horeb* 4th ed. (I. Grunfeld, Trans.). New

York, London and Jerusalem: Soncino Press.

9. Kitov, E. (1978). *The Book of our Heritage* (N. Bulman, Trans.) (p. 295). Jerusalem and New York: Feldheim Publishers.

10. Zohar, U. (1985). *Waking Up Jewish* (p. 164). Jerusalem: Hamesorah Publications.

11. Ewen, S. (1989). Advertising and the development of consumer society. In Angus, I. and Jhally, S. (eds.) *Cultural Politics in Contemporary America* (pp. 82-95.). New York: Routledge.

12. Dessler, Rabbi E. E. Ibid. p. 176.

13. Sforno, Rabbi O. In Dessler, Rabbi E. E. Ibid. (p. 190).

14. Rambam *Shemoneh Prokim* ch. 3.

15. Luzzatto, Rabbi M. C. (1981). *The Way of God* (A. Kaplan, Trans.) (p. 247). Jerusalem and New York: Feldheim Publishers.

16. Talmud Bavli *Shabbos* 55a.

17. Camus, A. (1955). *The Myth of Sisyphus.* New York: Knopf.

CHAPTER 18: BEYOND THE EGO (361-371)

1. Cardozo, N. T. L. (1988). *The Torah as God's Mind* (p. 18). New York: Bep-Ron Publications.

2. Wineberg, Rabbi Y. (1987). *Lessons in Tanya* (p. 96). Brooklyn: Kehot Publication.

3. Dessler, Rabbi E. E. (1978). *Strive for Truth* Vol. I (A. Carmel, Trans.). Jerusalem and New York: Feldheim Publishers.

4. Ibid. p. 98.

5. Gifter, Rabbi M. (1986). *Torah Perspectives* (p. 18). Brooklyn: Mesorah Publications Ltd..

6. Ibid. p. 19.

7. Dessler, Rabbi E. E. (1989). *Strive for Truth* Vol. III (A. Carmel, Trans.) (p. 20). Jerusalem and New York: Feldheim Publishers.

8. Dessler, Rabbi E. E. 1978 *Strive for Truth* Vol. I (A. Carmel, Trans.) (p. 89). Jerusalem and New York: Feldheim Publishers.

9. *Zohar* Part 1: 24a, Part II: 60a.

CHAPTER 19: HOW TO APPLY TORAH WISDOM TO YOUR LIFE (372-378)

1. The Ga'on of Vilna. Quoted in Fendel, Rabbi Z. (1986). *The Ethical*

Personality (p. 67). New York: Hashkafah Publications.

APPENDIX: A RATIONAL APPROACH TO JUDAISM (381-403)

1. Dessler, Rabbi E. E. (1978). *Strive for Truth* Vol. I, (pp. 82-83). Jerusalem and New York: Feldheim.
2. Gifter, Rabbi M. (1986). *Torah Perspectives* (p. 51). Brooklyn: Mesorah Publications Ltd.
3. For a thorough discussion of the validity of the design argument, read Ben Yosef, M. and Robinson, Gershon. (1983). *The 2001 Principle* Jerusalem: Hed Press Ltd.
4. *From Conception to Birth.* (1970). New York: Harper and Row Publishers.
5. Chazon Ish. (1944). *Emunah U'Vitachon.* Tel Aviv.
6. *From Conception to Birth,* Ibid.
7. Newton, I. (1952). *Opticks* Dover Publications (pp. 369-370). Cited in *Pathways to the Torah.* The Arachim Source Book, 5th ed. 1987 I: 41.
8. Einstein, A. *Comment Je Vois le Monde* (pp. 12-13) Cited in *Pathways to the Torah.* The Arachim Source Book, 5th ed. 1987 I:41.
9. Darwin, C. (1860). In a letter to Asa Gray in Darwin, J. ed. (1888). *Life and Letters of Charles Darwin* Vol. 2 (p. 273). London: John Murray.
10. Denton, M. (1985). *Evolution: A Theory in Crisis* (p. 342). London: Burnett Books.
11. Wald, G. (1987). The Origin of Life. *Scientific American,* Vol. 191, No. 4, p. 46. Cited in *Pathways to the Torah* The Arachim Source Book 5th ed. 1987 I:41.
12. Ibid. I:48.
13. Ibid. I:34.
13. Ferre, F. (1967). *Basic Modern Philosophy of Religion* (p. 161). New York: Charles Scribner's and Sons.
15. Hitler, A. (1943). *Mein Kampf.* Boston: Houghton Mifflin Company.

RABBI YECHIEL MICHEL TUCAZINSKY (1872-1955) wrote many scholarly works on a wide variety of Torah subjects, including the *halachic* aspects of sunrise and sunset (*Bein Hashmoshos*), the Sabbatical Year (*Hashemittah*), the International Date Line (*Hayoman*), the archeology, history, and geography of Jerusalem (*Ir Hakodesh Vehamikdosh*), the laws of married life (*Taharas Israel*), and the classic text on the laws and customs relevant to sickness, death, and burial (*Gesher Hachaim*). *Gesher Hachaim* (The Bridge of Life) was written in three parts. The first part contains the laws and customs pertaining to death, the second part consists of questions and answers regarding death, and the third part presents Rabbi Tucazinsky's uplifting *hashkafa* (world view). All the references in this book are from Part III of *Gesher Hachaim*.

RABBI ELIYAHU ELIEZER DESSLER (1892-1943) founded and sustained the first western European *kolel* (post-graduate institute for advanced Talmudic study) in Gateshead, England and Israel. He is considered to be one the foremost *baalei mussar* (master of the ethical principles of Torah). The series of volumes called *Michtav Me'Eliyahu* (the English version is entitled *Strive for Truth*), were compiled from notes and memories of his *talmidim* (pupils) and Rabbi Dessler's notes and letters. *Michtav Me'Eliyahu* has become a classic of modern Torah thought.

RABBI MOSHE CHAIM LUZZATTO (1717-1747) was regarded as a genius from childhood. He became an outstanding *Talmud Chacham* (Torah scholar) and had an unparalleled command of *Kabbala*. He wrote a series of works that display his remarkable ability to bring clarity and organization to the most abstruse teachings of the mystic tradition. Three of his best known works are *Mesillat Yesharim* (The Path of the Just), *Derech Hashem* (The Way of God), and *Da'ath Tevunoth* (the English title is The Knowing Heart). According to its translator, Shraga Silverstein, *Mesillat Yesharim* has been treasured for centuries for its "profound insight into human motives, its majestic overview of Torah, and the infinite wisdom of its counsels..." In *Derech Hashem*, Rabbi Luzzato brilliantly systematizes the basic principles of Jewish belief and teaches the dynamics of interaction between man and God. *Da'ath Tevunoth* is about how Torah knowledge can go beyond the intellect to influence the heart and exalt the soul.

GLOSSARY

Aleph-beis: the first two letters of the Hebrew alphabet. Often used to refer to the Hebrew alphabet

Am Yisrael: the Jewish people

baal teshuvah: male penitent, or one who becomes Torah observant (feminine singular is *baalat*, plural is *baalei*)

Bamidbar: the fourth book of the Torah (Numbers)

bechirah: free choice

beis midrash: study hall

Bereishis: the first book of the Torah (Genesis)

bris: circumcision

brachah: blessing

betzelem Elokim: in the image of G-d

chachmah: wisdom

chessed: lovingkindness

chillul Hashem: desecration of G-d's name, sacrilege

Chumash: the Pentateuch

davening: praying

Devarim: the fifth book of the Torah (Deuteronomy)

dveikus: union or closeness with G-d

frum: meticulous in Torah observance

Gemara: commentary on the *Mishna* (the *Mishna* and *Gemara* together make up the Talmud)

guf: the body

hakoras hatov: acknowledging and appreciating kindness

halachah: body of Jewish law

hashkafah: Torah outlook on life

kavod: honor

Kiddush Hashem: sanctification of G-d's name, martyrdom

kippah: skullcap

lishmah: doing something for its own sake, not for any personal gain

mezuzah: prayers written on a parchment scroll and affixed to doorposts in Jewish homes.

midos: character traits

Midrash: homiletic portion of the Talmud

mikveh: ritual bath

Mishnah: earliest portion of the Talmud

metamtem hanefesh: dulling of the soul

mitzvos: the Divine commandments

negius: personal, ulterior motives

neshamah: soul (the religious level in our model)

Oral Torah: oral transmission of the Torah, later written down as the Talmud

parnassah: livelihood

rodeif shalom: pursuer of peace

ruach hatumah: spirit of defilement

seudah: meal

shabbos: the sabbath

shiur: class, lecture

siyum: celebration of completing a unit of Torah study

shelo lishmah: doing something for personal gain

Shemos: the second book of the Torah (Exodus)

shleimus: completion, spiritual perfection

shomer shabbos: keeping the commandments of the Torah

shul: synagogue

sukkah: booth, or temporary dwelling used during the holiday of *Sukkos*

Sukkos: festival of the harvest

tefillin: phylacteries, containing portion of the Scriptures

Torah: specifically, the Pentateuch, but in its general sense refers to the whole spectrum of Jewish written and oral law

tov meod: very good

tumah: defilement, impurity

treif: non-kosher food

teshuva: repentance

tznius: modesty in conduct and dress

tzeddakah: charity

Vayikrah: third book of the Torah (Leviticus)

Yerushalmi: Torah observant Jews of eastern European descent

yeshivah: academy of Jewish study

yetzer hatov: good inclination

yetzer hora: evil inclination

Yom Kippur: Day of atonement

INDEX